(re)searching gothenburg

Published by Glänta produktion in 2010.

Translated by Brett Jocelyn Epstein,
except the texts by Barbara Czarniawska,
Bengt Furåker, Martin Letell, Abby Peterson,
Martin Peterson, Rolando Vazquez,
originally written in English.

Proof-reading by Simon Garnett.

Design by Richard Lindmark.

Printed by Exakta, Hässleholm 2010.

Published with financial support from Riksbankens Jubileumsfond (RJ)
and Swedish council for working and social research (FAS).

ISBN: 978-91-86133-20-7

www.glanta.org

(re)searching GOTHENBURG

ESSAYS ON A CHANGING CITY

Helena Holgersson, Catharina Thörn,
Håkan Thörn & Mattias Wahlström (eds)

Glänta produktion

INTRODUCTION

1. THE TRANSFORMATION OF THE CITY

2. SELF-IMAGE/S OF THE CITY

PHOTOGRAPHIC INTERMISSION

3. THE CITY'S PERIPHERIES

4. THE CITY AS STAGE AND PUBLIC SPACE

5. THE MENTAL STATES OF GOTHENBURG

INTRODUCTION

Helena Holgersson, Catharina Thörn,
Håkan Thörn & Mattias Wahlström

A CRITICAL VIEW OF GOTHENBURG

Who needs a book about Gothenburg? Is it a subject primarily for tourists and natives or could it be of more general interest? Does Gothenburg say something about general trends in urban change during the last decades? Is it even possible to view global urban developments through the lens of a peripheral city such as Gothenburg? At the most comprehensive level, international processes have influenced Gothenburg since its establishment, and today this is the case more than ever. During the 20th century, Gothenburg was also influenced by the Swedish, or Scandinavian, welfare model. As a harbour and shipyard city, Gothenburg was one of the first Swedish cities that experienced, in a fundamental way, the process of structural change that is often called "post-industrial". In the past decade, Gothenburg has been considered as one of the leading cities in Sweden by those who think that a closer collaboration between politics and business is the best way to meet the current challenges created by economic globalisation. Led by the Social Democrats, the city has allowed private actors to have a relatively large influence over developmental strategies.

The book *Undressing Durban*, edited by Rob Pattman and Sultan Khan, and published by the University of KwaZulu-Natal in connection with the World sociological congress in Durban, South Africa, in 2006, criticised the touristic image of Durban that the conference materials offered and presented a number of short, sociological analyses of the city written by students, Ph.D. students, researchers and professors. One of South Africa's leading sociologists, Professor Ari Sitas, contributed a short play.

In a similar spirit, this book examines Gothenburg with a critical gaze. Books about cities too seldom have such a starting point. On the contrary, the process of urban transformation during the most recent decades, which has been driven by the global competition to attract business, tourists and a cultural middle class with disposable income, has had the tendency to give rise to publications that uncritically celebrate the city. This can happen in diametrically different ways. On the one hand, the process of transformation has encouraged publications with aesthetically pleasing colour photographs that celebrate the "renaissance of the city", with its new cafés and landmarks. On the other hand, the transformation has led to books that eulogise and mourn what has been lost. As long as these books, with their historical perspectives, do not become completely wrapped up in an idolising and idealising nostalgia, they can make meaningful contributions both to urban historical documentation and contemporary criticism.

But a critical examination of the transformation of cities cannot stop at noting what has been destroyed. It ought also to analyse the process of transformation itself – its driving forces, ideologies and consequences. Today, this is taking place to a great extent within international, interdisciplinary urban research. Urban sociology, which took a central position along with the growth of sociology as a discipline not least via the Chicago school, has today been renewed and made topical. This book, which contains 37 essays by researchers from a number of different disciplines, most of whom are sociologists at the

University of Gothenburg, aims to offer an insight into critical urban research on Gothenburg.

We asked the authors to write a text that would not require previous knowledge of Gothenburg, but at the same time would also offer native Gothenburgers a new perspective on their city. The texts discuss and analyse developments and social conditions in Gothenburg from specific perspectives. But they also look beyond the local, towards more general and global processes of urban change. We also decided to include extracts from the stage play *The mental states of Gothenburg* by Mattias Andersson. It is to a large extent made up by interviews with youths from different parts of the city, made by sociologists.

THE TRANSFORMATION OF THE CITY

The city of Gothenburg has gone through many transformations since 1621, when it was founded upon King Gustav II Adolf's directive in the area now known as Gamlestaden (Old City). These are related to processes usually known as modernity and globalisation. Starting with the Dutchmen who were asked to design and construct the original inner city area with its system of canals, Gothenburg has to a large extent been shaped by groups with knowledge and experience from other countries and parts of the world (see Martin Peterson's chapter).

Most of the texts in this book discuss aspects of the most recent transformations in Gothenburg. There are good reasons to say that in the last decades, the city has passed from industrialism to post-industrialism. As one of northern Europe's most important harbour cities, Gothenburg became one of Scandinavia's leading industrial cities during the breakthrough of industrial capitalism. During the first decades of the 20th century, a "proletarian public sphere" was established, with its base in the centrally located working-class neighbourhoods. This created a strong foundation for the growing workers' movement (see Håkan Thörn's chapter), and gradually drove the Social Democratic party to power after universal suffrage was introduced in 1921.

In 1932, when the Social Democrats began their uninterrupted 44-year reign and began the construction of the modern Swedish welfare model, it was no coincidence that this model was christened "Folk*hemmet*" ("The People's *Home*") by the Social Democratic Prime Minister Per-Albin Hansson. Besides the concept's ability to appeal to both radical and conservative populations, it also refers to the central position of housing policy, which is something that distinguishes the Swedish welfare state from that of other Scandinavian countries. In this area, Gothenburg came to serve as a reference point and a model for the policy that was launched in full scale at the national level (see Tiiu Soidre's chapter).

During the second half of the 20th century, the number of people employed in industry in Gothenburg halved, which is a clear indication of post-industrial development. But the concept "post-industrial" needs to be problematised, since it suggests that we have found ourselves in a new kind of society radically different from the industrial capitalist one. Perhaps the term "post-industrial" conceals the fact that the process of change is actually an issue of an increased market economy in relation to the societal model created during the epoch of the welfare state (see Bengt Furåker's chapter). At any rate, the present and the future of "post-industrialism's new order" seem significantly less idyllic than what Daniel Bell led people to expect in 1973, with his pioneering book *The Coming of a Post-Industrial Society*, not least when viewed from the perspective of suburban[1] youths (see Åsa Andersson's chapter).

The city planning researcher Thomas Hall has claimed that there is good reason to be critical of the concept "post-industrial society", which implies too sharp a break with "industrial society". Nevertheless, the concept is "particularly apt in the context of planning and urban development" – and not least in regard to harbour cities.[2] In the 1970s, the shipyard crisis that

1. The term 'suburb' does in a Swedish context refer to socially marginalised and stigmatised areas, where today mainly people with immigrant background live in projects built for the working class in the 1960s (the million dwellings programme, see Tiiu Soidre's, Ove Sernhede's and Ulla Björnberg's chapters).

2. Thomas Hall (1991) (ed.) *Planning and urban growth in the Nordic countries.* London: E & FN Spon., p. 238.

hit Gothenburg meant that the city's docks gradually began to be transformed in the same way as in a number of other European cities, such as Glasgow, London and Barcelona. Hall suggests that there are striking similarities in terms of change between Scandinavian harbour cities, such as Gothenburg, Oslo and Copenhagen, and London, which has been seen as a "model" for urban post-industrialisation. It was as a description of the London borough of Islington that Ruth Glass, writing in the 1960s, coined the term "gentrification" – that is to say, the successive upgrade of old working-class neighbourhoods in connection with an increased interest in these areas on the part of a new middle class, which is rich in "cultural capital" and covets an urban lifestyle.[3]

But perhaps within modern urban research, such a central concept as gentrification ought to be problematised as well, or at least contextualised – that is to say, modified with its starting point in studies of social relationships at the local level. Some of the chapters in this book's first section show how neighbourhoods such as Haga (see Håkan Thörn's chapter), Stampen (see Mats Franzén's chapter), Östra Kvillebäcken (see Gabriella Olshammar's chapter) and Långgatorna (see Joakim Forsemalm's chapter) have undergone similar changes during the last decades; yet they also prove to have specific and different patterns. The transformations in these neighbourhoods have also faced opposition from social activists, volunteer organisations and small businesses. To the extent that the transformation of cities can be understood in terms of gentrification, it is about a complex interplay between local, national and global processes. For example, the old working-class neighbourhood Haga, which for a century was the centre for the city's social movements, in some ways shows almost "ideal" gentrification patterns.[4] At the same time, housing policies have thus far slowed down the type of extreme rent increases that have taken place along with gentrification in inner cities in other countries.[5]

3. Ingrid Martins Holmberg (2006) *På Stadens yta. Om historiseringen av Haga* (*On the surface of the city. About the historicising of Haga*). Göteborg: Makadam förlag.

4. Ibid.

5. At the time of writing, this is changing, because the tenants' organisation has accepted a "position factor" in rental contracts, which in principle means a transition to market rents.

SELF IMAGE/S OF THE CITY

The articles in the second part of the book, "Self image/s of the city", analyse different aspects of how what is called "the Gothenburg spirit" has put its stamp on Gothenburg through its consensus-building mechanisms. In recent decades, the Gothenburg region has become known for its many "partnerships", primarily between municipalities and the business world (which can also include parts of civil society). These collaborations can be understood with the help of the locally well-known concept of "the Gothenburg spirit", which describes an official self-image and spirit of mutual understanding with deep historical roots (see Gunnar Falkemark's chapter).

The Gothenburg spirit was established in the 18th and 19th centuries, along with the growth of a strong culture of donation, through which the city's bourgeoisie made significant contributions to the foundation of public institutions such as libraries, institutions for the care of the poor, and homes and organisations for workers. When these institutions were taken over by the state and the municipality at the time of the establishment of the welfare state in the 20th century, the character and function of the Gothenburg spirit also changed. Now the spirit was primarily adapted to the "Saltsjöbad spirit", which was established on a national level – another characteristic distinguishing the Swedish welfare model. The Saltsjöbad spirit is based on the agreement made at the Grand Hotel in Saltsjöbaden in 1938 between the LO (Landsorganisationen – the central trade union that organised 87 % of the Swedish workers in the industrial and public sectors in the mid-20th century;[6] up through 1991, union membership also meant membership in the Social Democratic party) and the Svenska Arbetsgivarföreningen (the Swedish Employers' Federation). This was an agreement about the game rules for the Swedish labour market.

Post-war, the Gothenburg spirit's political alliance between the municipality and the business world was primarily about creating good conditions for heavy and globally successful

6. Åsa Forssell, Anna Fransson, Mats Larsson and Ingela Goding (2007) *Synen på fackligt medlemskap och fackets uppgifter* (*The view of union membership and the union's duties*). Röster om facket och jobbet rapport 1. Stockholm: LO.

Gothenburg-based industries such as SKF and Volvo. Volvo has had a major influence on local politics,[7] something legitimised by the company profiling itself as being culturally responsible. In the 1980s, Volvo sponsored not only the city's symphony orchestra and its most internationally successful football team, IFK Göteborg, but also what was then considered the niched and cineastic Gothenburg film festival. In this way, "The Spirit of Volvo", also the name of a song that the company gave on a cassette to all its employees in the 1980s, was intimately linked with the Gothenburg spirit.

7. Gunnar Falkemark (1991) *Politik, lobbyism och manipulation. Svensk trafikpolitik i verkligheten* (*Politics, lobbying and manipulation. Swedish traffic policies in reality*). Stockholm: Nya Doxa.

As the chairman of the Swedish Metal Workers' Union at the ball-bearing factory SKF in Gothenburg, and as a member of Gothenburg's municipal council for 37 years, Göran Johansson, known as "the strong man of Gothenburg", encouraged the local variant of the Saltsjöbad contract between work and capital in the Gothenburg spirit. Yet as the chairman of the municipal executive board between 1993 and 2008, he also led the way for another transformation of the Gothenburg spirit that meant a retreat from Saltsjöbad.

From the 1970s, there has been a lot of criticism of and opposition to the Saltsjöbad spirit, first from the radical left and then more successfully from the right, as the latter pushed through a wave of privatisation and deregulation (much of which during the Social Democratic regime) from the 1990s onwards. Starting in the 1990s, the successive disassembly of the classic Swedish welfare model took place under very palpable pressure from a globalised world economy.[8] Yet it could not have been carried out without ideological components. In the 1990s and 2000s, as the right-wing/liberal and Social Democratic governments at the national level took turns carrying out deregulation, privatisation and cut-backs of the public sector, Gothenburg has often been one step ahead in the same process. Here, policies have been legitimised through the Gothenburg spirit. In Gothenburg, these changes can in part be credited to Göran Johansson, who managed to use local political traditions to

8. For an analysis that incorporates the Swedish reorientation in a global political, financial and ideological context, see David Harvey (2005) *A brief history of neoliberalism*. Oxford: Oxford University Press.

adapt the Gothenburg region to the new structural conditions that arose with the globalised economy. Gothenburg thereby fulfils two of the criteria mentioned in international research about the growth of the new "entrepreneurial city": a base in a historically established political culture of consensus and the arrival of a political leader with strong legitimacy.[9]

In concrete terms, the process of transformation has meant both the privatisation of large portions of the municipality's work and also a change in power relations between the municipality and the business world (and to a certain extent, civil society). According to political scientist Gunnar Falkemark, the local Business Secretariat, which was created in the late 1970s in connection to the shipyard crisis, has a direct line to Gothenburg's political decision-makers.[10] Through such partnerships between the municipality and businesses, Gothenburg has taken the shape of a "local state", creating its own foreign affairs policies independent of the national level, with the goal of building business relationships and attracting foreign investment. In recent years, these policies have been successful with regard to the new major financial power that is China.

A fundamental idea in the Social Democratic rule of Gothenburg has been to market Gothenburg as an "event city", as part of building a new identity for the city in a post-industrial or globalised world. A specific company (Göteborg & Co.) was created to adapt and market Gothenburg as the ideal location for sports and cultural events, with a centrally located "event area", bordered by the amusement park, a number of museums, a convention centre, two football stadiums and an ice hockey arena. It was also Göteborg & Co.'s congress company Congrex that took the initiative for the 17th World Congress of Sociology in Gothenburg. The connection between Gothenburg and the global "event culture", one of the key components in the marketing of cities/regions that in international urban research have been analysed as "cultural strategies"[11] for meeting the increasing economic globalisation, can be viewed

9. See Tim Hall & Paul Hubbard (1998) (eds) *The entreprenurial city: Geographies of politics, regime and representation*. Chichester: Wiley, and Stephen Quilley (1999) "Entrepreneurial Manchester: The Genesis of Elite Consensus", in *Antipode*, vol. 31, no. 2.

10. Falkemark, p. 181.

11. Sharon Zukin (1995) *The cultures of cities*. London: Blackwell.

as yet another modification of the classic Gothenburg spirit. Its happy-go-lucky state of mind now has as its primary symbol a green rabbit whose home is the amusement park Liseberg ("the Liseberg rabbit").

Today, there are also signs that things are changing. In the global financial crisis that began in the autumn of 2008, the very foundations of Gothenburg's economy and identity were again shaken when the Swedish government distanced itself from Volvo, which was forced to make mass layoffs. The solid legitimacy that the company had always had in Gothenburg was also seriously undermined when, amidst the crisis, the company decided to keep its bonus system for the management. At the same time, people saw a completely new and dark picture of Gothenburg in the advertising posters of the Gothenburg Traffic and Public Transport Authority. The pictures show a vision of the city in the future that is way beyond the "sweet and happy Gothenburg" that has been a constant of the city's public self-image over the past decades. The message of the campaign is that it is the responsible individual, rather than the government, businesses or the city, that must act if the city is to be saved from environmental catastrophe (see Martin Letell's chapter).

When the environment, culture and sports are used to serve growth, then democracy and equality are often subordinated to the dictates of marketing. For example, "election cottages", which symbolise ambitions towards a democratic culture, were removed in order not to disturb the urban scenography constructed when the World Cup in track and field was held in Gothenburg (see Catharina Thörn's chapter). When the East India Company's 18th century ship was "re-built" in the 21st century and set on a journey to China, a problematic colonial inheritance was transformed into a celebration of Gothenburg as a historically successful trade city (see Mikela Lundahl's chapter). As at the national level, the Gothenburg spirit's ideological rhetoric has also comprised a sort of modernism, not least as manifested in *Göteborgs-Posten's* (the Gothenburg Post newspaper's) visions of the future, where "change" has been seen as the goal itself (see Barbara Czarniawska's chapter). As in national politics, the concept of "change" in the rhetoric of the Gothenburg spirit during the past decade has been synonymous with "liberalisation". The photographs taken in Gothenburg by the Mexican-born photographer and sociologist Rolando Vasquez, published in this book, challenge this type of unreflected thinking about progress. Beyond marketing's homogenous fictions about the city, Vasquez seeks another picture of Gothenburg in the traces on its walls.

A central aspect of the last decades' transformation of cities in western countries has been that political rule has begun to place more weight on "shaping up" the public space through measures supposed both to beautify the city and guarantee safety for citizens. A project typical of the Gothenburg spirit is where government agencies, municipal companies, volunteer groups and businesses work together on the project *Safe, beautiful city* (see Ingrid Sahlin's chapter). When public space is not just to be made safe but also beautiful, homelessness becomes a central policy problem, which in turn becomes a subject both for intense debate and for new ways of governing. In line with the partnership's (new) logic, the municipality has begun to place part of the responsibility for homelessness policies onto volunteer organisations and private companies (see Cecilia Hansen Löfstrand's chapter).

The official picture of the city of the Gothenburg spirit also ignores how, beyond the visual examples of harmonic diversity, there is a normative centre connected to "Swedishness". The fact that Gothenburg, despite the secularism proclaimed by the Swedish society, is a Christian city is made clear not least by the controversies that arose regarding the building of a mosque (see Göran Larsson's and Åke Sander's chapter). A powerful demonstration of a new, hybrid Gothenburg youth culture took place in connection to the tragic nightclub fire in Kvillebäcken in Hisingen in 1997, when 63 young people, all from Gothenburg's suburbs and most with immigrant backgrounds, were burned to death. However, both the event and the demonstration revealed a number of conflicts with economic, political and cultural consequences, namely in terms of structural inequality and segregation (see Abby Peterson's chapter).

Gothenburg's ambivalent approach to immigrants also manifests itself in the missing link between, on the one hand, official statements regarding the need to increase the city's population in order to increase economic growth, and on the other hand the need to decrease the number of asylum-seekers in order to reduce segregation (see Helena Holgersson's chapter).

THE CITY'S PERIPHERY

Certain places in the city serve as obvious references in both Gothenburg's official history and its current marketing. Others do not fit into any of these stories. In public space, some aspects of history are made visible at the expense of others. What we have chosen to call the *city's periphery* are areas of the city that currently are difficult to talk about, areas that both tempt and scare. In this category, you will primarily find areas on the edges of the city, where the number of foreign-born residents is the largest. But the category also includes historical places that are forgotten and/or purposefully ignored when Gothenburg remembers its history, such as the Franska tomten (the French block) in Gothenburg's harbour, close to the casino and the Opera. What seems to be an unimportant area of land is actually a piece of Swedish colonial history. In 1784, King Gustaf III gave what was then a repository to the French regent Louis XVI in exchange for the little Caribbean island of St. Barthélemy (see Klas Rönnbäck's chapter). This and similar pieces of history have generally been absent from Swedish history lessons. That so many school groups visit Franska tomten is instead explained by the fact that "The House of Emigrants" is now found in an old customs building that was built here in 1866.[12] It was in Gothenburg in the late 19th century that the one million or so Swedes who emigrated to North America stepped onto the ships that took them over the Atlantic, and it was in this building where they had their emigration contracts signed.[13] The House of Emigrants can be seen as a textbook example of what the French historian Pierre Nora called *sites of memory*, in this case a building that has been preserved so that the memory of Swedish emigration is not forgotten. Yet the memory of Swedish colonialism remains suppressed.[14]

The House of Emigrants has the expressed ambition of tying together Sweden's emigrant and immigrant history. But as with Sweden's colonial history, there is as yet no consensus about how the latter can be understood. Negotiations about *what* is to be given a place in the collective memory continually take place, as well as about *where* and *how*. As a Swedish phenomenon, immigration is seen as fairly new; historical descriptions of it often start with the immigration of workers in the 1960s. In terms of numbers this is justified, but at the same time it risks hiding the fact that people from all over the world, or at least from Europe, have been a noticeable part of the city image ever since Gothenburg was founded. The city has never been ethnically homogenous. The photographic archives suggest that Romany camps have always been here, often on the edges of the city, but sometimes also right in the centre, such as by Bergslagsbanan's station building, behind what is today the Nils Ericson terminal. However, Romany camps have not been allowed to be part of Gothenburg's collective memory, which among other reasons can be related to the fact that generally cities remember their history in connection with buildings that can be declared historical monuments. While most Swedes researching genealogy can relatively easily find documents regarding people who made a stop in Gothenburg around the turn of the century before leaving Sweden for America, there is little information about the Swedish Romany, who passed

12. That it was not the neighbourhood that today is called Franska tomten that was given to the French king is another story. (See Klas Rönnbäck's chapter.)

13. The House of Emmigrants website, http://emigranternashus.se/, 2009-04-21.

14. Pierre Nora (1989) "Between memory and history: *Les lieux de mémoire*", *Representations*, no. 26.

In the summer of 2009, cars were set on fire for the first time in Gothenburg's suburbs. However, it is risky to compare this to what happened in France in 2005. In Gothenburg, protest forms other than fires and throwing stones are more common. In Gothenburg's stigmatised suburbs today, there is a hip-hop culture that, like youth culture in similar places in the world's big cities, comments on policies that seem to strengthen the spatial and mental segregation that has grown over recent decades. In their YouTube hit "I skuggan av den blågula flaggan" ("In the shadow of the blue and yellow flag"), the Gothenburg group Wordsilah ("silah" means "weapon" in Arabic) criticises a modern Sweden that shifts ever further from the visions of the welfare state. Dialogue about the failed integration policies of the last decades is still possible (see Ove Sernhede's chapter). What space – in history books and in Gothenburg's public spaces – these discussions get in the future when Sweden's history is told remains to be seen.

THE CITY AS A STAGE AND PUBLIC SPACE

A number of the processes described in this book are located in the city's public spaces. When one looks for *the public sphere* in a specific city environment such as Gothenburg, one soon realises that, just as in other cities, it cannot be referred to in the singular. To start with, the concepts of the *public sphere* and *public space* have several meanings. First, they refer to places for political discussion in the city, second to places that are the scene for common activities (demonstrations, carnivals, celebrations), and third to places for informal (often impersonal and anonymous) meetings between people.[17] In practice, these functions can coincide, but the city's public spaces are also divided geographically and, not least, subculturally.

17. Fran Tonkiss (2005) *Space, the city and social theory. Social relations and urban forms*. Cambridge: Polity.

In all three uses of public space, associations are made spontaneously with the city's central areas. Here people enjoy the greatest anonymity (even if Gothenburg sometimes can be experienced as a small city in this regard). It is where large-scale political demonstrations are held; according to Jürgen Habermas' image of the "bourgeois public sphere", public space is typically located in the cafés in the centre of the city. It can be parenthetically added that, compared to many other big European cities, Gothenburg's café life is still holding out fairly strongly against the monopolisation of the market by multinational coffee chains; it is, however, unclear to what extent the relative independence of cafés affects the free communication of ideas and opinions. The best examples of dynamic political discussions in public can be found in the slightly more organised events at Folkets Hus (The People's Building), or at Gothenburg Social Forum at Hagabion [the Haga Cinema].

The most ambitious attempt to create a political public sphere in Gothenburg in the last years was probably "Det fria ordets festival" ("The Freedom of Speech Festival"), planned in 2001 as the counterpart to the EU summit meeting held in the city at the same time.[18] This festival was unfortunately overshadowed by the violence between the police and demonstrators in other parts of the city. The exchange of opinions in the form of public discussions and peaceful demonstrations took place, tellingly enough, in parallel to the political violence and state repression (see Mattias Wahlström's chapter).

Even if, historically speaking, riots are a recurring event in Gothenburg, they are still an exception to the overwhelming majority of well-ordered demonstrations. But more peaceful forms of protest have not excluded creativity. The local environmental movement's campaign against motorism includes both bike demonstrations and sitting blockades. To a certain extent, protesters have followed an ever more individualised zeitgeist by shifting from the public and general to the individual and hidden, for example by sabotaging SUVs (see Olle Hagman's chapter).

If one is to find interesting political conflicts in Gothenburg's public spaces, one should not stop on the street. If you

18. For a critical discussion, see Sara Uhnoo (2002) "Demokrati i offentliga rum. En studie av Forum 2001 – det fria ordets festival" ("Democracy in public space. A study of Forum 2001 – the freedom of speech festival") in Micael Björk and Abby Peterson (eds), *Vid politikens yttersta gräns. Perspektiv på EU-toppmötet i Göteborg 2001* (*At the furthest border of politics. Perspectives on the EU summit meeting in Gothenburg 2001*). Stockholm/Stehag: Brutus Östlings bokförlag Symposion.

step into churches, for example, you will also find controversies. Gothenburg's diocese is said to be one of the more religiously conservative ones within the Church of Sweden. This did not stop the Annedal Church in central Gothenburg from being the second in the country to host the controversial photography exhibit Ecce Homo in 1998. This picture suite, in which paraphrases of classical religious motifs represent, among others, leather gays, transsexuals and victims of homophobic violence, aroused such anger locally that it had to have police protection. Perhaps *thanks to* the conservative faction in the Gothenburg diocese, the city has one of the more active groups of homosexual, bisexual and transsexual Christians, who among other things have contributed to pushing through the issue of homosexual weddings (see Daniel Enstedt's chapter).

If, after all, acceptance for homosexuality in the private sphere is on the rise in Sweden and Gothenburg, in relation to non-heterosexual family structures, the picture becomes slightly different when one looks at the degree of tolerance for homosexuals in the public sphere. Gothenburg distinguished itself during the 1990s for the high number of violent crimes against homosexuals committed on the city's streets. The situation seems to have improved, and for homosexuals today Gothenburg is a significantly safer city to be in than, for example, Stockholm, according to statistics of the BRÅ (the Swedish National Council for Crime Prevention).[19]

19. In 2008, 8 crimes per 100 000 residents were classified as hate crimes against homosexuals, as compared with 28 in Stockholm and 11 in Malmö; see Klara Klingspor & Anna Molarin (2009) *Hatbrott 2008* (*Hate crime 2008*). Sockholm: BRÅ.

From another perspective, homosexual practices can be said to have become more marginalised in public spaces during the past decades. An example is homosexual men's anonymous meetings in parks. Around the middle of the 20th century, the city park's public urinals were used as sexual meeting places, typically between men with a more overt homosexual identity and "real men" – not seldom working-class men who did not identify themselves as homosexual (see Arne Nilsson's chapter). As with working-class neighbourhoods, this public space can in part be said to have been "built away" (the urinals have been demolished, the bushes have been cut down and new forms of housing have made routes through the park less common. Gothenburg's male homosexual life has to a large extent moved to clubs and to settled family life.

Another male-dominated public space that has been built away in Gothenburg is the early 20th century proletarian public sphere in what were then working-class neighbourhoods such as Haga, Masthugget, Gamlestaden, Landala and Majorna. As opposed to the inner city's more anonymous civil public sphere, here, in a more collective spirit, a counter-public was cultivated that formed the base for a radical and anti-authoritarian faction of the worker's movement (see Sten O Karlsson's chapter). In practice, this environment was crushed when the old buildings in these neighbourhoods were torn down and replaced with modern but more anonymous building complexes.

The buildings themselves set the tone in the public spaces and also reflect social ideologies and power relationships. This relationship is confirmed if one looks at how buildings are talked about in public discussions, for example in the case of the new buildings in the 1930s on Gothenburg's main street – Kungsportsavenyn. The buildings' strict and controlled facades were discussed in the same terms as disciplined and unclothed women's bodies (see Michael Landzelius' chapter). In the pure and functionalistic aesthetic that blossomed, one can also find an important piece of the puzzle in regard to the wave of demolitions that occurred during later decades. As the previously mentioned discussions regarding gentrification show, it seems that today this aesthetic is mostly being replaced with an aestheticisation of the picturesque aspects of the buildings that survived the modernising demolitions.

When the city's public spaces are to be made attractive for visitors and residents, it is not enough to have aesthetic qualities. Safety and security are two related themes, whose importance to politics and social discussions in recent years has increased exponentially. Only seldom, however, is the relationship between actual security and experienced safety problematised; the same is true of *which* social groups' security is referred to in these discussions.

BRÅ collects annual statistics that show that Swedes generally are remarkably secure, in the sense that they are not particularly afraid of becoming victims of crime.[20] When Gothenburg youths discuss unsafe places, it is clear that unsafeness varies a lot, depending not just on *where* one is, but also on *who* one is. The public spaces of peripheral neighbourhoods are described both as more dangerous and less dangerous than the centre, according to whether the person has a connection to the place or not (see Sara Uhnoo's chapter).

20. Åsa Irlander & Jennie Wigerholt (2009) *Nationella trygghetsundersökningen 2008. Om utsatthet, trygghet och förtroende* (*National safety study 2008. On vulnerability, safety and trust*). Stockholm: BRÅ.

To return to gender and sexuality, personal safety in the city in general is worse for those who publicly reject the dominant heterosexual norm. An example is men who choose to defy the heteronormative clothing code in public places. Men who want to wear skirts in Gothenburg feel relatively safe only if they have clear markers – such as a beard – that are connected to heterosexuality. Anonymous places in the centre of the city are experienced as safer than places where they can be recognised (see Cathrin Wasshede's chapter).

While the men in skirts feel safest in the city's most anonymous environments, many women connect these places with unsafeness. It is also in the public space that authorities concentrate their efforts on stopping sexual crime. The public arena is incorrectly felt to be the most dangerous place for a woman. The flipside of this is that many women underestimate the risks connected with more private places, and their strategies for avoiding being faced with sexual violence are often focused primarily on public places. In the worst cases, these strategies can even turn out to be counterproductive (see Anne-Lie Steen's chapter).

GOTHENBURG – SPECIFIC AND GENERAL

It has not been difficult to find patterns that connect the different contributions in this book, and the reader will surely find more. Themes such as globalisation, gentrification, segregation and creating safety in public spaces recur and bind the essays beyond the book's already broad divisions. In contrast to the simplified and propagandistic pictures of Gothenburg that we criticised, the contributions reveal the reality of the city as complex, contradictory and hard to pin down.

In contemporary social scientific discussions, the big city is often referred to as the arena where the most important global oppositions and conflicts are played out. In these contexts, it is often referred to as "The City", in the singular, definite form. The focus is on global mega-metropolises such as New York, London and Tokyo, and on the general characteristics that these cities share. The contributions in our book show that general social processes can also be studied in smaller and peripheral cities, together with their unique aspects. By comparing the leading "global cities" with smaller cities, one can problematise and complicate the picture of what are often characterised as overarching processes of urban transformation. With this anthology, we aim to contribute to an increased sensitivity both to what is general and what is specific in contemporary processes of urban transformation.

1. THE TRANSFORMATION OF THE CITY

Martin Peterson

FOUR CENTURIES OF MULTICULTURE

The medieval walled city that became the standard in besieged Byzantium contained a mixed population of some significance. In any sea or river port city of a certain stature, several languages were habitually spoken. But one cultural level would prevail over another. Thus, deep in the DNA of any such city there is a recognition of asymmetric pluralism. A comparatively young port city such as Gothenburg is no exception. It was deeply affected by the immigration of specialists and a general transnational impact on its municipal development and integration into the economy of western Europe.

In Scandinavia, capitals such as Stockholm and Copenhagen fully met these prototypical criteria but both were turned eastward. Bergen, on the other hand, was a model for those turned westward, including the much later founded Gothenburg. Bergen was a major Hansa trading place from the 13th century onwards, largely owned by German multinational companies, which ruled as they pleased during the 14th and 15th centuries. After that, it served as the main city of Danish-occupied Norway until Sweden became the new occupier in the 19th century.

In spite of an excellent natural port position, Gothenburg was not established until 1621. Before that, it mainly served a defensive purpose against hostile sea forces. But compared to and in contrast with Bergen, it remained much less controlled from abroad. Its main feature was a steady recruitment of experts from other North Sea sources for the construction of its major institutions and supply services. In the mid-17th century, Jean de la Vallée, a famous French architect from a family that had migrated some years earlier to Sweden, was recruited to design the main fortress in the harbour – the fortress of Älvsborg.

EARLY MODERNITY: THE IMPACT OF NORTHERN SEA SHORES

As the town came into being, its founding industry was a shipyard and a shipping industry to which the Dutch branch expert, Albrecht van der Velden, was recruited, operating through other Dutch, German, Scottish and local business partners. Mid-century, a Walloon family called De la Gardie took control of the shipyard and made a deal with the Crown, which rented it to build a warship fleet there. First there were Dutch, and after 1660, increasingly British managers, since British marine interests had begun to outcompete those of the Dutch.

At the same time, a foundry was established in the centre of town to which an expert from Hamburg, Hans Ternant, was invited to operate. He in turn was succeeded forty years later by a younger associate from Bremen. A Dutch farmer and dairy expert, Johan van Buren, or Jan de Buur as he came to be called locally, came to supply the town inhabitants with food. He happened to have several Dutch namesakes, who were already settled in Gothenburg in various less visible and even menial positions. One food-supplying property was named Waterloo after the Flemish owners and labourers. In van Buren's treaty with the municipality, he became the major producer of dairy products. His name remains in, for instance, Burgården (Buur's estate) gymnasium. His closest neighbour and friend was another transnational recruit and the main brewer in town.[1]

1. See Sören Skarback (1992) *Göteborg på 1600-talet (Gothenburg in the 17th century)*. Göteborg: Tre Böcker, and Bertil Andersson (1998) *Från fästningsstad till handelsstad 1620–1820 (From fort to trade city 1620–1820)*. Meddelande från Ekonomisk-historiska institutionen vid Göteborgs universitet.

In the 1640s, the judicial and commercial president of Gothenburg municipality received higher civil servants and bureaucrats at his countryside mansion for conferences. This was located in Örgryte, now an upper class district. The town clerk, Claudius Kloot, studied law at a Dutch university and the exchange among political officials was reported to be relaxed and casual, conducted in a mixture of languages including Swedish, Dutch, German and English (with a mostly Scottish accent), confirming the linguistic and cultural pluralism the town was founded on.

However, Gothenburg was also a refuge from political oppression, for example in the case of the Irish rebels who in 1641 came from the Irish town of Kilkenny (Cill Choinningh in Gaelic), fleeing a British invasion. They were supported financially by a Scot named MacLear. This was recorded by a Polish doctor, who treated a sick woman in the Irish group. Similarly, German refugee immigration grew during the Thirty Years' War. In 1624, a German community with a salaried staff was formed around the German Church.

There were Scottish barbers doing occasional surgical operations. Others set up shops selling imported goods such as spices and chemicals for medicinal puposes, and they were in competition with German chemists owners. During the 18th century, an increasing number of Britons arrived as traders, labourers or simple shopkeepers such as bakers or as labourers. Some also came through the extensive and comprehensive smuggling of an assortment of goods via the dense archipelago to the north of Gothenburg. Larger waves of immigration regularly occurred during times of comprehensive warfare such as the Napoleonic wars.

However, no record of individual immigration existed until the first Jewish immigrants were registered in the 1780s. In the early 19th century, they made up one-tenth of the traders and a smaller number of the craftsmen in Gothenburg. They brought a new dynamism and a quest for quality to the markets in town. However, it took a parliamentary decision in 1870 for the implementation of their full formal citizenship, even though everyday behaviour towards them could still be both discriminatory and erratic.

THE BEGINNINGS AND TAKE-OFF OF HIGH MODERNITY

Gothenburg only surpassed Stockholm as the foremost export harbour in the 1850s. With increasing opportunities for trade and exports, Gothenburg attracted more professional immigrants, such as bankers, lawyers and physicians, who became decisive in modernising society. For instance, the gradual immigration of Jewish physicians brought with it a combined approach of healthcare and social policy aspects. They observed the deprivation brought to large social groups by incipient industrialisation and haphazard urban planning. At the same time, they noted that the local charity associations only reproduced an already miserable situation. They made the first steps toward public social policy measures, which a little later became the model for all of Sweden.

In the 1890s, with the worldwide general modernisation of industrial machines, tools and production methods, Gothenburg took an abrupt leap into industrialisation on a wider scale. Foreign investment and specialisation among credit institutions played a decisive part in this process. However, the class divide between a well-ensconced, sometimes opulent bourgeoisie of partly immigrant background, who had made good in this process, and the labouring classes, haphazardly recruited to the new industries, created segregation and antagonism throughout town. An immigrant architect contributed substantially to the launching of accessible quality housing as functionalism as the "new humanism" towards the late interwar period.[2]

During the first half of the 20th century, immigration re-

2. Torsten Hansson (1998) *Vi byggde Göteborg* (*We built Gothenburg*). Lund: Hjalmarson & Högberg.

mained steadily low at 7 000 to 10 000 per annum. It rose somewhat during the interwar period due to escapes from European totalitarian regimes. The comparatively modest figures for the 1930s had to do with stricter immigration controls; the fear of importing a problem that would inevitably provoke the German Nazi regime remains one of the shameful features of those days. Gothenburg had the largest Jewish community and was also more polarised than any other Swedish city at the time.[3]

Nevertheless, the number of Jewish officials on public or juridical boards was not reduced in Gothenburg except in one or two conspicuous cases. Jews often heard anti-Semitic threats from colleagues but mostly it stayed at the level of threat. Many public figures spoke with forked tongues and mostly in accordance with war tidings.[4] At the same time, Gothenburg housed as a refugee the world-class philosopher Ernst Cassirer, whose legacy to the town came in the form of an Ernst Cassirer society.

3. Sven Nordlund (2002) "Sverige – emigrationslandet som blev invandringsland" ("Sweden – emigrant country that became immigrant country") in Lena Andersson-Skogh & Olle Krantz (eds) *Omvandlingens sekel* (*The century of transformation*). Lund: Studentlitteratur, pp. 322–326, and Hugo Valentin (1964) *Judarna i Sverige* (*The Jews in Sweden*). Stockholm: Bonniers, p. 151.

4. Sven Nordlund (2009) *Affärer som vanligt. Ariseringen i Sverige 1933–45* (*Business as usual. Aryanisation in Sweden 1933–45*). Lund: Sekel förlag, pp. 108–132.

CONCLUSION

Up until to the first post-war decade, much immigration had been orderly, dominated by often handpicked labour, and at best was also humanitarian. It was limited to certain reliable populations, such as the Sudeten Germans, whose social democratic representation had close ties with their Swedish counterparts. Soon after the war, Italian and Balkan populations were handpicked to come to the major transnational industries in Gothenburg, such as Volvo and SKF. They were assigned certain quarters of town, which became theirs in practice, and they were only very slowly integrated.

Gradually growing multicultural conditions were a common feature of port cities, which then also accumulated an intensified exchange of information and ideas. That was the built-in condition in Gothenburg from the start. Hence, there were few if any palpable ethnic conflicts of the sort that were frequent elsewhere. The exchange of multicultural ideas was inherent and hence set its mark on the very gradual and seemingly harmonious growth of the town up to the phase of industrialisation, when more complex processes of urbanity unfolded.

The rapid and successful growth of export industries at the beginning of the 20th century, bringing with it the creation of new districts, created a first wave of more significant housing segregation. The centre of town still contained districts of very mixed class backgrounds, which vouched for relative civil harmony. The segregated conditions paved the way for the construction of still more new districts, causing processes of unintended and systemically generated large-scale future ethnic segregation (see Ulla Björnberg's chapter in this book).

Martin Peterson
is attached to the research department of Social Philosophy at the University of Bergen and the European Research Institute ICCR in Vienna and Paris.

Håkan Thörn

PROLETARIANS, PROGGERS AND PUNKS
Folkhemmet, Haga and a hundred years of social movements

I

On 4 November 1972, Swedish media reported that Hagahuset (Haga Hall), a municipal youth recreation centre in central Gothenburg, had been squatted by a group of young people. The action was a protest against the closing of the centre by the municipality, who claimed that the youth who were visiting the centre used drugs and disturbed the order in the city. One of the banners that the squatters put on display on the front wall of the house stated, "Struggle for Our Democratic Rights", and the squatters asked for a debate with municipal politicians in order to demand their own house in the city centre.

It was neither the first nor the last time that Haga has been the centre of national attention. For more than a century, the district has been a space for social movements, for struggles between different modernities and for pro-active responses to globalisation processes. Along with other working-class neighbourhoods in Gothenburg's inner city, Haga was singled out as an object for slum clearance by the municipality.[1] However, from the early 1970s, the inhabitants of Haga mobilised in order

1. Ingrid Martins Holmberg (2006) *På Stadens yta. Om historiseringen av Haga* (*On the surface of the city. On the historicising of Haga*). Göteborg: Makadam förlag.

to preserve the district. For 15 years, buildings were continuously squatted and Haga became the site of an "alternative culture", encompassing cultural, political and social movements of national significance. The last squatting of a demolition-threatened building took place in the autumn of 1986, and was carried out by youths who called themselves *Husnallarna* (The house snatchers).[2]

2. "Husnallarna" is a play with words as it means both "those who snatch houses" and "the Teddy bears in the house", the latter signalling the non-militant character of the squatting activists.

II

The Haga Hall was built in 1897 as the Dickson Public Library, financed by Robert Dickson. At that time, Haga was a working-class neighbourhood and the Dickson family, of Scottish heritage, was the leading family in Gothenburg's middle class. The Dicksons were engaged patrons who saw it as their mission to educate the working-class. They financed homes for workers in Haga and also supported the building of the liberal Workers' Union House.[3] The building expanded during the coming decade until it comprised a whole block in Haga.

3. The summary of the worker's movement meeting places in Haga is based on Lars G Strömberg (1996) "Arbetarrörelsens mötesplatser i Göteborg 1890–1920" ("The worker's movement meeting places in Gothenburg 1890–1920"), in Håkan Andréasson et al. *Vardag som vetenskap* (*Every day as science*). Göteborg: Etnologiska föreningen.

The Worker's Union, which was led by the editor-in-chief of *Handelstidningen* (The Business Times), S.A. Hedlund, did not welcome the working-class' self-organisation. From the 1880s, this manifested itself through an increasing interest in socialist ideas among workers, as well as through a growing membership in labour unions and in the Social Democratic Workers' Party. The tension between the liberal Worker's Union and the emerging worker's movement should be understood as an expression of a class-based political conflict, even if the leaders of the Workers' Union wanted to make it seem as though it was something else. In January 1882, the Workers' Union rejected an inquiry from the chairman of the Social Democrats, August Palm, who wanted to come to the Workers' Union building to hold the first Social Democratic speech in Gothenburg. When explaining the rejection, the Workers' Union argued that they could not "show solidarity with impractical positions", since "socialism's well-meant and in some cases good efforts lack the potential to be practically executed".[4] Instead, Palm gave his speech at the nearby variety show house Concert du Boulevard on Södra Allégatan street.

4. From Strömberg (1996), p. 343.

From the middle of the 1880s, however, the Workers' Union building began to open its doors more and more to labour unions. In 1886, the country's first socialist union banner was inaugurated in the house before a meeting in Slottsskogen, where thousands of workers gathered to hear Palm speak.

The worker's movement did however create its own centre in another part of Haga, near Skanstorget, below the old fortification Skansen Krona. In 1886, at Bergsgatan 24 (now Skolgatan 29), statutes were adopted for the Gothenburg's worker's commune, with representatives from 13 unions present. In the same year, an organisation was created for working-class women, with the goal of mobilising women to join unions and demand the same salary as men. The building strengthened its position as the centre for a growing proletarian public sphere in Gothenburg when it became the locale for the worker's movement's newspaper *Ny Tid* (New Times), and for the co-operative organisation Fram (Forward). This proletarian public sphere expanded even more when Folkets Hus (The People's Hall) opened in the building in 1899. It became the most important meeting place for the workers' movement in Gothenburg.

Not far from Folkets Hus, another important meeting place was created in Haga in 1905 when Verdandi, the youth and temperance organisation of the workers' movement, opened a café on Husargatan. Lively political discussions took place here. The radical young socialist wing that was associated with the newspaper *Stormklockan* (Storm Clock) had its own room at Café Verdandi, which was called the Red Room and had a portrait of Karl Marx decorating one of the walls.

III

In 1917, the year of workers' revolts in Europe, Folkets Hus moved to Järntorget. In Gothenburg, 40 000 hungry women and men marched through Haga in "the bread riot" that took place that year in a number of Swedish cities. Angry demonstrators smashed shop windows in Haga and the police's attacks with sabres and batons were met with cobblestones.[5] In this year, the Swedish Social Democrats split. Among the groups that went to the newly created Sweden's Social Democratic Left Party (from 1921, it was Sweden's Communist Party) was the group from *Stormklockan* at Café Verdandi.

The year of the end of the war can also be said to have started a period that included the highpoint and the big political breakthrough for the movement wave that broke out in Swedish society during the last decades of the 19th century. Fifteen years later, the Social Democrats began their unbroken 44 years of government rule and announced a welfare programme that, in a now-classic speech, Per-Albin Hansson christened *Folkhemmet* (The People's Home). Its rhetorical architecture and hegemonic claims were certainly built on the foundation laid by the culture of the people's movements and manifested in Folkets Hus buildings across the country. In reality, however, the Social Democrats' takeover brought along an institutionalisation and professionalization that separated parties and unions from the proletarian public sphere that had grown organically in Haga and other working-class neighbourhoods (see Sten O Karlsson's chapter in this book).[6] The belief in a carefree modernism within the party's leadership also created an active destruction of the material public space that had been one of the important conditions for the growth of the worker culture.

5. Hans Nyström (1994) *Hungeruppropret 1917* (*The hunger riot 1917*). Ludvika: Zelos.

6. Sten O Karlsson (1993) *Arbetarfamiljen och det nya hemmet. Om bostadshygien och klasskultur i mellankrigstidens Göteborg* (*The working-class family and the new home. On housing hygiene and class culture in Gothenburg between the wars*). Stockholm/Stehag: Symposion.

IV

During the most expansive phase of the Swedish welfare state in the 1960s, the so-called million dwellings programme was launched by the government. To solve the ever more acute lack of housing, a million new homes were built (see Tiiu Soidre's chapter in this book). The goal was to increase the standard of living for the Swedish working-class. The old working-class neighbourhoods were often falling apart after decades of bad maintenance, and the standards for the flats were far from the norms that were now established as the minimum requirements for good housing in a country that saw itself as a world leader in welfare. Therefore, the 1960s became the decade of demolition in Gothenburg. One by one, old working-class areas in the inner city were flattened. There was, however, opposition to the process in Annedal, Landala and, some years later and most successfully, Haga. As the working-class families moved out to the newly built suburbs, the old working-class neighbourhood received new residents. They were children of the welfare state, born after the Second World War. Many were university students – higher education expanded significantly at the time and was no longer an option only for the children of the privileged. Haga's new residents, who often had temporary rental contracts in places that were to be demolished, were as happy about their newly won simplicity and community in Haga as the working-class families about their new luxury in the shining flats in the suburbs Bergsjön, Västra Frölunda and Hisings Backa. In the old houses, there were once again collective ways of living, if with different conditions and forms than the collectivity that had characterised the working-class areas earlier in the 20th century.

Haga was now a local and national centre for the alternative culture that was created in the wake of the student and hippie revolts of the 1960s. After the police ended the squatting of Hagahuset in 1972, the municipality offered young people a locale on Sprängkullsgatan, where the organisation "Sprängkullen" became perhaps the most important stage in the country for the so-called "progressive music movement".[7] Haga was a strong base for the anti-Vietnam movement, which during the early 1970s dominated the new movement culture. Also, the Swedish pioneers of the new women's movement – Group 8 – had their first meeting in Hagahuset in 1971. Several hundred women came, and the next year the group opened its own space in Haga.[8]

The squatting of empty houses and other actions that took place during the 1970s also often brought attention to other political issues at the same time. At the most concrete level, there was a demand for cheap housing and public meeting places for youths. The squattings were also a protest against the planned demolition of the neighbourhood. People tried, by referring to the area's working-class history, to upgrade the neighbourhood from "inner city slum" to "historical cultural inheritance". An alliance was formed between the student-dominated Haga Group and an organisation run by older workers who still lived in the area. Along with this, there was general criticism of the transformation of the inner city by the "office-ising" and commercialisation of public spaces. In 1979, the Haga Group organised an international conference about city planning in Hagahuset. To a significant extent, critique was articulated in anti-capitalist Marxist terms, which raised the question of a larger democratic urban citizenship. The protests were also connected to the growing environmental movement (see Olle Hagman's chapter in this book), where the protection of Haga, with its narrow, pedestrian-friendly cobblestone streets, was viewed as a bastion against increased car use.

V

When the last occupation in Haga took place in 1986 by the so-called Husnallarna, a generational shift in Haga's alternative culture had occurred. Sprängkullen's stage had long ago been taken over by punk bands, the squatters' hair was coloured black,

7. David Thyrén (2009) *Musikhus i centrum. Två lokala praktiker inom den svenska progressiva musikrörelsen: Uppsala Musikforum och Sprängkullen i Göteborg* (*Music hall in the centre. Two local practices within the Swedish progressive music movement: Uppsala Musikforum and Sprängkullen in Gothenburg*). Stockholm: Stockholms universitet.

8. Eva Schmitz (2007) *Systerskap som politisk handling. Kvinnors organisering i Sverige 1968 till 1982 (Sisterhood as a political action. Women's organisation in Sweden 1968–1982).* Lund: Sociologiska institutionen, Lunds universitet.

red and purple, their leather jackets decorated with the symbols of anarchism. Now it was also clear how the mediathisation of politics, which in the 1960s was still in its infancy, affected the social movements' participation in public debates.[9] When the squatters invited politicians to a public debate at Allégården (previously Hagahuset), they dominated the room with their analyses and problematisations of housing policies. But when they were invited to a TV studio, they had trouble asserting themselves against the Minister of Housing, who had been trained to take advantage of all of media's opportunities. The highly aesthetised media dramaturgy transformed Husnallarna, with their punk style, into exotic and "cute" comic book figures. When, soon after, the squatted house was demolished, it meant that the No Future generation had lost the last battle for Haga.

9. Håkan Thörn (1991) "Rörelser i det senmoderna" ("Movements in the late modernity"), in Jan Carle & Hans-Erik Hermansson (eds) *Ungdom i rörelse* (*Youth in movement*). Göteborg: Daidalos; Håkan Thörn (2006) *Anti-Apartheid and the emergence of a global civil society*. Basingstoke/New York: Palgrave Macmillan.

VI

This text was written at the Department of Sociology, in the Social Science Complex along Sprängkullsgatan, on Haga's border with Vasastan. The Complex was opened some years after the last chord faded from Sprängkullen's stage. My window looks out on Skanstorget, which a hundred years ago was the place for the workers's movements' meeting place Folkets Hus and its newspaper *Ny Tid*. But today, as in other places in Haga, there are no traces of the century-long presence of social movements. Of course, the workers' movement history has been memorialised outside Folkets Hus on the other side of Järntorget, where a sculpture has been dedicated to the hunger riot of 1917. The global justice movement's protests against George W. Bush and the EU summit in 2001 did not get any closer to Haga than Järntorget (see Mattias Wahlström's chapter in this book). It is symptomatic that the new wave of squatting that swept through Sweden at the end of the 2000s in Gothenburg had its base in Gamlestaden, which is now subject to the same type of gentrification pressures that Haga faced in the 1980s.

The only visible trace of the alternative culture of the 1970s is the vegetarian restaurant Solrosen on Kaponjärgatan. Allégården/Hagahuset is still a public space, but it now houses, in comparison to the early political-related groups, a depoliticised civil society: yoga courses, pensioners' meetings, male choirs.

It is probably thanks to the Haga activists that Haga was renovated "carefully", and that its cobblestone streets and small-scale were preserved. But the lack of success for the social and democratic demands that were made has meant that the fruits of this victory, which are mainly on the aesthetic level, have primarily been harvested by the forces that were the objects of the movement's criticisms. In the global marketing of Gothenburg, Haga is now shown as a picturesque cultural inheritance, and the boutiques along Haga Nygata are increasingly exclusive. The proximity to the university influences café life. The gentrification of Haga that began at the end of the 1980s is now complete. In the 21st century, the social movements have moved out of Haga.

Håkan Thörn
is Professor of Sociology at the University of Gothenburg. His research concerns social movements, globalisation and urban processes of transformation.

Tiiu Soidre

GOOD HOUSING – FOR ALL?

THE INQUIRY ON THE SOCIAL CONDITIONS OF HOUSING

In 1945, there was a large housing exhibition, “Live Better”, at Guldheden in Gothenburg.[1] In the exhibition catalogue, one can read the following: “The lack of norms in today’s housing production means *functionally* there is a bad fit with the housing’s functions and the need of the residents, *economically* it is a waste of expensive space and technically there is an obstruction to *rational* production.”[2] The inquiry that was the basis of the exhibition was judged to be valuable for the continued development of plans for flats. They began to be created on the basis of housing research, and norms on overcrowding were designed and established. The potential housing consumer was the family and it was the (nuclear) family’s assumed needs that were the foundation of the development of “Good Housing”, which was the name of the collection of norms that the Swedish Housing Board published for the first time in 1954.

During the first decades of building of “the people’s home”, housing relationships in the typical working-class city of Gothen-

1. This very compressed historical description builds upon Tiiu Soidre-Brink (1987) *Boendets förändring och kollektivt handlande* (*Housing’s change and collective action*). Monograph no. 36 from the Department of Sociology, Gothenburg University, and Tiiu Soidre-Brink (1991) “Det goda boendet – vision och illusion. Exemplet miljonprogrammet” (“Good housing – vision and illusion. The example of the million dwellings programme”), in Sven E Olsson & Göran Therborn (eds), *Vision möter verklighet. Om social styrning och faktisk samhällsutveckling* (*Vision meets reality. On social steering and the actual development of society*). Stockholm: Allmänna Förlaget.

2. Soidre-Brink (1991), pp. 98–99.

burg were an important reference point for the formation of national housing policies. In the 1930s, the housing situations in Gothenburg were discussed in an inquiry that was carried out by architect Uno Åhrén and economist Gunnar Myrdal (also see Sten O Karlsson's chapter in this book). It laid the groundwork for what was later treated more in depth in The Social Conditions of Housing Inquiry (see below), in which both Åhrén and Myrdal were members. During 1932–1943, Åhrén was the head city planner in Gothenburg. He was a very active social debater as well as the initiator of, and first secretary for, the Sociological Association that was created in 1942 in Gothenburg. In 1947, Åhrén was made a professor of city planning at the Royal Institute of Technology in Stockholm.

The goals for Swedish housing policies were formulated in the inquiry on social conditions for housing in 1945. Research had shown that the lack of housing was all-encompassing. Overcrowding was common, especially among families with children, and the standards of the housing were insufficient. There was political unanimity about the overarching goals of housing policies, of which the foremost was that the housing shortage and overcrowded conditions had to end by the beginning of the 1960s. "Good housing for all" was the overarching political goal. With this new direction for housing policies, the municipalities had an increased responsibility for the provision of housing. An instrument of this was that politically run non-profit municipal housing companies were to contribute to providing the population with good homes. The market was not thought to be adequate.

Getting rid of the housing shortage and overcrowded conditions are still goals for housing policy, and there are non-profit municipal housing companies in most Swedish municipalities. In Gothenburg, there are currently (in 2009) five non-profit municipal housing companies that manage homes, particularly blocks of flats, and one that mostly produces small homes. All are part of the umbrella organisation Förvaltnings AB

Framtiden [Future Management Ltd], which is owned by the city of Gothenburg. Of the almost 200 000 flats in blocks in Gothenburg, around one-third are owned by these non-profit companies.[3]

3. *Göteborgsbladet* 2008. PDF 2009-03-20 (www4.goteborg.se/prod/G-info/statistik.nsf/3a1ad6102b0c4f0ac1256cdf004881c0/2a2cd9ed0d6eee46c125744b0026808d!OpenDocument).

The criteria for who can live in non-profit municipal housing are, in the Swedish model, as opposed to other countries' social housing, general and not selective. Anyone, even people with a good income, can rent a flat from a non-profit municipal housing company. But the thought behind non-profit municipal housing is to take social responsibility for the provision of housing, which means that even those with smaller incomes can have a good home. The housing standard in non-profit municipal housing is similar to that in other flats that were built during the same period.

OVERCROWDING NORMS AND INCREASED DEMANDS

The inquiry into the social conditions of housing rejected a flat with one bedroom and a kitchen as an adequate home for families with children. Overcrowding was judged to be when more than two people lived in one room, not including the kitchen. This norm was called the overcrowding norm 1 and it influenced housing production during the 1940s and 1950s.

In the inquiry that was the basis of the so-called million dwellings programme (see Ulla Björnberg's chapter in this book), it was decided that more rooms per flat should be prioritised over the size of the rooms. The home's differentiation and spaciousness were considered the first criteria for what characterises a good home. A new overcrowding norm – norm 2 – was launched. This meant that people should not have to have more than two people per room, not including the kitchen and sitting room. The expectations had been raised.

The goal of housing policy to fix the housing shortage and improve housing standards read: "Society's goal for the provision of housing ought to be that the entire population shall have healthy, spacious, well-planned and appropriately equipped housing of good quality for reasonable prices."[4] "Spacious" meant that the overcrowding norm 2 would be applied to the production of housing: to build bigger flats.

4. Proposition 1967:100.

As early as 1975, after more than a million homes were produced in Sweden over a ten-year-period, and where the non-profit municipal housing companies had a prominent role in making this happen, particularly in terms of the production of blocks of flats in the outer areas of the city, a new overcrowding norm began to be discussed. Now people thought that each child should have his or her own room, and that adults living together should have a shared room, not included the kitchen or sitting room. This norm – the overcrowding norm 3 – was made the goal for housing policy in 1987. This means that a family with two children needs a home with four rooms in order to not be considered overcrowded. The percentage of school children who have their own room has been used as a national overcrowding indicator. Overcrowding is seen as factor in bad welfare and is thought to cause physical and psychological health problems, giving children and youths bad conditions for growing up and having a family of their own.[5]

5. Boverket (2006) *Var finns rum för våra barn? – en rapport om trångboddhet i Sverige* (*Where is there room for our children? – a report on overcrowdedness in Sweden*). Karlskrona: Boverket.

FORMS OF TENURE AND TYPES OF HOUSING

In Sweden, there are three main types of housing tenure: rented tenancy, cooperative housing and ownership. These three have a strong connection with what type of home one lives in: if it is a flat in a block of flats or a (semi-)detached house.

Rented tenancy (with one's own contract, sometimes indirect contracts) means that one usually lives in a flat in a block of flats that is owned by a non-profit municipal housing company or privately. *Cooperative housing*, which is cooperative ownership, can occur for both flats in blocks of flats and (semi-)detached houses. *Ownership* of a home can only be of a small building. On average, small buildings are usually significantly larger than flats in a block of flats. To own a flat is (at the time of writing) a very unusual form of tenure in Sweden.[6] Cooperative housing, both for flats and buildings, like with owned homes, is run on market principles, that is, properties are bought and sold on the market like any other product. Rented tenancy, on the other hand, has no price on the market but rather is a contractual relationship between a tenant and a landlord and is regulated by law. Generally it is the landlord who decides who gets a rental contract.

6. Except for houses that had the forms of tenure in buildings built before 1930. The forms of tenure were reintroduced from May 2009.

To become part of the housing segment that is regulated by the market requires financial resources and credit. Those with low income, the unemployed, single parents, youths and immigrants need not bother. Nor do private property-owners want (if they can avoid it) to sign a contract with people from these categories. When there is a housing shortage, it is possible to ignore those who are not viewed as desirable tenants. In reality, it is the non-profit municipal housing companies that rent homes to households with limited financial resources, to those categories that from a property-owner's perspective are less desirable. Even if the Swedish non-profit municipal housing is thought to be general, in practice it tends to be selective, at least in some parts of the city.

HOUSING FOR ALL?

In the 1980s and 1990s, there were a number of empty flats in Gothenburg, particularly in the city's outer areas. In the last decade, however, the situation has changed. The percentage of empty flats in non-profit municipal housing at the turn of the year 2008-09 was around 0,0005 % of the total.[7] The houses built during the 00s has generally been either cooperative or owned homes. Also, a number of rented tenancies, particularly in the more central parts of Gothenburg, have been transformed into cooperative tenancies.[8] A large part of the new production of homes has so far been closed to large groups of those

7. Framtiden AB (www.framtiden.goteborg.se).

8. Statistisk Årsbok för Göteborg (Annual statistics for Gothenburg) 2009, 2009-03-20 (www4.goteborg.se/prod/sk/statistik/statistikR5.nsf).

looking for homes because of their lack of financial resources and/or their credit value. Even the relatively few rentals that have been built have high rents.

It is hard to know how many are without housing, since after 1992 there has no longer been a common housing agency in Gothenburg. Rental tenancies are mostly advertised via a particular organisation, Boplats Göteborg, where non-profit municipal housing companies and certain private property-owners list their available flats. In March 2009, there were around 87 000 registered people looking for flats and in 2008, the organisation listed 8 600 homes.[9]

9. Oral information from Boplats Göteborg AB, 2009-04-24.

SPACIOUS HOUSING FOR ALL?

Regarding the three norms for overcrowding, it is hard to comment on the situation in Gothenburg, since there are no statistics in this area. The Swedish Board of Housing, Building and Planning inquiry for 2004 shows that 16 percent of the population in Gothenburg lives in overcrowded conditions according to norm 3.[10] Overcrowding can be voluntary – one might want to live in a particular home in a particular location. Newspaper articles on "Compact Living" have launched it as an urban living style.

10. Boverket (2006).

Meanwhile, the housing situation could be significantly more serious for certain groups than what the Swedish Board of Housing, Building and Planning inquiry shows. The situation is probably different in different neighbourhoods in the city. In the neighbourhoods where the resource-weak people live – where non-profit municipal housing dominates as the owner of housing, and where the concentration of those with a low income, single parents, families with many children and/or immigrants is high – are also where overcrowding is greater. This is true even if one does not base this on the overcrowding norm 3, which is highly ambitious. "Overcrowding of flats", as was claimed in an investigation into the housing situation for poorer people in Gothenburg in 1911,[11] was thought to be the situation for certain households in Gothenburg one hundred years ago. Förvaltnings AB Framtiden, which owns non-profit municipal housing, decided in 2008 to "limit the number of residents in non-profit municipal housing in rental contracts from 1 June 2008. ... The limitation is based on the number of rooms and square metres."[12] Regarding the number of rooms, the limitation basically is the same as the overcrowding norm 1, the goal set for building in the post-war period, and which was replaced before the million dwellings programme and applied from then on. But now the norm has become a rule that excludes large households, often immigrant families, from signing their own contracts and getting their own homes. The result is, as it was a hundred years ago, that different types of emergency solutions exist for those most in need (see Helena Holgersson's contribution in this book).

The fantastic vision behind the million dwellings programme, that "society's goal for the provision of housing ought to be that the entire population shall have healthy, spacious, well-planned and appropriately equipped housing of good quality for reasonable prices"[13] remains a dream for parts of the population in Gothenburg.

11. Soidre-Brink (1991), p. 93.

12. Förvaltnings AB Framtiden (www.framtiden.goteborg.se).

13. Proposition 1967:100.

Tiiu Soidre
is Associate Professor in Sociology, University of Gothenburg. Earlier she was devoted to research on housing, but her most recent project concerns the situation of the elderly on the labour market.

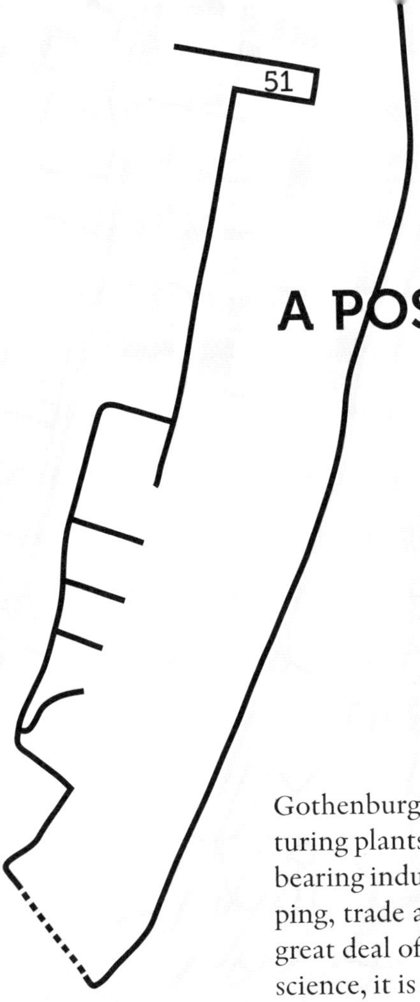

Bengt Furåker

A POST-INDUSTRIAL CITY?

Gothenburg has a long industrial history, with large manufacturing plants, for example in the shipyard, automotive and ball-bearing industries. The city has also long been a centre for shipping, trade and financing. As always in capitalist economies, a great deal of change has taken place over the decades. In social science, it is commonly argued that economically advanced societies have undergone – or are undergoing – a transformation to post-industrialism. Production thus presumably becomes oriented towards services rather than goods, and knowledge and information become key factors. The new stage is also called by other names, such as the "service", "knowledge" or "information" society. Employment changes are often taken as main indicators of the transition to post-industrialism. The simple question asked here is how employment developments in Gothenburg fit with this scenario.

POST-INDUSTRIAL THEORY AND SERVICES

In his characterisation of post-industrialism, Daniel Bell mentioned the expansion of services as a crucial feature. Before him, others had assumed a sequential employment shift, from agriculture to manufacturing and then to services.[1] A distinction is hence often made between a primary, a secondary and a tertiary sector. Bell underlined that the growth of the service sector is to some extent due to requirements in the production and distribution of goods. Transport, finance and insurance are typical examples. Another aspect – according to Bell – is that with rising incomes, people become increasingly apt to spend money on activities such as travel, entertainment, eating in restaurants and sports. They also become interested in improvements in healthcare, education and environment. The transition to post-industrial society thus entails an expansion of very different kinds of services.

Bell's theory of post-industrialism is modelled after developments in the US, neglecting the differences that exist across advanced economies.[2] It can be criticised on many other grounds as well; some have even argued that we have no post-industrialism at all, but only different kinds of industrial societies.[3] A crucial problem is how to define the concept of services. From Bell's discussion, we can conclude that his concept is broad. Others have proposed a narrow definition, treating services as immaterial, intangible and impermanent as well as produced in the presence of the consumer and consumed at the moment of production.[4] An obvious problem is, however, that many of the activities taken as illustrations – such as haircuts and dry-cleaning – hopefully have some lasting effects and imply changes in physical appearance (shorter hair and cleaner fabric).[5]

The narrow concept excludes a number of activities that most would count as services.[6] For example, when a consultant writes a report on how to improve the organisational structure of a company, this is likely to be called a service, although it

1. Daniel Bell (1976) *The coming of post-industrial society. A venture in social forecasting.* 2nd ed., New York: Basic Books, pp. 127–128; A G B Fisher (1935) *The clash of progress and security*. London: Macmillan; Colin Clark (1951) *The conditions of economic progress*. 2nd ed, London: Macmillan & Co.

2. Manuel Castells (1996) *The information age: economy, culture and society. The rise of the network society*. Vol 1. Oxford: Blackwell Publishers, ch. 4; Bengt Furåker (2003) "Post-industrial profiles. North American, Scandinavian and other Western labour markets," pp. 241–61, in Thomas P Boje & Bengt Furåker (eds) *Post-industrial labour markets. North American and Scandinavian profiles*. London: Routledge; Joachim Singelmann (1978) *From agriculture to services. The transformation of industrial employment*. Beverly Hills, CA: Sage Publications, pp. 85–107.

3. E.g., Stephen S Cohen, John Zysman (1987) *Manufacturing matters. The myth of the post-industrial economy*. London: Basic Books.

does not match the narrow definition. A wider concept is thus preferable, but just letting it be a leftover category also seems problematic. One way of proceeding might be to define different types of service.[7] Using official statistics, however, this is not an easy task, as the definitions are what they are. In the empirical section below, I stick to the statistical categories at hand, but try to keep an open mind in interpreting the data.

EMPLOYMENT DEVELOPMENTS IN GOTHENBURG

We will now take a look at the main employment developments in Gothenburg since the mid-20th century. To avoid some of the problems caused by changes in the statistical categories, I divide time into two periods. With almost the same categories over the decades, Table 1 shows employment by industry in Gothenburg in 1950, 1970 and 1990. The data merely cover the city's inhabitants, some of whom work in other municipalities; that is, commuters to the city are not included.

	1950	1970	1990	Diff. 1950–90	Diff. 1970–90
1 Agriculture	0.8	0.8	0.3	-0.5	-0.5
2 Manufacturing	36.3	28.6	19.1	-17.2	-9.5
3 Construction	7.6	9.0	5.2	-2.4	-3.8
1–3	44.6	38.4	24.6	-20.0	-13.8
4 Trade	22.7	18.8	15.9	-6.8	-2.9
5 Transport & communication	13.7	11.1	9.6	-4.1	-1.5
6 Finance, real estate & insurance*		6.9	11.4	-	+4.5
4–6		36.8	36.9		0.1
7–9 Public & other services*	18.8	24.6	36.6	-	+12.0
4–9	55.1	61.3	73.5	18.4	12.2
Non-specified	0.3	0.2	1.9	1.6	+1.7
Total	100	100	100		
Numbers	169 395	194 623	222 946	53 551	28 323

Table 1. Employment by industry among people living in Gothenburg, 1950–90, in percentages

* In 1950, Finance, etc. is included in 7–9.

Source: www4.goteborg.se/prod/G-info/statistik.nsf

4. E.g., Jonathan Gershuny (1978) *After industrial society? The emerging self-service economy*. London and Basingstoke: Macmillan, pp. 5–59; Claus Offe (1985) *Disorganized capitalism. Contemporary transformations of work and politics*. Cambridge: Polity Press, ch. 4; Andrew Sayer, Richard Walker (1992) *The new social economy. Reworking the division of labour*. Oxford: Blackwell, ch. 2.

5. Tom Elfring (1988) *Service sector employment in advanced economies. A comparative analysis of its implications for economic growth*. Aldershot and Brookfield: Avebury, p. 19.

6. Bengt Furåker (1987) *Stat och offentlig sektor* (*State and public sector*). Stockholm: Rabén & Sjögren, p. 128.

7. Castells, (1996), pp. 206–216; Singelmann, (1978); Elfring, (1988).

As can be seen, the number of employed increased considerably across the years in the table. Agriculture was, of course, a tiny sector all throughout, whereas manufacturing was large in the 1950s (and 1960s) but eventually started to decrease, with a total decline of more than 17 percentage points over the period. The figures for construction first go up and then down (even more). Across all decades, the proportion of those employed in the primary and secondary sectors (1–3) was lower than half, and the 1950–90 difference amounts to a substantial dip of 20 percentage points.

In 1950, employment in the trade sector was almost 23 percent but then fell to less than 16 percent in 1990. A similar development appears for transport and communication, although it was a smaller industry throughout. The finance category cannot be shown separately for 1950, but between 1970 and 1990, its relative volume increased by 4.5 percentage points. Public and other services, finally, grew more than that – by 12 percentage points – and had the same category been available for 1950, we would have been able to see its full expansion since then. The growth of the public service sector has supported the huge increase in female employment, which is one of the main characteristics of the period. Also, the class structure was significantly altered, with a decrease in the size of the industrial proletariat as perhaps the most important change.

Table 2 shows employment by industry in Gothenburg in 1994 and 2006. In this case, the information refers to those who actually work in the city. Moreover, for comparative purposes, I include data for Stockholm, the capital of Sweden, and for Sweden in its entirety. The industrial categories are slightly different from those in Table 1: trade, transport and communication form one category in Table 2, while public and other services are divided into three categories (7–9): education, research, health and social care: personal and cultural services; and public administration.

Table 2.
Employment by industry among people working in Gothenburg, Stockholm and Sweden as a whole, 1994 and 2006, in percentages

Sources: See *Table 1*; SCB database

	Gothenburg			Stockholm	Sweden
	1994	2006	Diff. 1994–2006	2006	2006
1 Agriculture	0.2	0.2	+/-0	0.2	1.8
2 Manufacturing	18.3	17.1	-1.2	8.1	17.7
3 Construction	5.3	4.8	-0.5	3.6	6.2
1–3	23.8	22.0	-1.8	11.8	25.7
4, 5 Trade, transport & communication	22.5	20.6	-1.9	18.9	18.4
6 Finance, real estate & insurance	14.3	20.1	+5.8	30.3	14.1
4–6	36.9	40.7	3.8	49.2	32.5
7 Education, research, health & social care	25.7	22.9	-2.8	18.2	27.5
8 Personal & cultural services	6.9	7.8	+0.9	12.1	7.3
9 Public administration	5.4	5.8	+0.4	7.6	5.8
7–9	38.0	36.5	-1.5	37.9	40.6
4–9	74.9	77.2	2.3	87.1	73.0
Non-specified	1.3	0.7	-0.6	1.0	1.2
All	100	100		100	100
Antal	232 590	292 014	59 424	537 449	4 280 768

Agriculture is not much to bother about, but we must note that manufacturing has continued to decrease in Gothenburg, although modestly. We also find some decline during the period in trade, transport and communication. The most expansive sector is finance, reaching 20 percent of all employment in 2006. In contrast, the category including education and various caring activities has fallen off, whereas the changes concerning personal and cultural services and public administration are small.

The comparison with Stockholm and Sweden as a whole reveals interesting differences. Taken together, the primary and secondary sectors (1–3) are much smaller in Stockholm but are clearly larger in Sweden. Most notably, while the proportion employed in manufacturing is very low in the capital, Gothenburg is quite close to the national proportion in this respect. Gothenburg has the lead regarding trade, but the main differences in terms of tertiary employment are found for finance, on which Stockholm scores more than 8 percentage points higher and Sweden more than 8 percentage points lower. Category 7 (education, etc) is relatively larger in Gothenburg than in Stockholm, but the national figure is much higher. Then again, Stockholm is number one for both personal and cultural services and public administration. In Sweden as a whole, the less commercial categories 7–9 beat the more commercial categories 4–6; in Gothenburg and Stockholm, it is the other way around.

It must be emphasised that the distinction between private and public sector employment is not visible in the tables. There was a great expansion of public services in Sweden through the mid-1980s,[8] but this trend was then broken as a consequence of both downsizing and privatisation. However, privatisation does not have to imply that services become entirely commercialised; they are still largely paid by tax money. Bell expected that the role of government and the public sector in society would increase and for some time this happened, but the tide has apparently turned.

8. Furåker (1987), ch. 6.

GOTHENBURG'S POST-INDUSTRIAL PROFILE

Summing up, we can observe that the proportion employed in material production was more or less halved in Gothenburg between 1950 and 2006. This must not mean that material production has become less important; an economic engine can become smaller but nevertheless stronger. However – in line with post-industrial theory – the tertiary sector has expanded, from a little more than half of the total employment in the mid-20th century to more than three-quarters in 2006. This transformation involves both an increased inflow of women into employment and important changes to the class structure. Interestingly, the most commercial parts of the tertiary sector (trade, transport and communication and finance, real estate and insurance) made up the largest subcategory in 2006, with about 40 percent of total employment. In this regard, Gothenburg differs from Sweden as a whole but also from Stockholm – in both cases above all because of the relative size of the category finance, which is smaller in Sweden and larger in the capital. We can also note that, in recent years, Gothenburg has seen a decline in the proportion of people employed in education, research, health and social care, largely organised or at least funded by public authorities. In sum, post-industrialism in Gothenburg is very much a matter of market-oriented activities.

Bengt Furåker
is Professor of Sociology at the Department of Sociology, University of Gothenburg. His research focuses mainly on issues related to the labour market and working life.

Åsa Andersson

"KNIFE IN THE HEART" Suburban mythology in the new post-industrial order

During the last months of 2004, a series of articles appeared in *Göteborgs-Posten* called "Future in the suburbs". One of the people quoted was a young woman at a youth recreation centre in Hammarkullen. She commented on the exclusion of Gothenburg's north-eastern neighbourhoods by saying that she felt that "politicians want to erase and cut off Gothenburg at Gamlestaden".[1] This pointed commentary can be said to capture and specify the social-geographical map in a city that is characterised by a clear correspondence between the social and spatial separation of different groups in the population.

The relationships in the polarised city and Gothenburg's north-eastern suburbs have also been the theme of a trilogy of drama productions for Swedish Television by the scriptwriter Peter Birro and director Agneta Fagerström Olsson, the last of which was *Kniven i hjärtat* (*Knife in the heart*) 2004. The series takes place and was filmed in the neighbourhood of Bergsjön. But it is not just this clear localisation that makes the drama interesting as a contemporary commentary. Certain aspects can also be read in relationship to a post-industrial new order and its effects on the city's social landscape.

1. Johanna Bäckström Lerneby (2004) "Hip hop hurra för Hammarkullen!" ("Hip hop hurray for Hammarkullen!"), *Göteborgs-Posten* 2004-12-02.

At the centre of the depiction is a gang of young men who are bound together by strong friendships and who are involved in various criminal activities. The tone of the drama's narration is realistic and is sometimes interrupted by musical features, when actors use song and dance numbers to comment on the events. The form and content of the series can be said to be faithful to the genre, in that expected and well-known motifs for a tale about the suburbs recur regularly. The drama also uses the popular mythology that has arisen regarding the suburbs of the million dwellings programme (see Ulla Björnberg's chapter in this book) and makes them into typical environments. It is a representational genre that has made *the concrete suburb* into a symbol with a powerful charge and more or less given associations. In his study of the Malmö neighbourhood Rosengård, Per-Markku Ristilammi has called this sort of typical suburban symbolic language "black poetry". Using the power of repetition and with a limited production of motifs, this black poetry has helped fortify the suburbs' status as inhuman and threatening environments. On a more overarching level, this arsenal of symbols has also served as a sort of negative reflection of modernity, as part of a social narrative with the aim of depicting the negative effects, setbacks and mistakes during the time of major planning.[2]

In accordance with the well-established discourse about the Concrete Suburb, which in *Knife in the heart* is heavily masculine, many threatening situations and social misunderstandings are depicted. There is drug abuse, illegal gambling at dog fights and young suburban men who go on raids to the centre of Gothenburg, where other youths almost regularly have their mobile phones and wallets stolen. Alienation from Swedish society and its institutions is shown as nearly total and is present in the Bergsjön of the drama nearly only in a repressive way, in the form of enemy policemen that the youths have to stay away from. Otherwise, Bergsjön seems to have been left to its fate, cut off from society. As an extra-obvious marker of this,

2. Per-Markku Ristilammi (1994) *Rosengård och den svarta poesin. En studie av modern annorlundahet* (*Rosengård and black poetry. A study of modern difference*). Stockholm/Stehag: Symposion.

the younger brother of the leader of the gang has a picture of Osama Bin Ladin above his bed.

All together, *Knife in the heart* presents a frightening image of a society and a city in crisis, where one part of the population seems to have been left to a permanent exclusion without much hope for improvement. By the depressing end of the story, one of the boys has died from drug abuse, two have gone to prison and one resignedly claims that he will probably never get any further than his hopeless job at the local pizzeria. Perhaps the most depressing picture is in the last scene, when a new, younger gang of boys, with the previous gang leader's little brother at its centre, is seen moving in the same way, in the same raw, dirty and poorly lit place. The group of characters in the new gang is similar to the gang that has just split up and, one guesses, has the same prospects for the future.

So far, *Knife in the heart* can be seen as a deeply pessimistic and, fictionally speaking, incisive commentary on some of the social incongruities that occur in Gothenburg and similar cities today. For the male youths of the drama, social reproduction seems just as predetermined as it is hopeless, and the joy and strength that they once experienced in the gang in the end becomes the weakness that drives them to ruin. But for two of the drama's gang members, things look better in the end; they are able to find ways out of the social dead-ends. One of them is saved by his football talent and recruited to a possible future as a professional sportsman in Barcelona. Besides showing the fulfilment of a typical dream for boys, what is also personified here is the classic individualistic story of success about a boy from the ghetto. It confirms the idea that it is only with the help of exceptional talent, preferably in sport or music, that one can win a place and a life where there are chances for dignity and honour. It follows that this place has to be far from Bergsjön.

The biggest surprise in the drama, and the most interesting development in terms of a contemporary commentary, comes in the figure of the gang's leader, Amir. His depressed and dejected father's suicide is the turning point for Amir, when he decides to radically change his life. He does this by applying for a job at the Volvo factory. Even if a job on the factory floor is a far more plausible opportunity for young people in similar situations than becoming a professional footballer, both of these situations are portrayed as equally implausible and unique. For an immigrant boy from the suburbs, then, something exceptional is required in order to become part of the industrial heart of Sweden and Gothenburg. And Amir has the exceptional characteristics that are needed. He is, it is true, relentlessly hard, but he also has something of the trickster's irresistible charm and skill when it comes to forming the image he wishes those around him to have of him. During the job interview, Amir manages to convince the recruiter that what she can expect from him is unswerving loyalty to his future employer, just as he previously had to the gang's code of honour. Against all odds, Amir gets the job that will presumably lead him on the right path, and he does this despite, or maybe thanks to, presenting himself as a hardened but changed criminal who comes from "a completely different world" than the one the recruiter lives in. What Amir does is that he makes it seem as though the qualities that make up the image of a typical suburban gangster can be exemplary for a loyal worker, through a sort of recoding.

Knife in the heart is not just part of the black poetry that has been around in various forms since the 1970s; parts of the series also dramatise and comment on the post-industrial situation, where to a great extent both resources and conflicts are about culture and the value of symbols. Volvo is no longer the Gothenburg-national heart it once was, but is instead a brand, a multinational company with an international ownership structure. Because of this, an ever larger part of its production has been outsourced to other countries. The Gothenburg Volvo factory in Torslanda no longer needs Bergsjön, one of the neighbourhoods that was once planned and built during the million dwellings programme with the goal of offering homes to the thousands of workers who were thought would continue to work on the factory floor. As a brand and symbol, Volvo still has a lot of importance for the city of Gothenburg, in a situation where cities, like companies, have to compete, market and sell themselves on a global market. Here, the city and the sustainability of large companies depend on one another, which makes its representatives, that is, its politicians and businessmen, in many respects united in the effort to market an appropriate and tempting image to interest investors and tourists.[3] In such a symbolic-economy, Bergsjön and similar neighbourhoods are more of a threat – to the city's image – than a possibility. Housing segregation, poor neighbourhoods, threatening slum-formation and criminality in the city space are defined as threats to investment and thereby growth. It follows that the young residents of Bergsjön and similar neighbourhoods are more often mentioned in speeches about crime prevention, such as efforts to survey and prevent new recruitment to criminal gangs, than in contexts that explore where the knowledge society's new workers might be. This can be seen as part of a global developmental pattern for city landscapes where certain population groups are thought to be structurally irrelevant for the societal or, rather, financial development.[4]

3. See Sharon Zukin (1995) *The cultures of cities*. Cambridge, Mass. and Oxford: Blackwell Publishers Ltd.

4. See Doreen Massey, John Allen & Steve Pile (eds) (1999) *City worlds*. London: Routledge.

To return to *Knife in the heart* and Amir's situation, it takes place at a time when big parts of the large-scale manufacturing industry are leaving Sweden. This means that the opportunity to become a faithful worker in this sector is not something that will be available to much of the working population. A more contemporary development for someone who, like the TV series' Amir, decides to follow the straight and narrow path, would be to go to school. Education and specialisation are formally the recipe for success in the knowledge- and education-society, as the post-industrial society is also called (see Mats Widigson's chapter in this book). But in Amir's successful transformation – from suburban gangster to faithful nine-to-fiver – the formula is more cultural. Here it is about the ability to handle and manipulate symbols strategically, so they respond to an always changing, individualistic and competitive symbolic economy. Because an unswerving but also flexible loyalty – the object of the loyalty can shift if the conditions so require – and a strong skill in social role-playing, probably work as well in what is nowadays a changing factory floor as in the suburban gang. This can seem to make the resolution of the drama comfortable in a reactionary way. The unique football talent gets his rightful reward and the nightmare from the Concrete Suburb can be conquered via socialisation and recoding from suburban gangster to an exemplary worker with flexible loyalty. The threat can be neutralised into a part of social reproduction that a post-industrial society needs. But in a situation where industry no longer requires so many workers, it can really never be so comfortable. And in a society where the traditional class cultures are dissolved at the same time that a large proportion of the population – both first-generation immigrants and their children – are facing intolerance and discrimination in many different situations, it can hardly be expected that the ever more shrinking industry sector is going to be the place where problems will be conquered and integration will take place.

But Amir of the fictional drama got his job in the end. Does this make him part of society and an equal member? The song Amir sings the last time we see him, dressed in work overalls on the production line on the factory floor, comments on the situation he now has to deal with, where, despite finding himself "deep inside the belly of Swea /. . ./ still cursed and transformed into something else", he is expected to be quiet and not complain since he has now obtained the security that employment represents. In other words, this is about conditional participation, which all participation is to a certain extent, but the conditions can be more or less evenly divided, the stakes higher or lower. For Amir, the stakes are high. He has to give everything by pledging his identity, to his employer, where his loyalty is now concentrated, and by distancing himself from his earlier neighbourhood-based community, which up until now meant everything for him. Besides the high price that Amir thereby has to pay on a personal level, the final song also takes notice of the generally uneven relationships and the lack of reciprocity that remain outside the workplace, where certain cultural symbols, despite their value for a large part of the population, are not allowed much space:

> You talk about integration on my TV
> "But build your mosque somewhere we won't see it
> otherwise we will burn it down."

Åsa Andersson
has a Ph.D. in Ethnology. She is currently working at University West in Trollhättan and does research on discourses of multiculturalism on film.

Mats Franzén

STAMPEN
On the eastern border

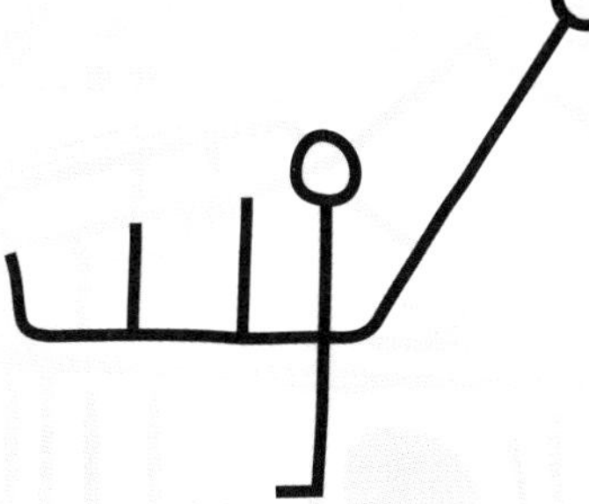

Although Stampen is one of Gothenburg's oldest and most centrally located neighbourhoods, it is surprisingly little known. There is something unfinished about Stampen. Despite its location, it has not been entirely exploited and built up. Nor does the district have a distinct identity. Rather, Stampen is extremely varied – it has something for everyone, but for that reason can be a neighbourhood that it is hard to identify with. Stampen is a neighbourhood for no one, and therefore is genuinely urban: arrestingly anonymous, characterised by such diversity that no one has managed to put their mark on it yet. Here, if anywhere in the city, you can really disappear.

The explanation for why Stampen became the neighbourhood it is now is not to be sought in the neighbourhood itself, but rather in Gothenburg's socio-spatial history. If one ignores Hisingen, which is easily done in Gothenburg, in social-spatial terms Gothenburg looks like a T. Inside the moat is still the city centre, which is located where the two bars of the T meet. From here, the city grew in three directions. Southwards – next to the monumentally built Götaplatsen – is still where the more fashionable quarters are. In the west, along the river, is where the working-class area developed. The harbour, and the shipyards, facing the western neighbourhoods from the Hising side, to which most workers got by taking the ferry across the river, together came to characterise the western neighbourhoods – not least the image of them. And in the east, there were also neighbourhoods for the city's workers, for those who worked at the slaughterhouse, at the SKF, and in the textile industry. Compared with the western neighbourhoods, the eastern ones were relatively anonymous. The image of working-class Gothenburg thus came to be dominated by the western neighbourhoods' casual harbour labourers and its comparatively independent shipyard workers, rather than the eastern neighbourhood, whose factory workers, especially the women, endured greater restrictions on their freedom. This cultural topography was already in place by the turn of the twentieth century and in some ways we still are living with it.

A special element in this topography is created by the two urban membranes that can be said to regulate the flow of people, goods and ideas between the centre of the city and the western and eastern neighbourhoods. The western membrane, Masthugget, has long been one of the city's most discussed and well-known neighbourhoods, but will be ignored here. The eastern membrane is Stampen. If not completely forgotten, it is relatively unseen, unknown and maybe sometimes notorious. This neighbourhood links the centre of Gothenburg with the eastern parts. If you stand on Drottningtorget with the Central Station behind you and face south, Stampen hides behind the large, fine post office building to the left, soon to be converted into a luxury hotel. Behind it is where Stampen begins: in the shape of an upside-down triangle, it stretches eastwards. Although there is something back there, which if by nothing else is shown by the traffic to and from the area, you are drawn in the other direction: into the city centre. If Stampen was and continues to be hidden behind the post office building, that is not the case for the Stampen triangle's eastern tip: a vital link to the eastern neighbourhoods is here in Olskrokstorget, with its lively square. In the 1960s, it was split brutally and effectively by an enormous motorway intersection connecting the E20 and E6. It is still possible to get from Stampen to the eastern areas by foot, bicycle or tram, but the traffic set-up does not encourage it. Its so-called barrier effects are very noticeable, even if they also significantly increased the tempo of the interregional motor traffic to and from Copenhagen, Stockholm and Oslo. Nonetheless, today it is still easier to get to know Stampen if you live in the eastern areas, because if you are going to the centre you usually have to pass this membrane.[1]

And you do not do that from the north: there the railway yards make a very effective barrier. To the south, in the sun and the light, across the Fattighusån canal, Stampen is not welcoming either, except for the through-traffic from Norra Allén and Parkgatan's ring road around the centre and from Skånegatan and Mölndal. That Gothenburg's so called "event area" is along the latter street does not change matters. Stampen's main orientation is clearly east-west.

Unfinished, unseen and unknown, Stampen squats behind the future luxury hotel in the post office building. Nevertheless, Stampen has never been so anonymous that the neighbourhood has been completely unknown by those who have never had a reason to go there. It is rather that Stampen has long – if not always – had a bad reputation. Many who never had to go there never got to experience Stampen themselves. Notoriety contributed to unfamiliarity.

The stigmata of poverty and misery is almost as old as the neighbourhood and older than the city plan from 1866 that gives the neighbourhood its shape even today. Before the monumental post office building was finished in 1925, there had been a poorhouse on this site, built in 1855 just before the railway came to Gothenburg. Had the railway come earlier, the poorhouse probably would not have been built at Drottning-

1. The picture of Stampen and its history I draw in this text has a number of different sources, primarily maps and pictures in various standard texts about and guides to Gothenburg, which capture the city's various historical layers, as well as letters from three informants. For more on this approach see Karl Schlögel (2003), *Im Raume lesen wir die Zeit*. München: Hanser.

torget. In the compound, there was also an orphanage, which can still be seen today. This was not Stampen's first poorhouse. In 1726, a poorhouse was provisionally established in a manufacturer's building, which in 1767 was replaced by a newly built wooden poorhouse, which still stands by Fattighusån and is remembered by slightly older Gothenburgers who visited the dispensary that was later established here in the fight against tuberculosis. This is also the site of the Mariakyrkan church, where the so-called poorhouse church used to stand. It is said that mortality amongst the poor was so high that a graveyard had to be constructed in Stampen. It opened in 1804; today you can still read over the entrance the famous *memento mori*: Tänk på döden. Much earlier, in 1742, in the eastern part of Stampen, a women's prison was established. It was closed at the beginning of the 20th century and turned into a home for single women with young children. Much later, in 1969, the buildings were used as offices for voluntary organisations. It seems logical that the editorial offices for the homeless newspaper in Gothenburg – *Faktum* – is in Stampen. If Stampen has any symbolic capital, it is not of the positive kind.

These institutions seem to have given Stampen its negative, unappealing reputation early on, and maybe there is nothing strange about it. From them, no positive symbolic capital was created. What is strange is that the reputation has hidden many of the other activities that have existed and still exist in Stampen, and that otherwise could have influenced the picture of the neighbourhood and given it a more exciting and less gloomy image.

Gothenburg's brewery, nowadays Pripps brewery, was here for around a century. It stopped operating in the 1970s; at the end of the 1980s the buildings were torn down to make room for offices, a hotel and housing. The brewery was connected to Gothenburg (Pripps is one of Sweden's older trademarks), but that it was located in Stampen seems to have been regarded as coincidence. *Göteborgs-Posten* (GP), the city's largest daily newspaper, moved to its new premises in Stampen, by the post office and the central station, in the middle of the 1930s. Yet it too was unable or unwilling to change the gloomy image of the neighbourhood, despite having the power of words. Modernity, in the form of cars and motorcycles, came to Stampen together with modernist buildings a few years later, along the north side of Odinsgatan and Friggagatan. Yet that did not manage to alter Stampen's negative reputation either – despite the fact that within a short time Gothenburg's car dealership district developed here. Over time, car dealerships moved out of central Gothenburg, and more or less shady businesses took their place. When much of the modernist buildings were torn down before Christmas 2008 in order to make room for new rental flats, GP had a classic slum-clearing headline about the event – "Clean House in Cradle of Evil" – and claimed laconically that "none of the former tenants has asked to return".[2] The demolition took place despite the buildings having been part of the municipality's preservation programme: in the end, it was more important to get rid of the pornography, graffiti, Harley Davidsons, illegal clubs and other things. A manly, partly criminal macho world fell prey to the demolishers wrecking ball.

2. Björn Hansson "Rent hus i syndanästet" ("Clean house in cradle of sin"). *Göteborgs-Posten* 2008-12-16, p. 5.

Stampen's negative reputation seems fairly robust. Businesses such as GP with high standing in Gothenburg moved in without really changing the image. Even more striking perhaps is that the Samskolan school took over the premises of the Östra Real school in Stampen around forty years ago. For a long time, clever boys from the eastern neighbourhoods attended preparatory school here. That the Gothenburg bourgeoisie's foremost private school, founded in 1901, could move here seems unthinkable. Just as little as GP has done, Samskolan does not seem to have contributed to making Stampen seen and known. Perhaps it is simply because the identity of both GP and Samskolan is connected to Gothenburg rather than Stampen.

What is unusual about Stampen, however, is that it is a very mixed neighbourhood, comprised of a number of different businesses. Housing is also mixed. As with Masthugget, Stampen is not a typical working-class neighbourhood. There was never built any "governor's houses" (landshövdingehus) here, so typical for most working class neighbourhoods in Göteborg up till WWII.[3] In Stampen, heavy blocks of brick were built, but slowly. The 1866 town plan is still not really completed, even if the building activities have intensified in the past decades. The building of housing has spread more since the end of the 1980s. In around 1990, a number of large and somewhat lavish houses were built in a postmodern style on the Pripps brewery property in the west, in the best southern location towards the Fattighusån stream. Later, several housing complexes in the typical Swedish new modernist style were built in eastern Stamp, also in the best southern position.[4]

The question is whether, despite the invisibility of the place, a sort of gentrification of Stampen can be discerned. In support of that, a certain upgrading of the housing has taken place in recent years. However the percentage of rental flats is still fairly high (around 60 %), even in the new buildings, and that speaks against it. The percentage of flats that are larger than three rooms and a kitchen is also rather low (10 %). The number of foreigners is, however, lower in Stampen than in Gothenburg in general, as is the figure for poor health and unemployment. This points to a certain degree of gentrification, as does the fact that the level of education is relatively high. The income level is just above the city's average, which roughly corresponds with a young population.

Above all, evidence against the gentrification of Stampen is provided by the fact that its symbolic capital has not yet been recharged. An explanation is that the 1960s leftwingers never came here as they did to western neighbourhoods like Haga, Masthugget and Majorna, which have now clearly been gentrified. In line with other differences between Gothenburg's western and eastern sides, gentrification was something for the former. Neither students, nor the social movements of

3. Recruited labour would preferably be housed in new housing schemes named after a governor of the province where Gothenburg was the capital. Their hall mark was a first store of stone or concrete to minimize risks of fire and then two flights up of wood, which occasionally expressed itself in a carpenter's joy. In 1940 almost half or 47 % of all inhabitants lived in these "governor's housing" districts. They lacked modern facilities such as toilets with shower and were like mass assemblies of crofter's housing.

4. Göteborgs Stadskansli. Göteborgsbladet 2008, p. 117 (and next section).

the 1960s onwards, both pioneers of gentrification, did come to Stampen; rather, it was a masculine, more or less criminal world. If some of the bearers of cultural capital settled here, they spent their capital elsewhere. Stampen was neither socially nor physically something to protect or preserve, revaluate or (re-)establish.

Stampen is all too anonymous a neighbourhood and that is why it is still relatively simple to find a centrally located home there. Businesses such as Bekväma skor (Comfortable Shoes), Gothenburg's specialist shop for drums, or businesses selling used white goods neither contribute to nor change it. Rather, they confirm the "anonymity of diversity"; in other words, many people have various errands to run here, but they do not appropriate the place. For how much longer this will be the case is an open question.

Mats Franzén
is Professor of Sociology at the Institute for Housing and Urban Research at Uppsala University. His research concerns the politics of public space.

Gabriella Olshammar

ÖSTRA KVILLEBÄCKEN
From informal industrial re-use to legitimised demolition

There is a place in central Gothenburg that is more and more deserted. The area is not far from Gothenburg's historical city centre but is on the opposite side of the Göta river, close to the Backaplan shopping centre on the island of Hisingen. From the beginning of the 21st century, it has been called Östra Kvillebäcken in city planning contexts. If you go there today, you find five torn-down blocks. Large piles of gravel spread out behind fallen fences. A few industrial buildings of indeterminate age stand alone. For a long time, this was a living urban environment with a large mixture of businesses: car repair shops, motorcycle stores, pet shops, immigrant organisations, lunch spots, cafés, junkyards, flea markets, antique shops and more. But since 2008, large portions of the buildings have been demolished and the businesses forced out. The destruction is the first step in a transformation into a housing and office area.

From the outside, it can seem to be an obvious development that some industrial areas are demolished to make room for the coming exploitation of an attractive location. What is harder to know is that the exploitation itself has dragged out almost three decades, pending decisions from property developers, planners at the city planning administration, and politicians at the planning and building and property management committees about what the buildings and the area as a whole will be used for.

In brief, the history is that an industrial area was established here at the beginning of the 20th century. By the middle of the century, it had shifted from industry to car dealerships and service. In an inquiry from the end of the 1970s, the area was judged to have served its time for industrial purposes. In 2008, a large portion of the buildings were demolished. Meanwhile, between the 1970s and 2008, businesses and organisations rented simple spaces in the area's small-scale buildings. Thanks to a simple re-use of the older industrial buildings, the condemned industrial environment created an unplanned area that was attractive to small businesses and organisations. Why couldn't this live on and be developed on a small-scale? What will happen now when so many of these buildings are instead to be torn down?

A COMPLICATED PLANNING PROCESS

When Östra Kvillebäcken was established as an industrial area at the beginning of the 20th century, it was on the edge of the city. Now the location is quite central, since the city has grown around it. The construction has always been sparse and small-scale, with buildings with one or two levels, in brick or with simple siding. As already mentioned, according to an industry inquiry, the area was seen as declining even in the 1970s. In 1986, in a motion to the municipal council, the area was said to have become a slum and to be in need of being put in order. Since then, various initiatives for transformation have been taken in turns.[1]

The initiatives have come from the planning and building committee, the city planning administration and the two property developers, Wallenstam and NCC, who own most of the land. In the middle of the 1990s, the business secretariat was asked by

1. For more about the planning process and its deadlock situation, see: Gabriella Olshammar (2002) *Det permanentade provisoriet. Ett återanvänt industriområde i väntan på rivning eller erkännande* (*The permanent-provisional state. A recycled industrial zone awaiting demolition or recognition*). Diss. Göteborg: Chalmers – Arkitektur, Institutionen för stadsbyggnad, pp. 61–95.

the city planning administration to investigate the area from a business perspective. At the same time, a group of researchers in workplace design from Chalmers University of Technology got involved. They established a "local academy" together with the city planning office and the two companies. The goal was to discuss an alternative and small-scale transformation. In 1999, the city planning administration presented a proposal based on the current buildings and operational structures, with the addition of residential blocks here and there in less sensitive locations. The proposal considered the current small-scale and mixed building area worth continuing to build on, but with some additions. The plan was not realised, in part because the engaged municipal officials at the city planning administration got new assignments, and in part because of the property developers' lukewarm interest. The property developers would rather have seen a larger exploitation than the authorities at the municipality, and primarily wanted to be able to build housing. In 2002, the city planning administration presented a new proposal for complete transformation with new buildings, which was approved by the planning and building committee. Despite this, nothing happened. Nowadays, the area is part of an expanded project assigned to the municipal company Älvstranden Utveckling by the municipal executive committee in 2004. A consortium of seven companies is to rebuild the area over a period of five years; the start of this was set for 2009.

A PERMANENTLY PROVISIONAL STATE

During the long drawn-out planning process, provisional solutions were made permanent. The property developers rented out simple space for low rents in buildings that they allowed to fall into disrepair. The geographic location, the rents and, in some cases, the sturdiness of the facilities suited the small businesses that established themselves here. The simple facilities were also viewed as useful places for meetings, and in 1990 there were 15 immigrant organisations here. Due to the proximity of the shopping centre Backaplan and the good public transportation, the area was also attractive for the establishment of retail trade, and they got support from the municipality for temporary building permission. However, a significant proportion of the area's businesses did not have this support, since the retail trade in central Hisingen was already seen as over-established.

With the short-term building permission, the municipality wanted to signal that the business that were allowed in Östra Kvillebäcken were only accepted because of their temporariness. Businesses and organisations were only given one-year contracts, which, according to the property developers, would check their hopes for remaining. The owners did not view their tenants as "serious", but rather felt that the mere existence of the resource-poor tenants was a hindrance to the development of the exclusivity that the attractive location suggested. Still, the one-year contracts were renewed for ten to fifteen years.

Entrepreneurs were therefore able to run their businesses and organisations could have their meeting places both in spite of and thanks to the insecurity of the conditions. One might ask if it would have been possible for a business to appear as serious under these uncertain conditions. The businesspeople I interviewed – within the framework of an empirical case study in 1998–2002 – explained that had it not been for the uncertainty, they might have fixed up their workspaces and paid for it themselves. Several had serious reasons for being in that location – they had a large enough customer base for their business to operate, the area was easily accessible by car and public transportation, the rents were suitable because they were low, even if they were high when one considered the low standards of the facilities.

Those who ran businesses in the area were devalued by both the real estate developers and the officials as a result of the simple and uncertain conditions under which they worked. In meetings and documents, the activities were not separated from the conditions, the short contracts and the lack of maintenance.

OBSTACLES TO MODEST TRANSFORMATION

In the 1980s, Wallenstam and NCC bought a large number of nearby properties. This served as the incitement for high exploitation, which has been a hindrance for more modest transformation plans for Östra Kvillebäcken, like the suggested plan from 1999. Another obstacle to renewal has been the likely presence of contaminated land from earlier industrial activities. In order to finance a clearance of this, the real estate developers would need high exploitation.[2]

Another obstacle to a modest transformation of the area is the opposition to start by using existing buildings as a resource. The modest and low-exploitation buildings never received any acceptance from the real estate developers as objects to base the transformation on: basic buildings in central locations are viewed as losses. They see buildings as objects for investment and refinement.[3] It can be pointed out that neither the Gothenburg City Museum nor the county administrative board have marked any of the old industry buildings in the area as worth preserving. The short contracts and building permission in turn implied that the activities were not accepted as anything other than temporary. Even the business secretariat – which, in an inquiry in 1996, was positive to the idea of this being a small-scale industrial area – claimed that the central parts of Hisingen "offer a run-down environment with the character of an industrial city in decline", which would impede the positive development of Gothenburg and the Gothenburg region.[4]

NEW PROVISIONAL STATE?

As already mentioned, today large parts of the Östra Kvillebäcken neighbourhood are deserted, without buildings. The renewal of the area was to begin in 2008 with support for a new plan from the city planning administration.[5] The plan was sent to the planning and building committee in the beginning of October 2008 and the property developers had buildings de-

2. Joakim Forsemalm (2007) *Bodies, bricks and black boxes. Power practices in city conversion*, Diss. Göteborg: Göteborgs universitet, Institutionen för etnologi, p. 146; Olshammar (2002), pp. 66–67, 95.

3. *Wallenstam, Årsredovisning* (*Wallenstam, Annual Report*) (2001), p. 36, *NCC, Årsredovisning* (*NCC, Annual Report*) (2001) pp. 24–26.

4. *Området vid Gustaf Dalénsgatan* (*The area by Gustaf Dalénsgatan*) 1996-03-04, Gothenburg Business Secretariat (1996), p. 1 and 8.

5. *Östra Kvillebäcken södra delen* (*The southern part of Östra Kvillebäcken*) (October 2008) Dnr 0965/04, detailed plan. Göteborg: Gothenburg city planning office.

molished on five blocks. The plan was, however, delayed until before Christmas, since the municipality and some of the small property owners in the area could not come to an agreement.[6]

A similar demolition in preparation for a coming exploitation took place at the turn of the decade 1999-2000. A large building was torn down then to make room for a cinema. The goal was for the cinema to attract visitors and to mark that a new era was beginning. This time the result was no more than some architectural sketches, attention-grabbing headlines in the local newspaper and a deserted area fenced in. A couple of popular second-hand markets were pushed out. Criminality is said to have escalated in the area since the beginning of 2000, via illegal clubs, illegal gambling and illegal selling of alcohol and drugs, weapons, stolen goods and other things as well as several murders.[7] The problem did not come about because the building was torn down and left an empty block in its place, but the empty plot can be seen as a symbol of all the failed attempts to transform the place on a large scale. One of the planners who worked on the planning process said resignedly when we met that the only thing that had had happened since the beginning of the 21st century was an increase in crime and that the buildings had fallen into disrepair even more.

One wonders what will happen in Östra Kvillebäcken this time. With the delay of the detailed plan, building can start at the earliest in the beginning of 2010. If it is delayed even longer, a new form of permanent provisional state will arise. However, the ravaged area of today rules out the sort of informal re-usages that were previously possible.

6. Gunilla Skoog, "Små fastighetsägare försenar lägenhetsbygget på Backaplan" ("Small property owners delay the building of flats in Backaplan"), *Göteborgs-Posten* 2008-12-29.

7. Gunilla Skoog, "1700 nya lägenheter i Kvillebäcken" ("1700 new flats in Kvillebäcken"), *Göteborgs-Posten* 2008-01-06.

Gabriella Olshammar is a researcher on urban issues at the Department of Conservation, University of Gothenburg, with focus on the re-use of industrial buildings.

Joakim Forsemalm

LÅNGGATORNA
Obstructed gentrification

In the beginning of May 2008, I am standing with a handful of people – including a property owner/developer who has renovated several older buildings in central Gothenburg, a researcher on social work and an architect – discussing the Gothenburg district of Långgatorna. The occasion is a seminar produced by the Centrum för Byggnadskultur (the Centre for the Built Environment) and the setting is an auditorium in a cellar in Gothenburg's city building office. Långgatorna is a neighbourhood in the western centre of Gothenburg that for a long time has been the place for a uniquely rich city life. During the 19th and 20th centuries, the proximity to the Göta river was important for this life: the Masthugg quay (today home to Stena Line's ferries to Denmark) was one of several places where ship cargo met land-based transportation of goods. Several historical studies record how harbour workers frequented Andra Långgatan's pubs and other pleasure spots.[1]

Gothenburg's western centre has historically been a changing and restless place, and a part of the city that has kept the police occupied.[2] Långgatorna was not a part of Masthugget,

1. Anders Gustavsson (1994) *Hamnens arbetare. En etnologisk undersökning av stuveriarbetet i Göteborg* (*The workers in the harbour. An ethnological investigation of dock workers in Gothenburg*). Stockholm: Nordiska museets handlingar.

2. Kjell Bergman (1990) *Poliser. Mellan klassförtryck och brottsbekämpning* (*Police. Between class oppression and crime-fighting*). Göteborg: Etnologiska föreningen i Västsverige.

with its old, now demolished wooden buildings, where the million dwellings programme's aesthetics are clearly visible today to travellers on the Stena ferries. Instead, it was a fully built brick city, comparable with Vasastan's fine houses. Even if there has always been cooperative tenured homes, there are also rentals and above all student housing, the latter important for the selection of stores available on the ground floors in the area. In Långgatorna, it is there it happens: the district has a long history of small-scale business, from suppliers and service providers to the harbour and the ships (there is still a small boatyard here, a good distance from the water!) through timber and the sale of wooden furniture, to today's various design companies. A number of well-established clothing companies started their operations here (Velour, Dem Collective, Elvine). Some have grown out of the small nooks available, but several are still here in office premises up above the street. *Camino*, Sweden's first ecological lifestyle magazine, is run from here, as is the international musical festival Clandestino. Despite the presence of shops selling pornography in the area, there have been celebratory articles in both local and international media, such as in the *New York Times* article "Sweden unzipped" in 2007.[3] The list goes on. In terms of type of business, the area has shifted from one craft to another, from one small-scale activity to another. It sounds like a nice picture, an area that lives and thrives, and not least creates employment opportunities for Gothenburg.

During the seminar, however, the atmosphere was heavy. What would happen to this area, which is viewed by more and more people as a unique part of Gothenburg, and as being important from a microeconomic perspective when the centre is growing and absorbing more of the areas on its borders? Some talk about gentrification (see the introductory chapter in this book). With geography's growth rings moving the centre ever further out, real estate speculation is expected to increase in this area too, where small-scale businesses require reasonable and manageable rents.

3. Stephen Metcalf, "Sweden unzipped", *NY Times* 2007-09-23.

Most of the seminar's participants thought that all the signs are pointing towards gentrification. If you want, you can find most of the signs of such a development in the area – which explains the general air of resignation during the seminar. When it was my turn, I said that concern about Långgatorna was, if not unwarranted, at least exaggerated. Långgatorna's transformation seems to follow something other than a given line with a predetermined result – the process does not necessarily generate the sort of change we imagine. In the discussion that followed, I was called naive. But if you really choose another point of view, if you do not just have "gentrification" on your mind, what kind of picture would you have of city transformation? If instead of asking, "How is the *gentrification* of Långgatorna taking place?", you asked: "How is the *change* of the area taking place?"[4]

4. For more on this, see Joakim Forsemalm (2007) *Bodies, bricks and black boxes. Power practices in city conversion*. Diss. Göteborg: Göteborgs universitet, Institutionen för etnologi.

In Sweden in the 1980s, there was a campaign against racism and hostility towards foreigners, "Don't touch my buddy!" (*Touche pas a mon Pote.*) This would be a good description for what has happened in Långgatorna at the beginning of the 21st century. Even if the celebratory articles can be seen as part of gentrification, they can also be interpreted as part of the opposition to it. The newspapers wrote, people went to lectures. And the planners listened and participated in different forms of knowledge-production. They were interested in understanding what it is that creates this *urban character* that the newspapers are writing about. It was understood by the planners as a large number of small things, which together created opposition against the idea of gentrification. But it was not just the newspapers that contributed to this. Tradesmen have contacted each other to make sure that friends with a clothes company, a retail contract or some other business get premises next to another with an adjacent clientele.

Much is going on, as it always has, in these eleven blocks, with their rich variation in terms of age, standards and height of buildings. The latter is something that in various contexts during the past years has been discussed as particularly interesting and important for the "feeling" of the space in Långgatorna. The way light slips in between the taller buildings creates air and light. Some of the lower buildings are in bad shape and some of them also house pornography shops. These have an important function as a "rent muffler", putting off exclusive retailers from renting available business locales and keeping the rent at a level affordable for small-scale businesses. A platform for ideas is created; there is space for things that are a little odd, alternative and independent. Instead of sharing the fate of the buildings described by Gabriella Olshammar in this anthology, the light and the airiness, as well as the insight that the area's character is to a large extent created by the meetings made possible in the boutiques on the bottom floors, offers opposition to gentrification. Such values were included in the planning documents that serve as guidance for the long-term plans. The local planning office documents say that the neighbourhood should be transformed on the basis of its own conditions.

There is no lack of theoretical support for the preservation of these buildings. Jane Jacobs' formula for a sustainable, safe and interesting city could be used as a model for Långgatorna.[5] The pavement, Jacobs believes, has an important function for safety and security. The more movement, the more meetings between people and the more secure city life is. In Långgatorna, small things have a major significance. Many small things, objects, and actions aggregate the bigger picture – a strong and enduring district identity. In winter of 2008, there were street parties called "Andra lång*dagen* 1 and 2", followed by an alternative Christmas fair, "Andra *juldagen*", happenings where the stores opened up onto the pavements, street and the yards in the back. A thousand people participated in this street festival. This made possible though the connection of people and objects – flyers and Facebook-grouped people.

Långgatorna lives, for better or for worse, all day long, and this makes us feel momentarily continental, according to many

5. Jane Jacobs (1961/1992) *The death and life of great American cities*. New York: Vintage Books.

comments in the media, planning documents and in various official debates. The popular Swedish artist Håkan Hellström has praised the neighbourhood in his songs. CDs, together with other things, such as planning documents, planning norms, popular city development theory, meetings, street fairs and telephone chains; all this has importance in a city's transformation process. In this case, this is what creates obstacles to gentrification.

Joakim Forsemalm
has a Ph.D. in Ethnology and works as a researcher at the University of Gothenburg and as a consultant at Radar arkitektur och planering in Gothenburg.

2. SELF-IMAGE/S OF THE CITY

Gunnar Falkemark

THE GOTHENBURG SPIRIT From donations to networking

Gothenburg was founded in 1621 and from the beginning it was an internationally influenced city. Dutchmen were invited to plan the city and Englishmen, Scotsmen and Germans established themselves early on – initially as businessmen and craftsmen. From the middle of the 18th century, the number of Scotsmen increased, and many of them significantly influenced business and industrial activities. During the 19th century, immigrating Jews also came to distinguish themselves both commercially and culturally.

It is often said that there is a special spirit in Gothenburg that is missing from other large cities, such as the capital Stockholm. The concept "the Gothenburg spirit" has been defined in a number of ways. What is usually mentioned is a particular kind of understanding that is thought to exist between the city's top politicians and the leaders from the business world and which refers to collaboration for the benefit of Gothenburgers. That there has been and still is a special climate of collaboration in Gothenburg's official life is hard to deny. It is also undeniable that this climate of collaboration has deep historical roots. It goes back more than 250 years.

RICHESSE OBLIGE

During the 18th century, a strong donation culture developed in Gothenburg. One of the pioneers here was Niclas Sahlgren, who, in 1731, together with Scotsman Colin Campbell, started the Swedish East India Company. Sahlgren made a very large fortune through lucrative trade with China. During his lifetime, he donated significant sums to orphanages and to the city's poor. In his will, Sahlgren donated a large portion of his remaining fortune to the building of a hospital. Today, Sahlgrenska Hospital is one of Scandinavia's largest healthcare institutions.[1]

1. Tore Frängsmyr (1976) *Ostindiska kompaniet* (*The East India Company*). Malmö: Bra Böcker, pp. 93–97.

During the 19th century, many rich people in the business world made donations. A number of these were for educational institutions of one kind or another. For example, William Chalmers – of Scottish ancestry and director of the East India Company – left in his will a significant sum for a new industrial school. Since its opening in 1829, Chalmers University of Technology has meant a lot to Gothenburg's development as an industrial city.[2]

2. Ibid, pp. 101–102.

The University of Gothenburg, which became a state university in 1954, was created at the end of the 19th century as an independent university by private initiative by the elite of the city's commercial aristocracy. A remarkable number were of Scottish or Jewish descent.

Initially, there were divided opinions about the direction of the university. Certain circles wanted a business school while others wanted to see a humanities-focused institution. The latter direction won. Many hoped that a solid education would prevent the sons of the city's rich men from surrendering solely to materialistic pleasure.[3]

3. Bo Lindberg, Ingemar Nilsson (1996) *Göteborgs universitets historia, I* (*The History of Gothenburg University, I*). Göteborg: Göteborgs universitet, pp. 11–31.

A number of the financial leaders also worked in the city's political government. Through their political engagement and donations to societal purposes – besides educational institutions, one can also mention libraries, museums, healthcare for the poor, and support of artists – the conditions for a new middle-class culture were created. According to historians of ideas, this was really the first time in Sweden's history that such a culture developed independently of the state and the church.[4] However, not everyone was impressed by what the middle-class culture achieved. The Norwegian Nobel-prize winner in literature Bjørnstierne Bjørnson commented ironically that, "In Gothenburg, no poetry is written; invoices are written."

4. Ibid, p. 12.

The donation culture that has been briefly described here can be seen as an expression of "richesse oblige". How did those large fortunes that made this generosity happen come about? Was Honoré de Balzac right when he claimed that behind every large fortune there is a crime? In the case of Gothenburg, Balzac does not seem to be completely wrong.

The wealth that the trade with China created was connected to the growth of Western colonialism. Mikela Lundahl notes in her contribution to this book that Swedish trade in the East Indies could not have taken place without the colonial structures other countries had established ("The simple Gothenburger"). There are also closer examples than trade with far-away countries. One of the most commented-upon wholesale families in Gothenburg – Dickson – built up a significant fortune during the mid and late 19th century by buying and felling very large areas of forest in Norrland. The methods of buying forest from farmers aroused great indignation. The farmers were tricked into selling their forest for a song and then the forest was devastated. This process created a hatred of companies amongst farmers that had long-term political ramifications.

INTERREGNUM

Around 1920, there was a democratic breakthrough in Sweden – on both the national and municipal levels. The right to vote for both men and women was introduced. At the municipal level, this political change had even more dramatic consequences than at the national level. Before 1920, within municipalities, there were graded voting scales depending on income and wealth. In 1907, this was limited so that no one could have more than 40 (!) times as many votes as someone else. Earlier, wealthy people could have thousands of votes.[5]

5. Gunnar Falkemark (2006) *Politik, mobilitet och miljö* (*Politics, mobility and environment*). Hedemora: Gidlunds Förlag, p. 118.

In terms of power in Gothenburg, the breakthrough of democracy brought with it a shift in political epochs. Before the conquest of democracy, political life was completely dominated by businessmen, industrialists and officials. Now something of a political landslide took place. The working-class had a decisive political influence. The breakthrough took place in the election of 1922 when the Social Democrats and the Communists got more than 55 % of the vote. During the period between the world wars, there was some strong political opposition in Gothenburg, not just between the middle-class and socialist parties, but particularly with the socialist camp, there were several party splits.[6]

6. Gunnar Attman (1963) *Göteborgs Stadsfullmäktige, I:2* (*Gothenburg City Council, I:2*). Elanders, pp. 225–234.

In the 1920s and 1930s, the donation culture continued but in a reduced way. A new view of governmental duties began to grow. The welfare of the population was seen more and more as an important political duty and not as something that could be taken care of by individual charities. As a result of this changed view of relations between the private and the official, a new type of Gothenburg spirit gradually formed.[7]

7. Ibid, pp. 238–242.

LARGE PROJECTS AND EVENTS – A NEW GOTHENBURG SPIRIT

It was after the second World War that the Gothenburg spirit as we know it today began to develop. Initially it was between the directors of the business world and the leaders of the three most important parties, the Social Democrats, the Liberal Party and the Moderates. The two latter parties were middle-class – the Liberal Party was socially liberal and the Moderates were a more rightwing liberal party. What is interesting is that there was often successful collaboration between the Social Democrats and the rightwing parties. In national politics, the former and the latter were ideological opponents and represented two different political blocks – a situation that is still the case in 2010. However, the new Gothenburg spirit did not include all the parties. For many decades, the Communists were left out.

The collaborative work between the directors in the business world and the parties has taken various shapes after World War II. For a number of years after the war, there were annual "budget dinners" at expensive restaurants in Gothenburg for the city's political leadership and the leaders of the large businesses in the city. These gatherings took place before the municipal taxation for the next year had been decided. With the coffee and cognac, the representatives of the municipality discussed the city's needs and problems while the directors talked about profitability, investment needs and similar topics.[8]

A more formalised arena for collaboration between the political leadership and the business world was established in 1977 when the business secretariat was founded in the wake of the serious global shipyard crisis, which especially affected shipping city Gothenburg. The main goal – then and now – was to develop business in the Gothenburg region. The secretariat was led by a political board that came to be dominated completely by the growth-hungry Social Democrats and Moderates. Through this organ, the business world has had a path right into the political system's inner core.[9] Since 2000, the secretariat has been called Business Region Göteborg and it has the same work as before. The board is still dominated by two parties – Social Democrats and Moderates.

In Gothenburg, this shared view has led to a long list of decisions made with significant agreement. An important area here was the overarching "city clean-up" in the 1960s and 1970s. In particular, a number of declining housing areas in the central parts of the city were slated for a rather brutal transformation. As a replacement, new areas were built along the city's periphery. This city transformation, which is often called a "demolition fury", was particularly comprehensive in Gothenburg.

8. Lars Ulvenstam (1999), *Göteborg* (*Gothenburg*). Stockholm: Carlsson bokförlag, pp. 101–104; Martin Åberg (1995) "'I vår lilla stad'. Om lokalpatriotiska strukturer och informella nätverk i Göteborg under mellankrigstiden" ("'In our little city.' On local patriotic structures and informal networks in Gothenburg between the wars"), in Lars Nilsson & Kjell Östberg (eds) *Kommunerna och lokalpolitiken* (*The municipalities and local politics*). Stads- och kommunhistoriska institutet, pp. 72–73.

9. Falkemark (1999), Chap. 6.

Here we have clear examples of "losers" when it comes to political agreement. The neighbourhoods that were demolished were mainly populated by the working-class. A hundred-year-old culture with well-established social networks was ripped to shreds. In the new outer areas that the residents were sent to, the previous networks could not be built up again. The idea to fix up and restore as an alternative to demolishing did not cross the minds of the decision-makers. Critics of the total transformation were met with the argument, which at that time was almost irrefutable, that "development must have its day". It is worth mentioning that when the newly built buildings were ready in the "cleaned-up" areas, it was just the better earning members of the middle-class who could afford to move in.[10]

Another field for collaboration has been to focus on various kinds of large construction projects. Among these, there is a new large sports arena – Nya Ullevi – which was finished in 1958, when Sweden hosted the football World Cup. In this arena, there has also been the world championship in track and field as well as annual summer concerts by the icons of the pop world, such as Bruce Springsteen, the Rolling Stones and Madonna. Similar projects have been an opera house and an indoor stadium for concerts and sports, which has also held spectacular events.

Among politicians and the business world, there has been a common endeavour to "put Gothenburg on the world map". A long list of building projects has been carried out in order to transform Gothenburg into an international event and trade fair city.

Often, a common spirit is facilitated by cultivating an "us against them" attitude. In Gothenburg's case, this is often directed at Stockholm and the central government. The government's traffic project in the city's larger cities, with the goal of minimising crowding and pollution, is a clear, but not unique, illustration. In the discussions in the beginning of the 1990s about accepting more traffic, the city's "strong man", Social

10. Kerstin Gustafson (2003) "Från fattig arbetarstadsdel till trendigt affärsstråk" ("From a poor working-class neighbourhood to a trendy business area"), Kulturtidskriften *Café Crème*, no. 5; Ulvenstam (1999), pp. 71, 283–285; Lars Wenander (2006) *Torsten Henrikson – stadsbyggaren* (*Torsten Henrikson –builder of the city*). Stockholm: Hjalmarson och Högberg, pp. 51–61. In many other cities, there were similar brutal interferences in the city environment. See Bengt O H Johansson (1997) *Den stora stadsomvandlingen* (*The big city transformation*). Regeringskansliet.

Democrat Göran Johansson, revealed to the city council his plans in regard to the national government. The goal was that "we should trick the state".[11]

11. Falkemark (1999), pp. 173–174.

Nowadays, it sometimes happens that people avoid talking about a specific Gothenburg spirit. Instead, people talk about building networks. In such situations, it is clear that not everyone can take part. A group that has long been kept outside the local power network is women. Gothenburg power has traditionally had a very pronounced male character. But maybe we are at the beginning of a shift. When the city's most powerful politician – Göran Johansson – recently left his most important positions, he was replaced by a woman, Anneli Hulthén. And she explained that for her, it is important to continue to cultivate the Gothenburg spirit.

Gunnar Falkemark is Professor of Political Science at the University of Gothenburg.

Mikela Lundahl

THE SIMPLE GOTHENBURGER

In October 2005, the East India ship *Götheborg* sailed off from the event city Gothenburg towards Shanghai. It was the culmination of a long reconstruction that was followed by publicity stunts, angry opinion pieces and political and diplomatic interventions. Thousands of Gothenburgers gathered on the day along the harbour to wave off the ship. Youths were engaged as volunteers, cultural workers were blogging from the boat and the city's daily newspaper was part of the event, both as a cheerleader and a financial sponsor. The route was to reconstruct the *original* route. Because this project gets it meaning in part from its use of history.

The boat in question is a replica of an 18th century ship that was built in Stockholm and used for the East India Company's trade, primarily with China. Around 20 years ago, some idealists, marine archaeologists and adventurers began diving after it and started building the replica. In the middle of the 1990s, the adventure became too expensive and complicated and they looked for partners. Meanwhile, these "partners" had another agenda; they held the idea, typical for the time, of benchmarking Gothenburg, which was in line with the current political belief that "events" were equal to culture.[1] The business world wanted to use the ship as a way of getting into the hard-to-conquer but growing Chinese market. The project gobbled resources and in an attempt to arouse interest to make sure the project really would be carried out, some ambassadors wrote an opinion piece:

> It is important to show that Sweden, including via, among others, the East India Company, has a long history as a successful trading nation. Today, when Swedish companies are among the world-leaders in, for example, the field of communication and transportation, the East India ship is a concrete symbol to represent international contacts and free trade. The picture of Sweden as a nation without a colonial past, but with a long history of international trade is strengthened. As representatives for Sweden, it is part of our job amongst hard, international competition to promote Sweden as an interesting country to work with, and therefore we see reasons to actively support the East India ship project in our work.[2]

This summarises the *official* picture of *Götheborg*, a picture that nevertheless hides central historical connections: European trade with China *is* indisputably connected with the colonialism that is denied above by the ambassadors. Of course, China was not a colony of Sweden (or any other European nation) in the 18th century. But the East India Company's success story (it is unknown how much they earned since the accounts are gone, but everyone agrees that they earned a lot) depended on how they could take advantage of other countries' successful colonies along the route and the development of trade that had already taken place. Sweden's lack of colonies was viewed as a real disadvantage at the time and not as the advantage that one can refer to when one portrays Sweden as neutral and peace-making.

1. See Johannes Samuelsson's texts and films about this theme: "Ett Modernt Äventyr" ("A Modern Adventure") no. 1, 2 and 3; "Ett Modernt Äventyr till 8 spännande marknader" ("A Modern Adventure to 8 exciting markets"), *Glänta* 1-2.08.

2. Those who signed this article are: Lars Andreasson, Mats Bergqvist, Peter Ekelund, Karin Ehnbom-Palmqvist, Lars Grundberg, Lennart Linnér, Börje Ljunggren, Helena Nilsson, Gunilla Olofsson, Ulf Sörmark, Teppo Tauriainen, Margareta Winberg (2004) "Ostindiefararen sätter Sverige på kartan" ("East India ship puts Sweden on the map"), *Göteborgs-Posten* 2004-04-03.

Sweden did not actively distance itself from participating in the colonisation of far-off countries. On the other hand, Sweden was not particularly successful in its colonisation efforts, perhaps because of its imperial ambitions in its region, particularly around the Baltic Sea. But there is, as we shall see, a direct line between Sweden's biggest colonisation *attempt* and the East India Company.

For example, in 1649 the Swedish African Company obtained the right to trade slaves, ivory and gold in West Africa. The next year, building was begun on a trading fort on the Gold Coast in what is now Ghana and it was named Carolusborg after King Karl X Gustaf. The small fortification was soon lost to other colonisers and it ended up as part of the British Gold Coast colony. Today, the fort, Cape Coast Castle, is on a cape in western Ghana, a frightening monument to the export of slaves that once took place here. In the permanent exhibition there, Sweden's role has not been covered up. Another example of Sweden's failed colonial history is the Caribbean island of Saint-Barthélemy (see Klas Rönnbäck's chaper in this book). A less known colonial project was Karl XII's attempt to colonise Madagascar in exchange for giving the pirates there a sanctuary on Marstrand. One of the participants in this enterprise was Henrik König. Twenty years later, he started the East India Company with the Scotsman Colin Campbell and Henric Sahlgren.

***

Then as now, one of the East India ships' way stations was the Spanish city Cádiz. One does not discuss why, if one wants to portray the East India Company as unsullied by Europe's colonial past. The Chinese were not too interested in trading with Europe. They had most things and did not really need the Europeans. But one good was interesting: silver. The Sala silver mine did not last long and it was forbidden to take silver out of

Sweden. But there was silver in Cádiz, silver from the colonies. Cádiz was a central point in the intricate colonial trading network. One of early colonialism's most important products was the silver that was taken from Latin American mines by Spanish and Portuguese colonists. In Cádiz, the East India ships could get the silver they needed in order to trade in China.

What we today label colonialism and distance ourselves from was not viewed in that way at the time. Colonialism took shape gradually. As conflicts occurred and the need of secure access to in-demand goods increased, countries tightened their hold on their possessions, which developed into colonies. The East India Company tried to established a trading station in India, but they were stopped by the stronger powers of England and France. The Swedes tried to do, and did do, the same things as the large colonial powers, but on another scale. This is why there was never a combined empire of the various projects.

Sometimes it is claimed that the colonial context is not important. For those who want to connect the East India Company's claimed non-colonial activities with the Swedish policy of neutrality, Swedishness and the defence of human rights, it is of course uninteresting or uncomfortable. Therefore *Götheborg* is portrayed as "an important link and symbol of good relations and trade between Sweden and China and all the countries that are visited on the voyage".[3] Historical facts are overshadowed by the fantastic possibilities that the ship is said to create. Hundreds of millions of Swedish crowns, of which a large part is public money, has been invested in the East India ship project. It is about marketing Sweden outwards, as well as assuring us Swedes that we have an honourable history to fall back on.

The history of Sweden as a non-colonial power can be said to contribute to "peace of mind".[4] But what worry is checked? What do we avoid seeing? What does it say about us, today? Maybe we cannot tell the story of the East India ship *Götheborg*'s colonial context without coming to terms with our self-image? Maybe we cannot look at the hidden side of our current self-image

3. The county director general, Göran Bengtsson, in the foreword to the recent official book about the project: Ingrid Arensberg (2005) *Ostindiefararen Götheborg seglar igen/The Swedish ship Götheborg sails again*. Sävedalen: Warne, p. 7. The book presents an idealised picture of the East India ship and of Gothenburg's middle-class public. The book project was undertaken by the officials behind it and written by someone without an agenda of her own. It is a tribute to a project that is based on its historical connection and at the same is completely without history.

4. Max Liljefors (2005) "Prime time trauma. Historia och television" ("Prime-time trauma. History and television"), in Catharina Raudvere, Anders Andrén & Kristina Jennbert (eds) *Hedendomen i historiens spegel. Bilder av det förkristna Norden* (*Paganism in the mirror of history. Pictures of the pre-Christian North*). Lund: Nordic Academic Press, p. 185.

because we are not prepared to give it up? Maybe it would be mean that we were forced to look at our "now" with new eyes, at the current national and international policies with another perspective? Our history and our now hang together; "to live as though our history has not influenced our culture and our way of thinking is a pure illusion, one of the most stubborn illusions today".[5] This illusion permeates our way of relating to uncomfortable events in our past, whereas there is a direct link between positive historical events and our present.

The Haitian historian Michel-Rolph Trouillot uses the phrase "the silence of the past" to show how unimaginable or uncomfortable events in history are written out or rewritten in order to suit current self-images.[6] With regard to the East India journey, we are talking about things that are known, but are systematically and actively forgotten or ignored because they are not considered important. Who has the power to decide that? What would all those who died in the service of this trade (and I am not referring to the sailors on board) think about this "scene for promoting Sweden", about this "symbol for the importance of international contacts and free trade"? All the slaves who were worked to death or died from diseases in the Latin American mines to get that necessary currency, silver; all those slaves who were part of and a prerequisite for the goods that were traded – would they agree that this is the "whole picture"?[7]

Why are the lies about the non-colonial background repeated again and again? There is no clear answer to this, but a repressed if insistent (lack of) consciousness about today's unjust world order, about today's treatment of new Swedes, can be more easily kept at bay if we can lean on a long history of work towards equality. To silence historical facts helps us maintain the myths and narratives that strengthen *contemporary* national and international policies.

Colonial thought patterns serve as a grid that together with patriarchal and capitalistic patterns arrange people and assets

5. Peter Kemp (2005) *Världsmedborgaren. Politisk och pedagogisk filosofi för det 21 århundradet* (*World citizen. Political and pedagogical philosophy for the 21st century*). Transl. by Joachim Retzlaff. Göteborg: Daidalos, p. 19f.

6. Michel-Rolph Trouillot (1995) *Silencing the past. Power and the production of history*. Boston: Beacon Press.

7. In the book, *Ostindiefararen Götheborg seglar igen* (*The East India ship Götheborg sails again*), they claim to give "a whole picture of the East India project." See Arensberg (2005), p. xix.

based on origin, identity and social status. As long as we do not admit the significance of colonialism, we cannot deal with the continuation of these thought patterns today. The Swedish self-image says that we stand for a sort of unshakeable humanism with long roots. Our long period of peace is seen as proof of that. The *folkhemmet* (the people's home), "the Swedish model", "the welfare state", equality, the supposedly liberal refugee policy, our image of ourselves as tolerant people who show solidarity, are further examples of this supposed humanism. But Sweden has an advantage in the world order that was established along with colonisation, a world order where Europe and the light-skinned, blond, Nordic is privileged.

In the story of *Götheborg*, modernity's contradictoriness is on display: on one hand is the modernity that is connected to obviously positive values: freedom, equality, fraternity, democracy and freedom from misconceptions. Modernity is a condition for and reason why globalisation gathered speed. On the other hand, modernity contributed to and depended on Africans being transported over the Atlantic to satisfy the Europeans' desire for sugar but also for the silver the Chinese wanted in trade for their goods. The East India trade was, therefore, dependent on the products of slavery. This tension was not unique to the 18th century but continues in other ways in today's globalisation. Trade and exchange are said to create prosperity and spread good ideals and knowledge. But the increased prosperity that Swedes see, in terms of easily gotten goods and ready money, has downsides, just as it did back then, in the form of environmental problems, child labour and the underselling of goods that force out local production, and so on.

Here comes the East India event and helps us to forget the downside of our time's successes. The cheerful image hides the downside of modernity – then and now. Imagine if instead it had been used as a tool for understanding our multicultural world, to understand how everything fits together? That today there are many Swedes who were not born here, or who have parents who were born elsewhere, fits with Europe's policies of conquest from the 15th century and forwards. The foundation was laid then for power relationships, borders were drawn, and ideas about us and them, and about development and underdevelopment, began to take shape. Europe polished its superiority complex, and sharpened an equivalent inferiority complex amongst the colonised and enslaved people.

We have not gotten rid of this superiority complex. We cannot get rid of it without many of today's disparities being seen as unreasonable. Therefore, we need all the support we can get to retain it. It is support for a one-sided and simplistic view versus a multi-dimensional and diverse one that *Götheborg* provides.

Mikela Lundahl
has a Ph.D. in History of Ideas, and works at School of Global Studies at the University of Gothenburg. Among other things she studies how images of Sweden are created and reproduced.

Barbara Czarniawska

A CITY OBSESSED BY CHANGE

In 1999, as the new millennium approached, I was asked by our daily newspaper, *Göteborgs-Posten,* to contribute a short piece on the theme "Gothenburg in 10 years". To a double immigrant like myself – an immigrant to Sweden and an immigrant to Gothenburg – it felt like receiving a certificate of citizenship. But the elation soon gave way to despair: I found I had nothing to say! My problem was that I did not want Gothenburg to change. I think that Gothenburg is a perfect city, at least for people like myself. This is why I moved to Gothenburg from Lund, and refused to go back to Stockholm, my first Swedish residence. Gothenburg combines, in a unique way, all the advantages of a big city and a small town. (With all respect to the countryside, I am a city person, and the country will remain for me an enchanting landscape, suitable for summer holidays.) Gothenburg is easy to move about in, aesthetically attractive through its combination of continental and Scandinavian architectures, enchanting with its wild and not-so-wild parks and canals, with a rich cultural life. And it is safe, despite of the excess of energy shown by some young men. The sea is just 10 minutes away, and it's a real sea at that, not like in the capital where the locals poke fun at poor tourists who never know what is sea and what is lake. Some of Gothenburg's Italian restaurants are better than in Italy, claim my Italian friends, who do all their shopping for Italian clothes here, because a shopping trip that takes 6 hours in Rome takes 2 hours in Gothenburg. And when they have taken a tour in the Padda and walked enough along the Avenue, I take them on excursions by tram to other parts of the city, so that they can see the variety of lifestyles that can be found here. This is why I want Gothenburg to remain as it is.

Upon reflection, it came to my mind that I was not actually asked to describe how Gothenburg could change. But, being the child of modernism that I am, I immediately reformulated the question thus. Future must mean progress and progress means change. Anything else would be "conservative", a negative word. The best thing would be to wipe a city and build it anew, as happened to Rabat.

Here, however, is one of many points that modernism has misunderstood. To conserve requires a lot of work and lots of competence, as all the curators and restorers can testify. In order to keep the buildings as they are now (read: beautiful), a lot of maintenance is required. In order to keep the city functioning as it does now, a lot of collective action is required, both from the city administration and from the companies involved in city life, not to mention the inhabitants. A living city requires all of them to cooperate in keeping it going.

But modernists love to build anew, to tear down the old, to reform and to innovate. Maintenance is boring and is the first item to go from the city budget. My Gothenburg in 10 years would therefore be a city where maintenance has priority, where no reform – either centralising or decentralising – is in the offing, where money would not be spent on quality assurances and bench-marking, not to mention branding. Games yes, gimmicks no. Ideally, striking new architecture, but not at the expense – aesthetic and financial – of the old one.

My contribution was refused, and after several discussions with the responsible journalists, the verdict was that I had "misunderstood the task". It was obvious – to them – that my text should include proposals for dramatic changes. It turned out that my first, modernist reaction was right, and my eventual answer wrong. Curious, I checked what other debaters wrote.

The general idea was that in 2010, Gothenburg will be much bigger and more beautiful, and will have more tourists. For all that, a lot of new investments are needed. A journalist, somewhat sceptical, asked if the city would have the money for all these investments. But this voice of reason was pushed away. Visions and money do not go together. A composer predicted that Gothenburg would become a city of art and culture, a testimony to which will be a new, big Cultural Centre (probably in the centre – in place of what?). An architect thought that Gothenburg would become a digital city, with a whole new district dedicated to information technology (here at least there was a district – the old docks – that could actually host this Gothenburg Silicon Valley). An art critic declared that what she sees in the future is a big modern city, not a small charming one.

This experience trained me in the proper ways of thinking, so that I now do not react with fright every time our local daily proposes a complete remake of the most central places in the city (which it does rather regularly). What struck me, however, was the contrast of this attitude with that expressed by the inhabitants of a city that I regularly visited on teaching assignments – Venice. I was also familiar with city studies conducted by my Venetian colleagues. It is not a great surprise that Venice lives off its past. However, in 1985, a select group of Venetians were asked to say something about the Venice of the future, which gave rise to a collection called "The roots of the future: 1985–2005" (*Le radici del futuro*). This somewhat peculiar expression made me do a Google check – an identical formulation has been used in Rome, Florence and Bologna. The contributors to the volume about Venice asked and answered questions that, in their view, were decisive for the future of the city. Here are some of them: "Is it possible at all to make a comparison of the cultural life of Venice thirty years ago and now? What elements of the history of *La Serenissima* [the Venice Republic] can be used in the re-birth of Venice? Is Venice mature enough to think about its future?" I especially liked the last one. But, jokes apart, Gothenburg is not Venice, and a contemporary city cannot be a museum. But a city can be comfortable according to contemporary criteria, and it can make its monuments live and be part of everyday life. It is a paradoxical goal, but possible to achieve, or at least strive to achieve.

To justify Gothenburg's obsession with change, one has to remember that the dream of a completely changed city is quite old, although perhaps not as old as Venice. Here is a modernist dream from the USA in 1939:

> The city of tomorrow, engineers say, will tend first to vastness; gigantic buildings connected by wide, suspended roadways on which traffic will speed at unheard of rates. … Traffic handled in huge underground tunnels, aerial ways, and in the air itself. Helicopter planes, capable of maneuvering about between buildings and roof-top airports, will take the place of the ground taxi. Each building will be virtually a city in itself, completely self-sustained, receiving its supplies from great merchandise ways far below the ground. Dwellers and workers in these buildings may go weeks without setting foot on the ground, or on the ground-level. In this city smoke will be eliminated, noise will be conquered, and impurity will be eliminated from the air. Many persons will live in the healthy atmosphere of the building tops, while others will commute to far distant residential towns, or country homes.
>
> Copyright: Amazing Stories, 1939.

Let us hope that this story will remain among the amazing stories, although I suspect that it could find many enthusiasts among Gothenburg-changers. After all, as pointed out in Gunnar Falkemark's contribution to this volume, the so-called demolition fury that afflicted Swedish cities in the 1960s and 1970s was especially acute in Gothenburg.

My vision of Gothenburg – admittedly seen from the privileged point of view of an inhabitant of its centre – remains that of a city that goes slowly, because it does not want to lose that what it has. Milan Kundera says that slowness is on its way to becoming fashionable again. So, apart from slow food, and slow movement, we will have slow cities (*cittaslow*). Hopefully, Gothenburg will be one of them. After all, by sticking to its trams, it reached the top of city fashion when many others cities were digging tram tracks from the asphalt in haste. Thus, not a city that is immobilised by its past, and not a city that looks only in the future, but, possibly, a city that keeps its past up-to-date, and moves into the future not by drastic jumps but by strolling into it.

Barbara Czarniawska is Professor of Business Economics at GRI, School of Business, Economics and Law in Gothenburg. She was responsible for the Research program Managing Big Cities 1995–1999.

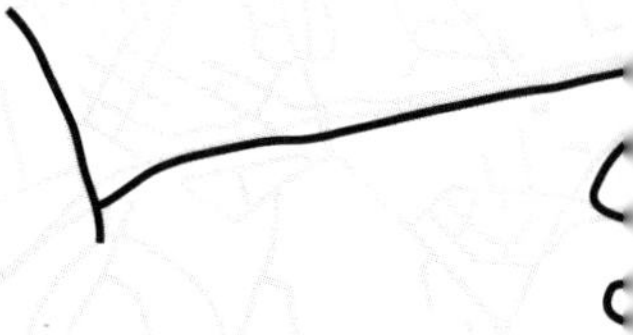

Helena Holgersson

"HIDDEN REFUGEES" AS MUNICIPAL HEADACHE

In the debate about housing for asylum-seekers, Gothenburg is described by local politicians as a segregated city without much to offer. People will be able to find neither reasonable housing nor work here, they say.[1] However, in the separate discussion about how Gothenburg is to be transformed from a harbour and industrial city to an event and knowledge city, the city is described as a place with enormous potential, often by the same politicians (see Catharina Thörn's chapter in this book). The municipality emphasises the need to *decrease* the uncontrolled inflow of asylum-seekers – and thereby in the long-run the number of "hidden refugees" (as people who live under the threat of deportation are often called in Sweden) and "immigrants" – while at the same time stating the ambition to *increase* the city's population by tens of thousands to become a large city region. "Size is decisive for growth", claimed the then-chairman of the municipal executive board, Göran Johansson, in an interview in 2006 in the *Göteborgs-Posten*.[2]

It is just as hard to verbally describe people who do not have the legal right to live in the country in which they are resident

1. Christer Lövkvist (2007) "'Flyktingmottagande skapar misär'" ("'The reception of refugees creates misery'"), *Göteborgs-Posten* 2007-06-04.

2. TT (2006) "Göteborg för litet, tycker Johansson" ("Gothenburg is too small, thinks Johansson"), *Göteborgs-Posten* 2006-06-25.

as it is to deal with them politically within the framework of the welfare state. This issue is today being brought to a head in larger cities around the world, because it is often urban environments that these people go to. Their presence is always paradoxical, but as the anthropologist Nicholas De Genova emphasises, non-citizenship, as with citizenship, is always context-bound.[3]

3. Nicholas De Genova (2002) "Migrant 'illegality' and deportability in everyday life", *Annual review of anthropology*, no. 31: pp. 419–437.

NON-CITIZEN PARADOXES[4]

4. The examples are taken from my fieldwork in 2005–2007, where as part of my Ph.D. project I interviewed a number of asylum-seekers and "hidden refugees" in Gothenburg.

"Hidden" | visible

A man around 35-years-old works in a small neighbourhood shop in one of Gothenburg's suburbs. I have spent some afternoons there with him. On the way home from work, people stop to buy cigarettes, snuff, soda and maybe an evening newspaper. They never need to say what they want. When he sees them in the doorway, he immediately picks out their items, and then he writes how much they have shopped for in a notebook that he keeps under the counter. Probably none of these customers has ever thought that he could be a "hidden refugee". The concept is clearly linked to expressions such as "underground" and "outside society", which makes the presence of this group in Gothenburg seem almost mythical. (Compare this to Ingrid Martins Holmberg's chapter in this book.)

"Illegal" | law-abiding

As a "hidden refugee", one always has to have a valid ticket on the tram. If someone gets caught by the ticket inspector and cannot be identified, the police are called in. Although "hidden refugees" are often referred to as "illegal", they are probably among Sweden's most law-abiding citizens. At any rate, they are if you ignore the fact that they have not accepted their deportation orders and have to live and work on the black housing and labour market. They cannot take any risks. A man I interviewed laughingly told me how he had trouble getting his friends to keep to the speed limit when they drove somewhere together.

Political object | political subject

On 7 May 2005, the campaign *Flyktingamnesti 2005* (Refugee Amnesty 2005) organised protests in cities around Sweden. When the Utlänningsnämnden (Aliens Appeals Board) was replaced by the Migrationsdomstolar (Migration Courts), the campaign's goal was to get the government to give residence permits to those asylum-seekers who had been refused by the previous system. Thousands of people participated. In Gothenburg, the protest march started at Götaplatsen on the main street Avenyn and went to Gustav Adolfs torg. I met two people in the crowd I had previously interviewed. Today, "hidden refugees" are a subject of heated political discussions, but at the same time they themselves can be very politically engaged. Another of my interviewees had done volunteer work with homeless people in Gothenburg during his "hidden" time.

Refused | retained

A man said that during the years he had been "hiding" from the Swedish authorities in order to avoid being deported, he had successfully focused on his music. His video – filmed in a park in Gothenburg filled with summer flowers – had been shown on international satellite channels from the region where he had grown up, which had led to offers of concerts in Canada, the US, Germany and England. Various TV shows had also invited him to perform and be interviewed, but since he did not have a residence permit, he was forced to say no. "Hidden refugees" have no right to live in Sweden but at the same time they are stuck here (if they want to continue applying for asylum, that is).

Guest | resident

After each interview with a "hidden refugee", I asked the person to draw a map of "his or her Gothenburg". The man who drew the map below had lived here for over five years, mostly in Hisingen, when I met him. The map stretches over large parts of the city and includes stores, a sports hall, a market, parks, two shopping centres and a number of places where he and his friends live and have lived. He is not recognised as a resident, but he is hardly a guest. (See Minoo Alinia's chapter in this book.)

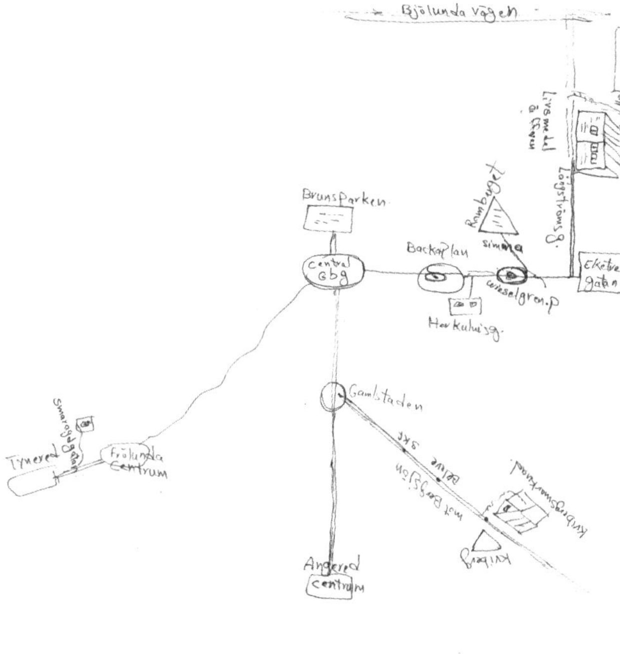

Human | citizen

Sighing, one woman recounted how she was once asked for her national identity number when she was picking up a wristwatch that she had had repaired at a watch shop in Gothenburg. Another interviewee had been refused the purchase of a computer in instalments for the same reason. The *last four digits* of the identity number can be said to symbolise Swedish citizenship (or in any case a residence permit). Without them, a person has very limited access to the fine-meshed social security net. What makes "hidden refugees" so hard to handle bureaucratically is that they are people without being citizens. Judging from the stories of my interviewees, it seems that in a Swedish context, exclusion is not limited to the public sector.

Gothenburg as a space for negotiation

It is in this mess of paradoxes that the Swedish government and Gothenburg municipality have to handle the presence of "hidden refugees". Today, thousands of people live in Sweden without legal permission to do so.[5] "I don't want it to be this way", said the Social Democratic then-minister of health Ylva Johansson in 2005 during a radio debate about the right of "hidden refugees" to get healthcare. From the state's perspective, the ideal situation would be that everyone whose asylum applications are rejected accept the fact and willingly leave the country. However this is not the case. Since the end of the Second World War, Sweden has grown accustomed to its role of international role model and tries to get *other* countries to agree to and follow various conventions regarding human rights. A few years ago, however, the Swedish government was heavily criticised by the UN's special reporter Paul Hunt because it offers "hidden refugees" emergency healthcare only and also makes them pay for it themselves. Hunt said that this did not follow the guidelines set out by the UN's Committee for Economic, Social and Cultural Rights (CESCR).[6]

But Swedish policy is completely understandable within the frame of the Scandinavian welfare model, which, more than other systems, is built around *the citizen*. In the radio debate mentioned above, Johansson explained that if Sweden were to offer "hidden refugees" education and healthcare, as is the case in many other European countries, there would be a risk of

5. Pia Fridén (2005) *P1-morgon* (*P1 Morning*), 2005-12-01.

6. Paul Hunt (2007) "Implementation of General Assembly resolutions 60/251 of 15 March 2006 Entitled 'Human Rights Council.' Report of the Special Rapporteur on the Right of Everyone to the Enjoyment of the Highest Attainable Standard of Physical and Mental Health, Paul Hunt. Addendum. Mission to Sweden" A/HRC/4/28/Add.2. *The Office of the United Nations High Commissioner for Human Rights.*

creating a society with first-class and second-class citizens, a development she does not want to see in Sweden. In order to avoid what Johansson calls "parallel systems", the country is using a lot of resources to *enforce* the rejections; that is, to make sure that the rejected asylum-seekers actually leave the country. The consequence is that *because of* general welfare – which was created to guarantee everyone the same provision – it is in many respects more difficult to live in Sweden without legal permission than it is in other countries.

Scholar of cultural studies Ien Ang suggests that while nations can be viewed as imaginary communities, cities can be understood as *concrete realities*. They cannot control their borders, but are nevertheless to some degree responsible for the people who reside there. Even if the setting of laws on immigration and asylum takes place at a national level, it is in big cities that the consequences become visible.[7] Here one cannot wish away the group. Like the geographer Monica Varsanyi, I have looked for examples of how the presence of "hidden refugees" (or "undocumented immigrants" as she calls them in the American context) is dealt with at the local level.[8] I found that governmental authorities in Gothenburg, at the same as offering "hidden refugees" a certain amount of provision, attempt to make it harder for them to settle.

In 2006, without a national directive, the Sahlgrenska University Hospital decided to offer every patient the emergency care required, regardless of his or her ability to pay. At seminars, the staff got information about how this would impact routines.[9] Also, with reference to the Convention on the Rights of Children, many headmasters in the Gothenburg municipality welcome "hidden" children to their schools, even though they are not paid for this.[10] At the same time, Gothenburg, primarily along with Malmö and Södertälje, is pressuring the government to minimise the opportunity for asylum-seekers to arrange their own housing, because in practice this system leads to many people moving to "immigrant-dense suburbs" in big

7. Ien Ang (2006) "Nations, migration and the city: Mediating urban citizenship." Paper presented at the ESF-LiU Conference *Cities and media: Cultural perspectives on urban identities in a mediatized world*, Vadstena 25–29 October.

8. Monica Varsanyi (2008) "Immigration policing through the backdoor: City ordinances, the 'Right to the City', and the exclusion of undocumented day laborers", *Urban geography*, 29(1): pp. 29–52.

9. Ann Louise Leikin (2006) "Gömda flyktingar ska ha vård efter behov" ("Hidden refugees shall have healthcare as needed"), *suMagaZinet*, no. 3.

10. Anne Sjögren (2007) "Mödosam kamp för de gömda och papperslösa" ("Difficult struggle for the hidden and paper-less"), *Barnbladet*, no. 4.

11. Göran Johansson, Anders Lago, Ilmar Reepalu (2007) "Alla måste ta emot flyktingar" ("Everyone must accept refugees"), *Dagens Nyheter* 2007-03-02.

12. Förvaltnings AB Framtiden (2008) "Begränsning av antalet boende" ("Limit to number of people in a home"), Nyheter 2008-04-09, URL: http://www5.goteborg.se/prod/framtiden/dalis2.nsf/vyPublicerade/843D6772A6BD2F40C1257426004234ED?OpenDocument.

cities.[11] In the spring of 2008, the municipal housing companies introduced laws regarding how many people can live in each flat, a measure clearly justified in terms of refugee-policy.[12]

The local authorities' various – and often contradictory – ways of handling the presence of "hidden refugees" in Gothenburg cannot be easily summarised. It is hard to see a linear development. The situation can instead be characterised by continuous negotiations. Thus, the *municipal headache*.

Helena Holgersson
works at the Department of Sociology and the Department of Cultural Sciences. Her research focuses on non-citizenship, exclusion and urban experiences of everyday life.

Abby Peterson

THE FIRE CATASTROPHE IN GOTHENBURG
Ritual performances of multiculturalism

On the eve of 30 October 1998, a fire that swept the premises of an immigrant association during a party organised by local Gothenburg youth resulted in the deaths of 63 young people and injured over 200. This was the worst fire catastrophe to hit Sweden in the modern era. Most of the youth, although far from all, had what in Sweden is commonly designated as an "immigrant background". Initially, the youth and ethnic minority communities expressed rage over the efforts of the police to find the perpetrators behind the arson. Rumours abounded as to who the guilty people were and the motives behind their crime. In short, the content of the rumours was that rightwing extremist youth with racist motives were responsible for the fire. The catastrophe dramatically brought the official Swedish model of multiculturalism and the self-image as a tolerant ethnically integrated society into question. (It was during the spring of 2000 that charges were brought against four young ethnic minority men for the crime.)

In this essay, I will analyse the discotheque fire in neo-Durkheimian terms as a sacred moment of epiphany, where unexpected violence disrupted the everyday lives of the people of Gothenburg and opened a space for a reiteration of the social construction of order and collective identity. The memory work that recalled and re-enacted the event as a collective trauma was structured and re-structured through the performances of rituals. Instead of describing the meaning of their grief and loss, performances sought to achieve their meaning by "doing". They created social reality by doing something, and through their actions they attempted to frame the extraordinary event of the catastrophe and to cope with their overwhelming sense of loss and grief.[1] These social performances of ritual attempted to construct and convey in various ways, and with varying degrees of success, a sense of multicultural community in metropolitan Gothenburg.

1. Abby Peterson (2006a) *Att minnas saknad och dela sorg. Brandkatastrofen i Göteborg i ett kollektivt minnesperspektiv (Remembering loss and sharing grief. The fire disaster in Gothenburg in a collective memory perspective).* Department of Sociology: Göteborg Studies in Sociology.

SPONTANEOUS RITUAL PERFORMANCES

The sites for memory work and the ritual performances of collective identity were many in the aftermath of the fire catastrophe – the cathedral, local churches, grave sites, the bedroom of one of the girls who died in the fire, school auditoriums, etc. In short, the sites for memory work ranged across the public, semi-public and private spaces of metropolitan Gothenburg. But more than any other of these spaces for collective mourning, the site of the fire in an unattractive semi-industrial area of Gothenburg – Backaplan – became the focal point for the first spontaneous ritual performances of collective grief. In the days and nights immediately after the fire, and during the following weeks, crowds of youth gathered – instating and reinstating a sense of multiethnic community. The local government official appointed to coordinate the municipality's long-term support efforts described the scene at the site with the following words: "Everyone contributed to maintaining dignity out there; there was a powerful atmosphere of solemnity."[2] The young people lit thousands of candles and sat in their glow, weeping and reflecting on the calamity that had unexpectedly befallen them. They left flowers, notes and letters, photographs, furry toys and other small tokens of memory for

2. Ibid, p. 79.

the young people who had perished or who lay injured in the hospitals. Ultimately, these memorial artefacts created a 150-meter-long embankment surrounding the site.[3] In these initial days and weeks after the catastrophe, grief and a sense of loss knew no ethnic boundaries. While we cannot measure the lasting effects of these first spontaneous rituals of collective identity, at that time these rituals forged powerful social bonds between many of the young people of Gothenburg, transgressing ethnic boundaries in a community mourning the deaths of compatriots. The unexpectedness of the catastrophe, which took the lives of fellow youth, disrupted their lives and opened a space for reflection on the fragility of the meaning of life. The scope of the catastrophe – so many perished and so many were injured – opened up and even demanded collective forms for memory work, for coping with what was perceived as a collective trauma.

3. Ibid, pp. 80ff.

THE ORCHESTRATED RITUALS OF COMMUNITY CONSTRUCTION

Immediately, on the following day, "official" Sweden mobilised ritual performances of grief and loss. On 30 October 1998, municipal offices and institutions in Gothenburg were closed, sports events were cancelled and flags were flown at half-mast across the city. The Prime Minister, mayor and other government officials participated in a ceremony held at the cathedral. Perhaps even more orchestrated was the official ceremony held at the cathedral the following Saturday. The King and Queen, together with government officials, attended a memorial service presided over by a bishop from the Swedish Lutheran church, an imam from the Muslim community, a Jewish rabbi, a Catholic priest and a Serbian-Orthodox priest. This was a potent performance of the official version of Swedish multiculturalism. The King repudiated those who sought to use the fire catastrophe in order to kindle conflict between Swedes and ethnic minorities. "He reminded us that the discotheque that had ended in a tragedy had begun as a broad meeting place for young people from Sweden as well as from many other countries, religions and cultures."[4] Later, in his annual Christmas speech to the nation, the King highlighted the fire catastrophe in the following words:

4. *Svenska Dagbladet* 1998-11-08, p. 4.

> The catastrophe in Gothenburg was not only a great tragedy for relatives and friends but for an entire nation. ... Let us see in the midst of the darkness that took place that October evening a hope for the future in that these young people with such diverse backgrounds had gathered for a common party. I believe that tomorrow's Swedes, with ties to many cultures and religions, will find new ways to live together in Sweden.[5]

5. www.royalcourt.se/kungafamiljen/hm-konungcarlxvigustaf/tal/arkivhmktal19951999/hmkonungensjultal1998.5.19ae493103f9816b7080002426.html.

This is a concise version of the sanctioned Swedish model of multiculturalism, which was performed in orchestrated rituals at the official memorial ceremonies in the immediate aftermath of the fire.

ORGANISED RITUALS OF MULTIETHNIC COMMUNITY

The Association of Fire Victims (BOA) is a constructed memory community of fate; that is, it gathered together many of those who experienced direct losses – relatives and friends of those who perished as well as young people who survived the catastrophe. It was the event of the catastrophe that brought them together, and the victims of the catastrophe came from nineteen different national origins. The Association has organised annual ritual performances of memory on the eve of the catastrophe. They have commemorated the tragedy through moving events of remembrance incorporating torchlight marches from the city centre to the site, music, poetry and short narratives in well-choreographed performances of mourning. The rituals perform their utopian vision of multiethnic community with their idealisation of the community of young people who gathered on that fateful night in 1998. The image they wish to convey through their ritual performances is that of a loving, tolerant community that transgresses Sweden's multiethnic diversity. Narratives of troubles, conflicts and other "awkward" aspects of the party are suppressed. For example, suppressed in this idealised account of multiethnic community is the fact that four young men with ethnic minority backgrounds were later tried and sentenced for arson and murder – the motive for the crime was that they were angry that the organisers had demanded that they should pay the entrance charge.

By remembering an idealised ephemeral community, a moment of belonging is frozen in time. A memory image of a culturally transgressive community is defined and fixed, giving it a stability, whereby one can evoke "the finest specimens of fossilised duration".[6] But an imagined community is not the same as an actually lived community; it is a reconstruction after the event, which often is necessarily idealised so as to help its members cope with trauma.[7]

6. Gaston Bachelard (1994 [1958]) *The poetics of space. The classic look at how we experience intimate spaces*. Boston: Beacon Press, p. 9.

7. Abby Peterson (2006b) "Minnesresor. Mellan försök att minnas och glömma" ("Memory journeys. Between attempts to remember and forget"), in Diana Mulinari & Nora Räthzel (eds), *Bortom etnicitet* (*Beyond ethnicity*). Umeå: Boréa, pp. 47–60.

THE CRITERIA FOR PERFORMATIVE SUCCESS & FAILURE

The goal of ritual performances is to create an emotional connection between the audience and the ritual participants/actors and their text (the message they wish to communicate) and thereby to create conditions for projecting cultural meaning from performance to audience – to fuse a collective identification and a cultural extension of meaning.[8] The various ritual performances in the aftermath of the fire catastrophe attempted to create a new social reality – a cultural extension of meaning – in the face of an ethnically segregated Gothenburg, where the ethnic minority population is disproportionally relegated to the urban periphery in socially and economically depressed communities. The housing estates are characterised by a high rate of unemployment, a high degree of social welfare dependency, a disproportionate number of "underachievers" in the school system, a large part of the population under the age of 24, and

8 Jeffrey C Alexander (2006) "Cultural pragmatics. Social performances between ritual and strategy" in Jeffrey C Alexander, Bernhard Giesen & Jason L Mast (eds), pp. 29–90. Cambridge, UK: Cambridge University Press, pp. 55ff.

above all, a high percentage of residents from ethnic minorities. Between approximately 40 and 85 per cent of the residents of housing estates have immigrant backgrounds. The reality of ethnic segregation, together with ethnic discrimination in the labour market, stands in glaring contrast to an image of Gothenburg as a vibrant multiethnic community.[9]

9 Abby Peterson & Mikael Hjerm (eds) (2007) *Etnicitet. Perspektiv på samhället (Ethnicity. Perspectives on society).* Malmö: Gleerups.

The initial spontaneous performances of ritual mourning most closely fused audience with participants/actors and text. In these ritual performances, we can say that audience and participants/actors were more or less one and the same, in stark contrast with the "official", far more complex mode of orchestrated ritual political performances. Giesen emphasises that in these forms of ritual performance, the audience, in this case "the nation", is invited into the ritual as participants. In other words, the political actors in these types of ritual performances pretend to include the people in a community of participants who all share "the same reality".[10] The very size of the addressed group, i.e. the nation, which was invited to participate in a reinstatement of the Swedish nation as a multiethnic community, makes the distance between audience and participants/actors so great that the truth claims of Swedish multiculturalism are virtually impossible to establish – the emotional connection between the audience and the actual participants/actors in the ritual and their text is implausible.

10 Bernhard Giesen (2006) "Performing the sacred. A Durkheimian perspective on the performative turn in the social sciences", in Jeffrey C Alexander, Bernhard Giesen & Jason L Mast (eds), pp. 325–367. Cambridge, UK: Cambridge University Press, pp. 355ff.

Finally, the "organised" annual rituals staged by the Association of Fire Victims recalls the tragedy of the original event and re-enacts the original party by interpreting their community through a mythical narrative of an idealised multiethnic community – thereby attempting to give meaning to the meaninglessness of the violence that claimed 63 young lives. Their rituals are inwardly directed towards reinstating the Association's collective identity as a multiethnic community of fate – participants/actors and text are fused. Audience is secondary to their performances, rather playing a role as background relief and mediated witness to the authenticity of their grief.

Abby Peterson
is a Professor at the Department of Sociology, University of Gothenburg. Her research interests tangent cultural sociology and political sociology.

Göran Larsson & Åke Sander

FROM CELLAR TO DOME AND MINARET

Fifty years ago, Gothenburg was ethnically and religiously a very homogenous city. For most Gothenburgers, Islam, Hinduism, Buddhism, Sikhism, etc. were in principle unknowns with which few people had direct contact. Today, the landscape is completely different. No one can walk in the centre without seeing a Muslim or a Sikh, and in certain neighbourhoods people with Christian backgrounds are the minority. Gothenburg has become a multi-religious city with mosques, temples and gurdwaras. What is described below is just one example of this development.

The first Muslims came to Gothenburg during the second half of the 1950s. Up through the middle of the 1960s, there were no formally organised religious activities amongst them. They only met "spontaneously" at someone's home for Friday prayers, major holidays (*Eid*) and other festivities. During the second half of the 1960s, the Turkish Cultural Association were given a space that was used as Gothenburg's first Islamic prayer space. The number of visitors increased gradually. During the second half of the 1970s, the number of people who used the locale was estimated to be around 1 000. In 1997, they created their first formal religious organisation or "congregation", the Islamic Centre in Gothenburg. The year before, *Islam's Ahmadiyya Djama'at in Sverige* was established in Gothenburg with Sweden's first "real", purpose-built mosque – the Nasir Mosque.[1] This was before Islam and Muslims got media attention, which started with the Islamic revolution in Iran in 1978–79. There were no objections or protests, except for from some people who lived nearby, who complained about the fact that it was painted pink.

From the 1980s forward, the Islamic institutionalisation process accelerated in Gothenburg. As new groups of Muslims came to the city, the need for religious institutions and mosque premises increased. At the end of the 1970s, the Islamic Centre formed a mosque-building committee and applied for building permission. During the following years, they made various attempts to organise the building of a "real" mosque. Three of these attempts got so far that they received suggestions for locations from the municipality. However, these were met by "storms of protests" from people who lived nearby and so they did not get planning permission. "Of course Muslims should be able to built a mosque – but not here", seems to have been the general point of view. But it was not just reactions from the majority that created an obstacle for the building plans. There has always been a problem with working together within the Muslim group and financing was a problem. The majority of today's 15 or so Islamic congregation locales are still located in spaces that are not suited to the purpose, often in industrial or cellar locations.

Most of Gothenburg's approximately 60 000 Muslims[2] would agree with Abd al Haqq Kielan, imam and secretary of the Swedish Islamic Academy, when he says:

> It is important to be able to move up from the lower level and into a real mosque. As long as we are in a cellar, we do not really exist. It is important to leave the cellar, partly for practical reasons, because down there it is crowded, poorly ventilated and has bad lighting, but also for status reasons.

1. Ahmadiyya represents what can be described as an Islamic reform movement. It was founded by Mirza Ghulam Ahamd al Qadiani in India at the end of the 19th century. As the main part of the movement ("the *Qadians*") claims, among other things, that the founder was a prophet and *al-masih* (and not just a "new interpreter" or "reformer" (*Mudjtahid*)), it was considered by other Muslims as "heretical." Many Muslims distance themselves from this variety of Islam and thereby would not visit their mosque.

2. On the basis of previous research (such as Åke Sander [1993] *I vilken utsträckning är den svenske muslimen religiös? Några överväganden kring problematiken med att ta reda på hur många muslimer som deltar i verksamheten vid de muslimska "församlingarna" i Sverige* (*To what degree is the Swedish Muslim religious? Some considerations regarding the problem of finding out how many Muslims take part in activities at Muslim "congregations" in Sweden*). Kim-Rapport no. 14. Göteborg: Göteborgs universitet), it seems that 15–20 percent of Sweden's ethnic Muslims live in the Gothenburg area. The total number of Muslims in Sweden is estimated today to be around 400 000. In 1930, there were around 15, in 1970 around 10 000, in 1985 around 50 000, in

1990 around 120 000 and in 2000 around 325 000. Göran Larsson, Åke Sander (2008) *Islam and Muslims in Sweden. Integration or fragmentation? A contextual study*. Berlin and Münster: Lit Verlag, p. 70ff.

> A visible mosque wins prestige and means a lot for integration. Muslims would then feel that we are also part of society and it would be easier to socialise on equal terms.

In 1996, a mosque-building project led by Sveriges Muslimska Stiftelse (Sweden's Muslim Organisation, SMS) got permission to built a mosque on Myntgatan by Ramberget in Hisingen. A variety of factors, including the fact that the political climate regarding Islam and Muslims had worsened, particularly after the terror attacks on 11 September 2001 and the following events (the war against terror, the bombings in Bali, Madrid and London, to name just a few), meant that it took until 2007 for the financing to be secured (via the Saudi Arabian government) and for Bashar Ghanoum, the chairman of SMS, finally to be able to declare that Gothenburg was going to get a purpose-built Sunni mosque. So the "mosque issue" has a long history in Gothenburg.[3]

Ghanoum's announcement got a mixed reception. On the one hand, there was a positive reception from, for example, Brämaregården's congregation, which, after the fire catastrophe on 30 October 1998, when many young people died (see Abby Peterson's chapter in this volume), started to actively develop, in part with other Christian congregations, a religious dialogue between Christians and Muslims. A leading person here was assistant vicar Marika Palmdahl, who was assigned by Bishop Lars Eckerdal to write a so-called priest meeting paper for a priest meeting in 2005. It was titled *Det Nya Landet – kristen och muslimsk dialog som utmaning och möjlighet* (The new country – Christian and Muslim dialogue as a challenge and opportunity).[4] The basic idea of this work is that ethnic, religious and other diversity and pluralism – correctly managed – should be seen as a possibility, an asset, rather than as a threat.

On the other hand, this announcement got a negative reception from other places. A group that called itself *Action group stop the building of the mosque* put up posters in the area, includ-

3. Åke Sander (1991) "The Road From *Musalla* To *Mosque*. Some reflections on the process of integration and institutionalization of Islam in Sweden." In W A R Shadid & P S van Koningsveld, (eds) *The Integration of Islam and Hinduism in Western Europe*, Holland: Kampen, pp. 62–88; Åke Sander, Göran Larsson (2002) "The mobilisation, organisation and institutionalisation of Islam in Sweden 1990–2000. From green to blue and yellow Islam?" In W A R Shadid and P S Van Koningsveld, (eds) *Religious freedom and the neutrality of the state: The position of Islam in the European Union*. Holland: Pharos, Kampen, pp. 91–112; Larsson, Sander (2008).

4. Marika Palmdahl (2005) *Det Nya Landet. Kristen och muslimsk dialog som utmaning och möjlighet* (*The new country. Christian and Muslim dialogue as a challenge and opportunity*). Lund: Arcus.

ing on the walls of the Brämaregården church, with the text: "Stop Islam, do not build a terrorist nest in Ramberget!" On the poster there was also a picture – inspired by the conflict regarding the Danish Mohammed caricatures – of an Arabic-looking man with a beard, a turban and a bomb in his turban. The Sweden Democrats also quickly launched a campaign, "No to the mosque in Ramberget", on the internet, via leaflets left in mailboxes in Hisingen and posters in public areas.[5] The main message of the campaign was that a mosque is a foreign element in the city image and it ruins it. The mosque will be a breeding ground for terrorists, a propaganda centre for Islamic values and a threat to "our" view of democracy, equality and women. It was also seen as an expression of Saudi/Islamic cultural imperialism. The mosque was viewed, along with other kinds of ethnic and religious diversity, as a threat to Sweden and Swedishness. It is harder to say who is behind the more distasteful protests, such as placing pigs' heads on the planned building site. It is clear that the building project arouses strong feelings and also that the protests against the mosque are not only from the extreme right. In a study, Pia Karlsson and Ingvar Svanberg show how basically every attempt to build a mosque has been met with upset feelings, opposition and protests at in principle all levels of Swedish society.[6] Existing studies on Swedes' attitudes towards the presence of Islamic symbols in public clearly confirms this: negative responses vary between 50 and 75 percent.[7]

5. www.ramberget.com.

6. Pia Karlsson, Ingvar Svanberg (1995) *Moskéer i Sverige. En religionsetnologisk studie i intolerans och administrativ vanmakt* (*Mosques in Sweden. A religious ethnographic study on intolerance and administrative powerlessness*). Tro & Tanke no. 7. Lund: Svenska Kyrkans Forskningsråd.

7. Larsson, Sander (2008), p. 208ff.

ONE MOSQUE – TWO DISCOURSES

One of the primary thoughts within the oppositional discourse seems to be that they want to "maintain Sweden as Swedish" – and in this case "maintain Gothenburg as Gothenburgian". In this discourse, people view the site where the mosque is to be built as Gothenburg's old precipice. The location has been portrayed as a pagan cult place, which is why it is seen as a scandal to use it for something as foreign and non-Swedish as a mosque. The argument is based on a sort of essentialistic historical view of what is Swedish. There is something “typically” Swedish and it can be identified and should be protected. That this kind of thinking is related to classical racism, and even more with so-called new racism, is not hard to recognise. It is a kind of thinking that is based on the idea that one can separate different cultures, ethnicities and religions from each other and stick them into closed boxes. The qualities that make them different decide the other characteristics which form the basis for and legitimise how they are separated. It is often implicit that different groups with their specific characteristics are differently valued. One’s own group always has its own intrinsic value. Added to this is often the idea that cultural, ethnic and religious purity and unity is a necessary condition for the survival, development and success of a culture, ethnic group or religious group. It leads to the idea that any kind of cultural, ethnic and religious mixing must be opposed, because it leads to decline and ruin. So it follows that members of the group not only have the right but also the duty to protect, take care of, look after and develop their specific group and its purity.

The other discourse takes as its starting-point Esaias Tegnér’s famous comment that “only barbarism is our true heritage” and dismisses the idea about an essential Swedishness as a bad genealogical construction. We are all immigrants! Sweden and Swedishness are seen as an ongoing historical process that is created and re-created by its elements. For example, within the Swedish kingdom’s borders, which over time have varied, there have always been Sami people and so-called gypsies, as well as people from our neighbouring countries. Walloons and Scotsmen, who came to Sweden in the 17th century, helped shape our country and culture. A major part of the Swedish nobility has its origins outside the country’s borders, and the same is true for the royalty. This is not just the case for people. Technology, crafts, music, religion, food and much more have always been affected by things from outside the country. The Santa Lucia holiday and the Christmas tree, Santa Claus and pizza – all of these things were imported, but today are viewed as "Swedish". Dutchman troubadour Cornelis Vreeswijk is probably seen by most people as being as Swedish as Carl Michael Bellman. Analogously, religion, especially folk or unofficial religion, has never been uniform or invariable, something that literary fiction – such as Vilhelm Moberg's series on emigrants – shows. Sweden and Swedishness can only be characterised as a historically continuing and always changing project. Islam, Muslims and mosques can – if we allow them to – with time became as Swedish as Christianity, the Christmas tree and pizza.

As opposed to the first discourse, with its essentialising historical view, the second is characterised by history being seen as an ongoing and dynamic process. Ethnicities, religions and identities are human, social, societal phenomena or constructions. Every expression of religion is understood as a product of the social, economic, cultural and political situations that people in a certain place at a certain time find themselves in. When these situations change, religion also changes. Religious traditions (as with other social and ideological phenomena) get new functions and meanings and take on new shapes when they have to respond to new questions and legitimise and confirm new identities within the frame of new social and societal situations.

Naturally, both discourses are ideological. Both can be said to assume a genealogical view of history, where history functions as a source for resources, from which various participants can take different pieces in order to legitimise their various claims. It is a question of the re-conquering of traditional elements in a creolised or hybridised form, a question of developing or creating history rather than discovering it. The focus is not really on what has been or happened in history, but rather on how history can be used for current purposes. All in accordance with the known formula: those who control history control the present, and those who control the present control the future.

Göran Larsson
is Associate Professor in Religious Studies, University of Gothenburg. His doctor's thesis dealt with Muslim theology in Andalusia during the Middle Ages.

Åke Sander
has a Ph.D. in Philosophy and is a Professor of Religious Studies with Special Emphasis on the Psychology and Sociology of Religion at the Faculty of Arts at the University of Gothenburg. 1990–2001 he was Head of the Centre for Studies of Cultural Contacts and International Migration at the University of Gothenburg.

Ingrid Sahlin

A SAFE AND SECURE CITY?

"We are working throughout Gothenburg to make you feel safe", says Gothenburg municipality's website, with reference to a number of partnerships for increased safety. In *Safe, beautiful city*, "administrations, municipal companies, organisations and businesses (are) engaged … together to make a more pleasant city environment and to increase safety in the city." *Safer and more humane Gothenburg* will "contribute to intensifying the efforts to ensure safety, in terms of the social arena as well as the physical environment". The University of Gothenburg and Chalmers University of Technology have a *Forum for research on the safe and secure city*. The security manager of The Framtiden Group, comprising the city's five housing companies, has initiated the partnership *Young and safe*, where "schools, recreational services, housing companies, social services, the police and the prosecution authority in Gothenburg" work together to stop recruitment to youth gangs. For visitors and conference planners, Gothenburg has been launched as a safe and secure city. But what kind of safety is it that is desired?[1]

As the social security system has weakened, it seems that

1. This is one of the issues in the research project "Allmännyttan och den lokala tryggheten" ("Public housing and local safety"), financed by the Swedish Research Council Formas. Also in the research group are Ulf Borelius, Jenny Stenberg, Ulla-Britt Wennerström and Johan Öberg.

unsafety is associated more and more with crime. The then-chairman of the city council, Göran Johansson, captured the change in the safety discourse rather well in a comment in the *Göteborgs-Posten* newspaper on 13 September 2008: "When we built [the million dwellings programme], it was traffic that was seen as not safe, and safety was in the subways. Today it is people who cause the lack of safety, so tunnels are dangerous." Walking *across* a trafficked road is seen by many people today, despite the risk of being run over and injured or even killed by a car, as safer than walking *under* it. When policemen, security companies, CCTV, burglar alarms and locks are associated with safety, it is in the sense of the absence of crime. But when the police claim in their "basic values" that their assignment is to "increase safety and decrease crime", it suggests that these two tasks are not identical.

The association of Gamlestaden's property owners was created in 2001 to increase safety in the neighbourhood. The initiative was taken by a municipal housing company, which owns around half of the flats in the area. Some of its employees explain what the safety measures comprise:

> – Above all, what we have done is to improve the outdoor lighting in the whole area a lot. We have added gate locks in the whole area.
> – Yes, and we have put up gates where there were closed yards, with locks, to prevent just anyone from entering at any time, and we have also improved the lighting indoors, in the stairwells and cellars to a certain extent, we have cut down many tall bushes and trees, and the last thing that we are doing now is to offer everyone the chance to buy a security package with a security door." (Group interview with janitors)

There are similar stories in other housing areas in the city. Lighting is improved, gates are set up and locks are installed. Bushes and trees are trimmed or cut down so they cannot hide shady people and intentions – crime prevention through environmental design (CPTED). No one should be able to hide, be unseen in the darkness of night or get into a yard uninvited. Security doors are offered as protection against break-ins and unwelcome visitors.

Positively charged concepts are often diffuse. An old insight for both researchers and planners is that security and the lack of security are emotional conditions that can emerge even when they are not "objectively" justified, and that can be influenced without criminality changing.[2] This means that security can motivate efforts that are not related to crime or to the fear of crime.

2. See for example BRÅ (2008) *Otrygghet och segregation. Bostadsområdets betydelse för allmänhetens otrygghet och oro för brott* (*Insecurity and segregation. The residential area's impact on public insecurity and fear of crime*). Stockholm: Brottsförebyggande rådet; Gordon Hughes, Eugene McLaughlin and John Muncie (eds) (2002) *Crime prevention and community safety. New directions*. London etc.: SAGE and The Open University; and Carina Listerborn (2002) *Trygg stad. Diskurser om kvinnors rädsla i forskning, policyutveckling och lokal praktik* (*Safe city. Discourses about women's fear in research, policy development and local practices*). Göteborg: Chalmers arkitektur.

According to the property-owners' organisation, the vision of a safe Gamlestaden demands a "diverse demographic composition". According to ownership directives, the municipal housing companies in Gothenburg have no particular social responsibility; their job is to contribute to the development of the municipality. Instead, it is the social services that are to arrange housing for the homeless, which they attempt to do by renting properties and flats that are then sub-let with special conditions to homeless clients. Although the property owners are guaranteed rent, supervision, the management of disturbances and fast evictions in the case of problems, several of them claim that such tenants create an unsafe environment.

The Gamlestaden property-owners' organisation and the municipal housing company aim to decrease the number of flats that the social services rent out. These tenants do not get offers of security doors but instead are expected to contribute to the safety of the area by moving away. Some of the evicted have received new sub-lets elsewhere, but only "people who were judged to have the chance to succeed", as the municipal housing company's personnel say. Of course the homeless should be taken care of, but "then it is better if they are separate". But even when they are gathered together in "special-housing units", they are accused of creating insecurity. Therefore, the municipal housing company has attempted to cancel these contracts and encourage the tenants to leave the neighbourhood, in order to "increase safety for those who live there".

Additionally, the municipal housing company has carried out "safety purchases" of "difficult" properties, whose tenants are exchanged for "regular people". At the same time, they have "gotten rid of a number of suspect landlords who don't care what kind of tenants they have". The idea, therefore, is to get rid of certain categories of tenants to increase others' safety. So a building with 180 small flats was purchased and then turned into a student's housing. No one knows where the old tenants went, but they are no longer in Gamlestaden.

***

So what is safety? If subway tunnels, bushes and trees are said to impair safety by lowering visibility, it means that, inversely, the possibility of oversight and control of nearby places creates safety. When locks, alarms and gates are installed, safety is instead placed behind firm barriers against trespassers with criminal intentions. These physical measures project an image of other people with evil intentions, while at the same offering residents a chance to ensure their distance from them.

But there are also people whom the housing company wants to avoid in the name of safety, regardless of whether they are completely visible and if locks and gates prevent them from coming into other people's yards, and regardless of what kinds of intentions they are thought to have. Those who are sent to "special-housing units" or who, according to the municipal housing company, should not have been approved as tenants, are thought to create insecurity as a category. How else can collectively depriving them of their homes be called an effort for increased safety?

Together, these three types of safety measures in the neighbourhood – improved visibility, physical barriers and changed population – mean that the area's unsafety is equated with the risk that the (desirable) tenants run of meeting "the wrong kind of people", undesirable residents who are not necessarily dangerous. And it is the municipal housing company that hereby increases its control over who can be not only in their buildings, but also in others' properties and on streets, and in open areas and yards in the area.

Perhaps the driving force behind what is called safety work is not primarily a desire for the residents to feel safe. At its statutory meeting on 4 September 2001, the Gamlestaden property-owners' association decided that it should work towards the *vision* that "Gamlestaden shall be a safe, pleasant and well-functioning neighbourhood to live in, work in and visit – an attractive part of Gothenburg with a good reputation", but that the overarching *goal* of safety work was "to positively influence the value of rental properties and tenant-owner apartments."

This goal is in line with the city's decision to make safety part of its brand name. Since it is ideas and reputation more than the actual situation that influence peoples' choices about where to move and visit, as well as companies' and conference-planners' location decisions, with time the concept of safety has come to be relatively disconnected from both the risk of being a victim of crime and the experiences of residents. This is illustrated by the following extract from an item in the newspaper *Svenska Dagbladet* on 9 November 2008:

> GOTHENBURG'S REPUTATION THREATENED
> ... All told, ten people have been injured in connection to shooting in the past months. The question of whether Gothenburg can be called a safe and secure city is now being discussed at the event and marketing company Göteborg & Co.
>
> "There are discussions. We think it is important to have respect for the issue, but *to change the brand would be to give in to criminality*," says Claes Bjerkne, chairman of Göteborg & Co. (Emphasis added)

When all is said and done, perhaps the goal of safety work is neither to decrease the risk of being a victim of crime, nor to increase safety amongst the residents – at least not amongst those who have been forced to move. Instead, the aim is that financially important people and companies from outside get an *image* of the city or neighbourhood as safe and tidy. It is the image that sells and increases the value of the properties. Neither high criminality nor the residents' sense of insecurity is a risk for the launching of Gothenburg as a safe and secure city, as long as the brand works.

Ingrid Sahlin
is Professor of Social Work at the University of Gothenburg. Her research concerns, among other things, processes of exclusion and urban safety.

Cecilia Hansen Löfstrand

PSEUDO-SOLUTIONS AND FAÇADE RENOVATIONS
The Gothenburg version of homelessness

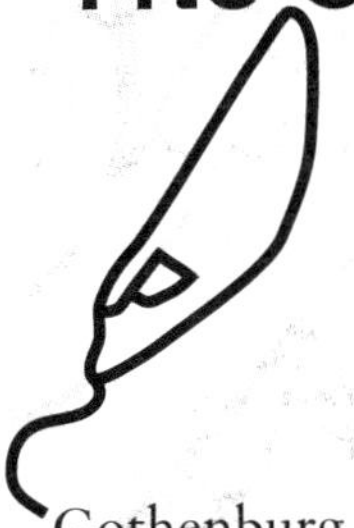

Gothenburg is usually portrayed, both by others and by itself, as a forerunner when it comes to measures for dealing with homelessness.[1] And yet, since the beginning of the 21st century, the number of homeless people and the costs of special-housing units have both increased, and the city's efforts to deal with these problems have not led to the desired result.[2] For a while, there has been a definition struggle in terms of the homeless problem – a fight where each interest group tries to make their definition the relevant one, which in the long-term affects how the problem is viewed and (thereby) which measures are taken. For example, politicians in Gothenburg reacted to the National Board of Health and Welfare's recent census of the number of homeless people, which showed that in 2005, Gothenburg had 2 620 homeless people, which was the largest number per resident in the country's municipalities. The city's leading politicians claimed that that the number was around 50, plus around 200 people who sometimes slept outside at night.[3] Research shows that during a period of around ten years, the number of spots in special housing for the homeless has increased from

1. Cecilia Löfstrand (2006) "Counting the homeless and explaining homelessness in Sweden". Executive summary of commissioned working report on the measurement of homelessness in Sweden to the European Commission; Cecilia Hansen Löfstrand (2007) "'Vi är oerhört unika' Träning i boende som åtgärd mot hemlöshet" ("'We are unbelievably unique.' Training in housing as a solution for homelessness"), in Cecilia Hansen Löfstrand & Marie Nordfeldt (eds) *Bostadslös! Lokal politik och praktik* (*Homeless! Local polices and practices*). Malmö: Gleerups, pp. 177–194.

around 1 300 to around 3 000.[4] The number of homeless people and the definition of homelessness – as something that only includes those who sleep outside or anyone without a home – is therefore a hot political issue.

Gothenburg's special housing for the homeless has changed during the second half of the 20th century. Instead of an improved situation for the homeless, the reforms have just contributed to the homeless problem being cemented in the city. During periods when the differences between the organisations' formal structures and their informal, daily practices have been so comprehensive that they create problems of legitimacy, reforms have been strategically launched to retain or strengthen legitimacy. To launch a reform means to concede that that current way of handling homelessness has not worked in the way that was hoped for. However, it is hard to change anything other than the formal structure, the official *picture* of the organisation, through reforms. Still, the launching of reforms itself is a way of affecting the situation and creating legitimacy: the organisation shows that it is willing to change and improve, something that at least temporarily protects it from criticism from various interest groups. An organisational reform can be described as a façade renovation when it does not change the daily practical work for the organisation's target group, the scope of the problem or the real situation for homeless people. Launching a reform can strengthen legitimacy, but the reform is only a pseudo-solution so long as the underlying problems are not fixed.[5]

GOTHENBURG'S WORK ON HOMELESSNESS IS REFORMED

At the beginning of the 20th century in Gothenburg, there was the Salvation Army and the municipality's night shelter and hostel. Towards the end of the 1960s, the municipal night shelters were closed while the hostel system – eventually called social hotels – was expanded. During the 1970s, it was noticed

2. Göteborgs Stadsrevision (2005) *Sociala boendelösningar i Göteborgs stad* (*Social housing solutions in Gothenburg city*). Göteborg: Göteborgs Stadsrevision. Socialstyrelsen (2006) *Hemlöshet i Sverige 2005. Omfattning och karaktär* (*Homelessness in Sweden 2005. Extent and character*). Stockholm: Socialstyrelsen; Ingalill Balheden, Juan Navas, Lena Säljö, Kerstin Wadman, Arne Wiik (2008) "319 miljoner – socialtjänstens nota för brist på bostäder" ("319 million – social services' bill for lack of housing"), *Göteborgs-Posten* 2008-10-05.

3. Socialstyrelsen (2006) *Hemlöshet i Sverige 2005. Omfattning och karaktär* (*Homelessness in Sweden 2005. Extent and character*). Stockholm: Socialstyrelsen; Socialdemokraterna i Göteborg (2006) *Vi uppmanar Socialstyrelsen att i samråd med kommunerna se över definitionen av begreppet hemlöshet* (*We encourage the National Board of Health and Welfare and the municipalities to define the concept of homelessness*). Press release, Social Democrats in the municipal executive committee, Gothenburg, 2006-03-02.

4. Cecilia Löfstrand (2005) *Hemlöshetens politik – lokal policy och praktik* (*The politics of homelessness – local policy and practice*). Malmö: Égalité.

that the social hotels had a tendency to be permanent solutions for homeless individuals, who were led to believe that these placements were temporary, emergency solutions while they were waiting for something better. The closing-down of social hotels, which were thought to make the situation worse, started in 1981 in connection to an alcohol policy program – in which the abuse of alcohol and drugs was described as causes for homelessness – started by the municipal executive committee. The system of hostels was criticised heavily during the second half of the 1980s by the media, the public (engaged citizens) and Parliament's ombudsmen. The last social hotel was closed in the beginning of the 1990s.[6] During the same period – and as an answer to the criticism – new special-housing units for the homeless were built, according to the model of a housing staircase, where the individual would move from more collective to more individual forms of housing, and where the highest step would be one's own flat on the regular housing market. The housing staircase would be a road to normalisation and one's own home. The model has since spread to other parts of the country.[7] The major news was that in practice, access to temporary housing was now connected to a prohibition on bringing in and consuming alcohol and drugs, on having pets and receiving visitors.

Towards the end of the 1990s, a debate arose on emergency homelessness – reasons and possible solutions as well as the number of affected individuals. Church-based non-governmental organisations were portrayed, by both politicians and municipal officials, as though they could and should take care of the municipal help system's "leftovers" – those who were completely excluded as well as those who were evicted and shown the door. The plan *Höjd kvalitet i arbetet för hemlösa i Göteborg* (Increased quality in the work for the homeless in Gothenburg), launched in 2002, had as one of its several ambitious goals to enable all of the city's homeless people access to some type of permanent housing before the end of 2002.[8] Two years later, some of the

5. Nils Brunsson, Johan P Olsen (1997 [1993]) *The reforming organization.* Bergen: Fagboksförlaget; John W Meyer, Brian Rowan (1977) "Institutionalized organizations: Formal structure as myth and ceremony", *The American Journal of Sociology* 83(2), pp. 340–363.

6. Riksdagens Ombudsmän (1988) *De bostadslösa i Göteborg – socialnämndens ansvar för dem som av sociala skäl möter särskilda svårigheter att få en bostad* (*The homeless in Gothenburg – the social welfare board's responsibility for those who, for social reasons, have particular difficulties finding a home*). Stockholm: Riksdagens Ombudsmän; GKF (1993) Proposal for a care resource plane for 1993–1995. Gothenburg municipal council; Marie Nordfeldt (1999) *Hemlöshet i välfärdsstaden. En studie av relationerna mellan socialtjänst och frivilliga organisationer i Stockholm och Göteborg* (*Homelessness in the welfare state. A study of the relationships between social services and volunteer organisations in Stockholm and Gothenburg*). Uppsala: Institutionen för kulturgeografi, Uppsala universitet.

7. Ingrid Sahlin (1997) *The staircase of transition.* European Observatory on Homelessness. National Report from Sweden; Mats Blid (2008) *Ett folkhem för alla? Kommunala*

city's volunteer organisations and an editorial in the *Göteborgs-Posten* criticised how this so called "zero-vision" had not yet been accomplished. The municipality's response to this criticism was based on the story of the closure of social hotels and the simultaneous development of municipal special housing according to the housing staircase model. In this "standard tale"[9] about how the old social hotels were replaced by something qualitatively new and different, the reform came across as a major success.[10] In response, the representative for the municipality emphasised that the municipality also had a goal of "maintaining the housing staircase" and continuing to develop municipal special housing according to this model, as well as buying beds in purchased volunteer organisations.[11] The tale about a(n old) reform process was used to influence critical groups and handle the problems of legitimacy raised by the criticism. Legitimacy was strengthened, but without the underlying problem – the occurrence of homeless people excluded not only from the regular housing market but also from the particular housing sphere comprised of housing for the homeless – being solved.

Three years later, in 2007, the municipality's official line suddenly changed. The *Göteborgs-Posten* reported that the municipality had decided to scrap municipal special housing based on the housing staircase model, which was portrayed as obsolete.[12] The decision had been made, said the politician responsible, to deal with the "rounds" in the system, including the tendency to exclude those whose existence motivated the system and whose success would legitimise the system. Instead of moving homeless clients up a housing staircase, they would now be immediately matched to the right housing – the staircase was replaced by a lift as a metaphor – and getting their own home was no longer described as a goal (the official goal). Instead, the goal was now launched that the homeless people could continue to live there (permanently). This reform too can be described as a façade-renovation: the official image of the organisation, its methodology and ideology are changed but the daily practical work with

insatser mot hemlöshet (*A folkhem (people's home) for everyone? Municipal efforts against homelessness*). Östersund: Institutionen för socialt arbete, Mittuniversitetet.

8. GKF (2002) Proposal for a plan for "Höjd kvalitet i arbetet för hemlösa i Göteborg" ("Increased quality in the work for the homeless in Gothenburg"). Gothenburg municipal council.

9. Charles Tilly (2002) *Stories, identities and political change*. Maryland: Rowman & Littlefield Publishers. The standard tales communicate collective images that build on (re)constructions of events.

10. Cecilia Löfstrand (2005) *Hemlöshetens politik – lokal policy och praktik* (*The politics of homelessness – local policy and practice*). Malmö: Égalité.

11. Pelle Berglund, Owe Nilsson (2004) "Vi har inte gett upp" ("We have not given up"), *Göteborgs-Posten* 2004-02-19.

12. Per Sydvik (2007) "Boendetrappa för hemlösa skrotas" ("The housing staircase for the homeless is scrapped"), *Göteborgs-Posten* 2007-10-16.

the organisation's target group and their actual situation remain unchanged. Today, homeless people are still excluded, evicted and shown the door from the municipal system. Interviews with municipal employees in the social service show that the practical social work with the homeless has not been changed, although a *new picture* of the solution has been launched.

Another acute legitimacy problem that was intensely discussed during the mid-2000s was that two-thirds of the municipality's costs for special housing, in direct contrast to the official policy, were used on placements for housing run by private or non-purchased companies for whom homelessness was a business idea. In order to deal with this problem, bans were issued, before many of these companies entered into formal agreements with the municipality in 2008 by the municipality, which meant that it became legitimate to use them. This (pseudo-)solution has not solved the underlying problem of legitimacy: whether it is socially acceptable for private actors to earn money from other people's need and what can be viewed as a legitimate use of tax revenue. For companies with homelessness as their business idea, which establish themselves as providers of special housing, tax money generates profits. But even municipal and charitable providers make a profit. The difficult question is what the profits will be used for. It is, as Paula Blomqvist and Bo Rothstein have pointed out, not legitimate to do just anything with tax revenue.[13]

13. Paula Blomqvist & Bo Rothstein (2000) *Välfärdsstatens nya ansikte. Demokrati och marknadsreformer inom offentlig sector* (*The new face of the welfare state. Democracy and market reforms in the public sector*). Stockholm: Agora.

SPECIAL SOLUTIONS FOR "THE HOMELESS" – MAKING THE PROBLEM PERMANENT

Is it reasonable and right that certain people should not have the right to their own home? That access to *temporary housing* comes with conditions and is used as a way of motivating change in the individual? And that, paradoxically enough, it is now also a goal in and of itself? The housing staircase as a model implied at least the promise of access to one's own home on the regular housing market – even if the road to achieving this was long for some and impossible for others. Now the municipality says that a place in municipal special-housing units is a *permanent* solution to an individual's problem – and in the long run to the city's homeless problem. The question is whether this solution is not just another in a list of pseudo-solutions, because can those who live in housing for the homeless be described as something other than homeless? Does the existence of a large and particular sphere for special-housing units for the homeless mean that the homeless problem has been solved? The existence of the sphere itself can be seen as part of the problem.

The homeless problem is made permanent and nothing is done to counteract exclusion from the regular housing market. An institutionalised myth in Gothenburg and Sweden today is that homelessness is best solved through particular solutions that comprise different types of temporary housing that are given with special conditions, instead of through an improved access to and allocation of regular housing.

Cecilia Hansen Löfstrand has a Ph.D. and works at the Department of Sociology, University of Gothenburg. Her research concerns how society deals with homelessness and victims of crime.

Catharina Thörn

FISHING FOR AUTHENTICITY
The city as theatre

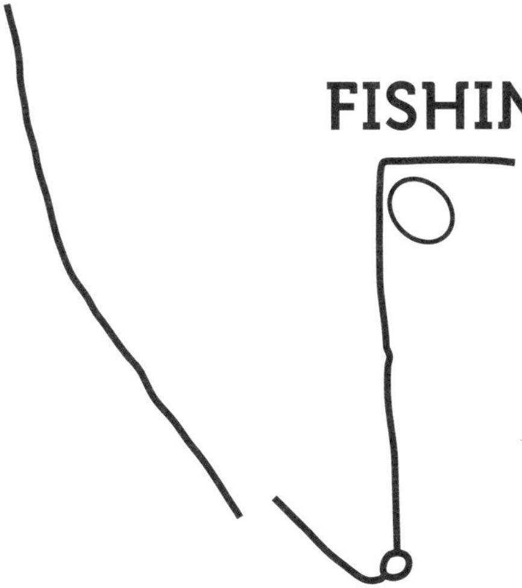

Gothenburg, August 2006. For several weeks, cleaning and fixing has been going on in the city. Facades have been washed free of dirt and graffiti and flower arrangements have been set out. Street vendors and cheap falafel stands have been removed and replaced with carefully chosen food stands offering "a taste of Gothenburg". No one can avoid the European Athletic Championship in track and field that is coming to town. When the competition is inaugurated with pomp and circumstance at Götaplatsen, Europe's TV channels are there, broadcasting pictures from picturesque Gothenburg, with cycling policeman on the streets and people (pretending to) fish in the river. That it is also time for an election in Sweden is not noticed. The politicians in Gothenburg were in complete agreement that the election campaign should be postponed and not begin until the competition was over. The traditional "campaign election cottages", symbols of democratic dialogue, have been forbidden, with the reason being that they make an untidy impression on TV. Politics and democracy are subordinated to the marketing of the city. But what exactly has made such a development possible?

SPORT EVENTS AS URBAN GROWTH PROJECTS

> The political and economic core of practically every town is growth ... the demand for growth creates the main motivation for consensus amongst the political elite, no matter how divided they are in regard to other questions.[1]

1. Harvey Molotch (1976) "The city as a growth machine. Toward a political economy of place," *The American Journal of Sociology*, 82(2) pp. 309–310.

The quote is from Harvey Molotch's now classic essay "The city as growth machines" from 1976. The trend that Molotch could see in big American cities such as Baltimore is now visible in the smallest Swedish city. Cities should not longer just provide service and care in accordance with traditional municipal policies, but also create the conditions for growth. Today this makes it as important for a city to invest in iconic buildings or new sports arenas as to build infant schools. This requirement has resulted in the development of a new type of politics – a politics that is not primarily run in the city hall but also in so-called public and private partnerships that together develop the city. Central to these partnerships is to create an attractive city to lure capital investments, tourism and, not least, the creative class. Sport plays a central role in this development. Large events not only bring financial income but also an opportunity to carry out large urban transformation projects and to market the city. This is important not least for formerly industrial cities whose images are often associated with chimneys and harbour cranes – today signs of unemployment and poverty. Global competition means that cities must market themselves in a recognisable way *at the same time* that the city's unique qualities, its authenticity, are promoted. Sporting events are very suitable for this because of their collective character – the possibilities to use the events to create social loyalty to a place. This is something that Mari Paz Balibrea focuses on in her analysis of the Olympic Games in Barcelona. She points out that the Olympic Games were portrayed as a project "for everyone and by everyone", and thereby comprehensive transformations of the inner cities received legitimacy.[2]

2. Mari Paz Balibrea (2001) "Urbanism, culture and the post-industrial city. Challenging the 'Barcelona model,'" *Journal of Spanish Cultural Studies* 2(2), pp. 187–210.

Just like many other cities, Gothenburg was hit by the shipyard crisis in the 1980s. Something had to be done. Today Gothenburg has managed to create a reputation for having handled the crisis in an innovative way and for getting things done, not least via alliances between politics and the business world. Alliances where various actors with different interests have a common main interest in adapting Gothenburg to the global economic politics by transforming the harbour city into an event city. Therefore, in 1991, Göteborg & Co was created. It is a company that is owned and run jointly by the municipality and the business world, and its mission is to market Gothenburg in order to attract business investors, large events, conferences and tourism. Since then, a number of larger events have taken place in Gothenburg – everything from major concerts with Madonna, U2 and the Rolling Stones to world congresses (like the sociology congress) and sports events such as the World Championship in track and field in 1995, the UEFA European Football Championship 1992 and the European Athletic Championship in track and field in 2006.[3]

3. This text is based on research that was carried out as part of the project "Vem får rätt till staden" ("Who has the right to the city?") together with Mats Franzén and Nils Hertting, Uppsala University. A longer text about the EC in track and field is Catharina Thörn (2009) "Governing the entreprenurial city. Implications for the meaning of public space" in Frank Eckhardt and Ingemar Elander (eds) *Urban Governance in Europe*. Berlin: Berliner Wissenschafts-Verlag.

THE CITY AS THEATRE: THE EUROPEAN ATHLETIC CHAMPIONSHIP IN TRACK AND FIELD 2006

When the European Athletic Championship in track and field was going to take place, Göteborg & Co. came up with a number of strategic goals for their work:

- Make Gothenburg and the region more attractive for people to live and work in and to visit.
- Strengthen Gothenburg and Sweden as brands.
- Improve Gothenburg as a tourist destination, event city, conference city, culture city, business location and environmental city.
- Stimulate tourism in Gothenburg, the Västra Götaland region and Sweden and thereby create a large incoming tide of money and new jobs.

- Create a festival in Gothenburg that contributes to increased happiness for the residents of Gothenburg and the region.
- Stimulate the development of track and field in Sweden.[4]

4. Annual report 2006. Göteborg&Co, p. 25.

These goals show how the emphasis of the event was *primarily* placed on strengthening the city's brand and increasing the city's appeal. An important part of the arrangement was that which took place at the same time as the competition and was called a "people's festival", a number of events in the city such as outdoor concerts, children's theatre, art exhibitions, etc. Everything took place in the city's central neighbourhoods and most events were free. The goal was said to be that anyone could take part in the "European Athletic Championship atmosphere". The whole arrangement was therefore marketed as "more than just a sporting event" and "this is our EAC". The collective support from Gothenburgers was also emphasised in the information given to foreign guests on the website.

> Over the past 20 years, Göteborg [Gothenburg] has made its name as the city where major sporting, entertainment and cultural events take place. Göteborg's large arenas, loyal audiences and carefully planned strategy have made the city a leading events venue. When there is something big on, the whole city joins in the party.[5]

5. www.goteborg.com

Another aspect that was focused on is that in Gothenburg, the city itself *is* the arena. In other words, the competition would not take place in arenas outside the city centre, but the arena was in the middle of the city while parts of the centre were also used for competitions. This was emphasised by the official posters that were created to market the events. The three pictures showed five of Sweden's most successful athletes in strategic locations in the city, using the city as an arena. The pictures can be said to represent a highly driven aesthetization of the urban environment, where the city is the scene.

SWEDEN
SWEDEN
NORDIC
NORDIC

SWEDEN

In the first one, we see heptathlon star Carolina Klüft ready to throw a javelin from a roof in Gothenburg's harbour. In the background, one can see the opera house and the small craft harbour, and further back one can glimpse the harbour's cranes. The sunrise in the background spreads a certain light over the harbour, which sets off the sports star's body and the buildings nearby, but covers the rest of the city in a pleasant haze.

In the second picture, we see the twin Kallur sisters jumping hurdles down the city's main street, Avenyn. At the end of the road, one can see Götaplatsen and the Art Museum.

In picture three, high jumpers Kajsa Bergqvist and Stefan Holm are seen observing the city from a fictional outlook spot (on the Lion which is otherwise in Brunnspark near the Central Station), where Liseberg and Gothenburg's only skyscraper – Gothia Towers – are in view. In the background is the proud Ullevi, the sports arena, brightly lit.

In contrast to what usually is traditional for track and field competitions, this time the opening ceremony of the event took place in the city centre, in Götaplatsen. The choice of location was both strategic and symbolic. Götaplatsen was created and completed before the World Fair in 1923 in Gothenburg, and was planned as the city's cultural centre. Today, the City Theatre, the Art Museum and the Concert Hall are in Götaplatsen, and for the opening of the EAC a transparent stage was built so these buildings would be visible. In this way, the event was marketed as a festival for all, as well as a sporting event. On the last day of the competition, a marathon took place outside the arena, and the athletes ran along a route that showed many important landmarks of the city: the Avenyn, the Opera, the canal, Järntorget square and finally Götaplatsen. In that way images of Gothenburg were broadcast all over Europe and contributed to the marketing of the city.

AUTHENTICITY AND PUBLICITY

For Gothenburg, the European Athletic Championship meant that the city's public places were both transformed *before* the EAC and performed *during* the EAC. In this performance, public space as a spectacle was prioritised before its function as a public sphere, which the ban of election cottages obviously shows. Large events can be used to change a city's spatial, cultural and social geography for a long time. In the case of Gothenburg, it is very clear that the World Fair in 1923 created the conditions for the area in the city that today is called the event area (around Korsvägen with Liseberg, Universeum, the Museum of World Culture, Scandinavium, the Swedish Exhibition and Congress Centre, Bergakungen halls and Ullevi). But the event changes not only the city's geography, but also the political view of public space. The staging that temporarily takes place when the city is to be marketed during large events has a tendency to remain and be normalised via a continued aesthetification of public space. When the city is seen as a theatre, its residents are reduced to viewers of and participants in the play that aims to create an attractive city. Neighbourhoods are beautified, made pleasant and easy to consume. Despite promises of authenticity and local colour, neighbourhoods and environments are standardised the world over. Whatever does not fit into the aesthetics and the order of things, such as rough sleepers and beggars, is removed.[6] An example is the law forbidding street music, which a business association in Gothenburg had passed in the summer of 2009. Although well-known musicians protested on the streets that summer, no one was fined. In an article in the *Göteborgs-Posten*, the neighbourhood policemen commented by saying that there are two kinds of street musicians: those who can play and those who beg. They clarified:

> The new law was about one guy, Big Papa, who played his two songs on his accordion day in and day out on Avenyn. Now he's gone.[7]

6. See Catharina Thörn "Soft policies of exclusion. Entrepreneurial strategies of creating ambience and control of public space in Gothenburg" (forthcoming).

7. Gunilla Granh-Hinnfors "Gatumusiker trotsar förbud" ("Street musicians defy ban"), *Göteborgs-Posten* 2009-08-17.

Catharina Thörn has a Ph.D. in Sociology and works at the Department of Cultural Sciences. Her research concerns urban transformation.

Martin Letell

FREEDOM IN AN AGE OF RISK

Steering one's way through the neighbourhoods of a mid-sized northern European city like Gothenburg, the potential moments of authoritative address are numerous and multifarious. As the public space of the city is entered, there is the familiar plethora of messages crowding in on the individual: traffic signs and signals (not to mention the speed humps or "sleeping policemen" conducting the traffic flow) call for attention, while billboards are virtually bursting, marketing the same old new goods, services and lifestyles, in an endless attempt to attract the flow money. This is the plural terrain of the city. While this terrain can be reduced to an infrastructural space of logistics, it can also be conceived of as a theatre of war, as a battleground for market shares and profits, and as a combat zone for the wars on subjectivity. It may be seen as a terrain of contestation, an arena for the politics of individual conduct. Given the plurality of the public space of the city, by what means of propaganda do local authorities attempt to produce new road habits and re-plot the common course towards more sustainable ways of urban life?

One answer to this question can be found by looking at the evocative imagery that belonged to the governmental mobility management campaign – New Road Habits – administered by the Gothenburg Traffic and Public Transport Authority (TPTA).

***

While the newly imported Italian trams occasionally break down due to the Nordic cold, a central Gothenburg hit by a blizzard is a very rare sight indeed. A manipulated image resembling the dramatisation found in a popular film like *The Day After Tomorrow* might therefore strike a chord of doom (see picture 1). The familiar statue of Poseidon, a symbol of the seaport city, is covered in snow and ice. A rescue party is trudging through the deep snow covering one of the major city squares (Götaplatsen) and the downtown avenue (Kungsportsavenyn). When buses and cars are snowed under, it becomes difficult to move about at all on the city streets. The scenario in the first image displayed here is an odd sight, no doubt. An image of a Gothenburg damaged by rainstorms may resonate more with the locals, since the city is blessed, and cursed, for its temperate and humid winter months (see picture 2). The second image depicts a flooded Gothenburg, with the opera house submerged under water and a floating lifebuoy in the foreground.

A message conveyed by these images is of course that the local impact of severe weather events and rising sea levels may turn out to be disastrous, thus underscoring what many scientists and prominent sociologists have been claiming in the recent decades.[1] For this reason, it may come as no surprise that the local authorities seek to govern individual conduct in the name of risk. More interesting, perhaps, is that the imaginary presence of the infamous "world risk society"[2] is taken as an opportunity for re-inventing the local politics of conduct based on freedom.

1. IPCC (2007) *Climate Change 2007. Synthesis Report* (Contribution of working groups I, II and III to the fourth assessment report of the intergovernmental panel on climate change). IPCC, Geneva, Switzerland.

2. Ulrich Beck (2008) "Living in the world risk society", *Economy & Society* 35(3): pp. 229–345.

Picture 1.

Picture 2.

While calling to mind the broadcasted images of large-scale catastrophes, it is not the victims of a tsunami in south-east Asia that are shown, nor is it the people of New Orleans in the wake of the hurricane, or the so-called climate refugees of the Arctic whose villages are swallowed by the sea as the ice melts. If there is a confrontational logic at work in these images it is a logic that seeks to bring the world risk society to our very own backyard. Enacting a threatening and frightening urban dystopia, thc imagery seems to be saying that the city, rather than the deprived people in a faraway place, needs *you* to make a choice – preferably before it is too late. A message emphasised by the large font caption of the latter image: CLIMATE CHANGE – WHAT ABOUT YOU?

Wherever they have been displayed, these images are accompanied by the trademarked logotype of New Road Habits and a smaller piece of text that reads: "The campaign for a more sensible way to move about in traffic." New Road Habits is a long-term endeavour meant to exert influence on the personal, everyday choice of transport, in order to bring individual conduct in line with the Swedish Environmental Code and a handful of European Directives. The campaign images have been seen in the public advertising spaces of the city, on buses and trams, and at stops, in newspapers as well as in information leaflets distributed to households, offices and other workplaces.[3] Since the campaign is now mushrooming in and around Gothenburg with the support of the Swedish Environmental Protection Agency, this is a good occasion to reflect upon the question of how we are governed in this age of risk.

3. All four pictures included here are produced by advertising agencies (1 and 2 by Stormen Kommunikation, 3 and 4 by Frank & Earnest) on commission of the Gothenburg Traffic and Public Transport Authority, from which the author has obtained copyright permission. At the time of writing (2009-06-04) all images and leaflets were available at http://www.nyavagvanor.se

***

As a further step in such an exercise, one may ask about the kind of limits and prohibitions the authorities seek to impose in order to avoid an urban disaster. Indeed, many governmental measures to combat the detrimental effects of certain emissions are prohibitive in nature (such as the environmental zone inside of which specified vehicles are forbidden). However, the campaign imagery does not draw on allegories of prohibition. While the imagery certainly moralises individual choice by enacting the potential death of the city, the real political problem addressed seems to be an *epidemic of the will*, i.e. an almost pathological and infantile individual inability to take care of the self. Hence the imagined target of the campaign: an estimated 1000 individual travel choices per person and year. So, if it is obvious that the authorities seek to govern in the name of global, urban and individual risk, the most interesting aspect of the campaign is the attempt to *govern in the name of freedom*.[4]

This may seem like a contradiction, at least at first glance. One can, for example, ask if a known and accepted risk *undoes* freedom or if freedom is always fundamentally constrained where and when a risk is believed to be real. Nevertheless, it is possible to trace a politics of conduct that seek to govern by enabling and making use of individual freedom. When enacting a Gothenburg at risk, the confrontation with the polluting externalities of the welfare society takes the form of a confrontation with the self.

Another image of the campaign (see picture 3), depicting what looks like a runaway herd, provides an illustrative example of such a politics. Here dust whirls around and, as the animals pass by the lens at full speed, individuality almost dissolves. The most conspicuous element of the picture is the text, which reads: DO NOT BE LIKE EVERYBODY ELSE. First the text comes into view, then the herd and then, in the foreground, an individual emerging, standing out from the rest. Given the appeal not to be like everybody else when moving about in the city, it looks like an individual faced with a choice, or even an individual free to choose his or her own unique trajectory. An interpretation close at hand is to view this individual as an *emerging* individual, and the image as an enactment of a moment in the process of individualisation. The enactment might

4. The interpretation is inspired by the so-called governmentality literature, e.g. Graham Burchell et al. (1991), *The Foucault effect. Studies in governmentality*, Chicago: University of Chicago Press; Andrew Barry et al. (1996), *Foucault and political reason. Liberalism, neo-liberalism and rationalities of government*. London/New York: Routledge; Peter Miller & Nikolas Rose (2008), *Governing the present. Administering economic, social and personal life*. Cambridge: Polity Press.

as well have succeeded in capturing the moment preceding the constitution of the political subject of a specific will to govern. Interpreted in this way, the image depicts an individual about to control him- or herself, about to make a choice and become an autonomous, self-governing individual. The image seeks to establish a free individual governed by his or her own rational decisions. In a sense, the imagery of the campaign destabilises

Picture 3.

the authority of the campaign. However, the campaign is still an attempt to govern individual conduct.

In this image as well as in others (for example, an image depicting the blood vessels of a translucent part of the body), congestion on the roads and in the veins is associated with a lack of common sense, a herd mentality and a lack of willpower. If the automobile was ever the symbol of freedom, the imagery

Picture 4.

of this campaign frames the car as an iron cage for humans. The scientific risk assessment is readily available, but in this imagery we seem to be unable to kick the habit, break free and step out of that old twentieth-century cage. However, taken as a whole, the campaign is not trying to make up and get across a helpless creature of habit, but an individual able to shoulder the rational calculation of risk, and act accordingly – reclaim individual responsibility and do the right thing.

TOMORROW I WILL TAKE MY BIKE! is the caption of the last image displayed here, depicting a happy man riding his bicycle on an empty street with trees in the background (see picture 4). Relaxed, with both hands in the air, the suit-wearing man is smiling, as if savouring the sweet taste of victory when crossing the finish line. The celebration of life, success, enjoyment, satisfaction and, above all, freedom: these are the connotations of the imagery, these are the positive, nearly existential, values associated with bicycling in this image. The impression is given that we are already there, in the utopia of this will to govern. Freedom can be imagined as the final moment of liberation, as the very end of government, perhaps literally, as the end of rule, and indeed, as the advent of the no-risk society. Complete freedom, in contrast to the death of the city, is the prospect of tomorrow; tomorrow is the day when you do not need to take the helm (hold the handlebars) in order to lead your life and move through the streets of Gothenburg.

Although the freedom of riding a bike is depicted as achievable, freedom seems to remain an aspiration, at least as far as the textual appeal is concerned. If appealed to with the freedom of riding a bike (freedom meaning no risk, no specific responsibility and no government), those targeted by the campaign are suddenly faced with the freedom of choice, the rational calculation of risk, individual responsibility, autonomy, and the government of the self. In this sense, freedom is not only framed as an *end of government* but also as a *means of government*.

According to this "advanced liberal" strategy of government, the practice of freedom is an instrument of power, which is another way of saying that the governmental campaign is framing and targeting individual choice. This is not freedom as opposed to government (i.e. a form of resistance), but freedom as the means through which the ends of government are sought. It is a therapeutic politics of conduct that seek to govern through individual projects of lifestyle maximisation. Through information campaigns, educational empowerment schemes and travel-coaching projects, the politics of risky conduct becomes a matter of encouraging people to use their freedom and shoulder their individual responsibility.

Combining the arguments of two well-known sociologists like Nikolas Rose and Ulrich Beck, it may be said that the local authorities seek to govern by inviting city-dwellers and rural residents to claim citizenship in the *advanced liberal risk society*.[5] By creating a responsible citizen with a proactive attitude and a sustainable behaviour, the governmental address seems to be saying that you may, rather than that you may not, make an urgent moral choice today and enjoy the day after tomorrow, i.e. break free from the epidemic of the will and make the vision of a healthy and sustainable urban future come true. The prescribed remedy to the pathological road habits of today is a particular configuration of risk and freedom: risk as a confrontation with the self and freedom as the reclaimed government of the self. Seeking to produce new road habits by hailing the man on the street, Gothenburg invites you to govern yourself and steer freely through the neighbourhood.

5. Nikolas Rose (1999), *Powers of freedom. Reframing political thought*. Cambridge: Cambridge University Press; Ulrich Beck (1992), *Risk society. Towards a new modernity*. London: Sage; cf. Mitchell Dean (1999), *Governmentality. Power and rule in modern society*. London: Sage.

Martin Letell
has a Ph.D. in Science and Technology Studies and works at the Department of Sociology at the University of Gothenburg.

PHOTOGRAPHIC INTERMISSION

Rolando Vázquez

RE-IMAGINING GOTHENBURG
Critical photography

In the photographs that follow, the camera has been used to subvert the "totalising eye" of technology. The camera was put at the service of walking in Gothenburg, in an effort to bring to view an urban text of multiple times and multiple bodies, to signal the traces of everyday life that remain inscribed in the city walls, in the city's skin.

Our experience of the modern city is heavily mediated by the visual, just as are our experiences on the internet, our habits of consumption, our construction of the self. Visual culture, visual economy and self-image are all part of a thriving vocabulary in the social sciences. These pages bring together text and photography to question the way in which the visual dimension of the modern city is constituted and experienced. The technologies and the interests of the advertising and the tourism industry hold their hegemony over the visibility of the city, over the city's visual experience. In his famous study, *The Practice of Everyday Life*, Michel de Certeau[1] shows us how the technical procedures that have transformed modern society have also taken control of the visible. According to de Certeau, technical

1. Michel de Certeau (1984) *The practice of everyday life*. Berkeley: University of California Press, pp. 92–93.

procedures, the instrumentalisation of the world, have achieved an "all-seeing power", a totalising eye.[2]

2. Ibid, pp. 92–93.

The visual imagination of the city-dweller is continuously targeted by the ever-present images of marketing. Our visual environment is also turned into a commodity; we are visual consumers not only of entertainment but also of the city. The city has been made visually consumable through the images of the tourism board and its accompanying postcards. In the realm of the visual, the city is not only the place for shopping but itself becomes a ready-made landscape for visual consumption. By rendering the city into a visual totality configured by the city map and the series of postcards that constitute an inventory of its monuments and vistas, the logic of tourism turns the city into a commodity, into a readily-legible text, a simulacrum.

> The panorama-city is a "theoretical" (that is, visual) simulacrum, in short a picture, whose condition of possibility is an oblivion and a misunderstanding of practices.[3]

3. Ibid, p. 93.

The visual simulacrum of the panorama-city implies the oblivion, the veiling, of other practices, other aesthetics that belong to the city. When the visibility of the city is controlled by the simulacrum of a totality, we become blind to the multiplicity of practices that constitute the "other visuality" of the city. Photography has long been a technical tool for the inscription and reproduction of the totalising eye of technology. Photography brought the image under technical control; it enabled the visual simulacrum that is endlessly reproduced in the postcards and the web portals that make a city's fixed identity out of a series of perspectives and visual monuments.

The power of instrumental reason is also exercised in the visual; it extends its hegemony over the visual. De Certeau mentions the map as a mechanism that means the submission of places, of localities, to the spatial control of technical representation. Today, tools like Google maps have given a concrete dimension to the idea of achieving a total-view of the world, a total-representation.

We could ask, "What is the problem with attaining a total view of the world, or a fully readily legible image of the city?" The problem is precisely that of bringing the visible under the control of totality. These total images of reality are the visual equivalent to the social and political idea of universality. They stop us from thinking, they exercise a hegemony, they erect a simulacrum that hides, that marginalises the other knowledges, the other *visualities*.

But what precisely is being lost? What goes missing under the visual hegemony of the commodity or of tourism are everyday practices, the memories that belong to each locality, to each street, to each body that inscribes itself in the urban space. How can we subvert the simulacrum of the total image of the city, of its hegemonic touristic representation? How can we re-imagine the city? How can we look away from the images of marketing and tourism? How can we move away from the technical imaginary produced by the media, the corporations or the state? Is it possible to find another aesthetics, another image of the city? Is it at all possible to use photography, which is a foremost technology of representation, to subvert the very simulacrum it has helped to produce?

De Certeau hints at walking as a practice that can unveil other *visualities*. "The ordinary practitioners of the city live 'down below', below the threshold at which visibility begins. They walk – an elementary form of this experience of the city; they are walkers, *Wandersmänner*, whose bodies follow the thicks and thins of an urban 'text' they write without being able to read it."[4]

4. Ibid, p. 93.

The walker subverts the total image of the city. The walker opens other *visualities*, other temporalities. The practice of walking can be deployed as a critical exercise, as a way of exploring the contours, the thresholds of hegemonic visibility. Michel de Certeau finds in the *pedestrian rhetoric* a possibility to subvert the "technological system of a coherent and totalizing space", in other words, he finds an aesthetics of walking that challenges the image of the city as a totality:

> the figures of pedestrian rhetoric ... are the acts of ... [a] stylistic metamorphosis of space. ... These "trees of gestures" are in movement everywhere. Their forests walk through the streets. They transform the scene, but they cannot be fixed in a certain place by images. If in spite of that an illustration were required, we could mention the fleeting images, yellowish-green and metallic blue calligraphies that howl without raising their voices and emblazon themselves on the subterranean passages of the city, "embroideries" composed of letters and numbers, perfect gestures of violence painted with a pistol, Shivas made of written characters, dancing graphics whose fleeting apparitions are accompanied by the rumble of subway trains: New York graffiti.[5]

5. Ibid, p. 102.

The objective of this critical photography was not to comment on or reproduce the hegemonic image of the city, nor to photograph its practices of daily life; rather, these photographs are about showing the very impossibility of achieving such visual certainties. They are about showing how the skin of the city is flowing, always changing, always other, always escaping the total-eye, the need for certainty, the power of space, the colonisation of technology. Somehow these images aim to show the borders of the visible and the absurdity of affirming a visual totality. They denounce the simulacrum. In other words, they show themselves but only to affirm the impossibility of capturing the invisibility that constitutes the life of the city. Beneath visual totality, beneath the total legibility of tourism, of the commodity, there is another aesthetics. The borders of the rhetoric of totality appear as fragments. The fragment becomes critique.

> It is as though the practices organizing a bustling city were characterized by their blindness. The networks of these moving, intersecting writings compose a manifold story that has neither author nor spectator, shaped out of fragments of trajectories and alterations of spaces: in relation to representations, it remains daily and indefinitely other.[6]

6. Ibid, p. 93.

These photographs of Gothenburg bring into question the image-industry that invades and rules our visual experience. They are a call to divert our sight, a call to stop and subvert the totalities, to stop the train of progress that is blinded by its race towards the ever new, the unattainable. In contrast, these images tell us to direct our gaze towards a past that despite its withdrawal is always alive and in proximity; a past that is not fixed but signifies multiplicity and uncertainty. The images say: stop the chronologies, the fictions of continuity and individuality; look at the discontinuous, at the forms and colours made by various hands, in a coming together across multiple times. Look at the city's skin as an interstice, as the celebration of the swaying of time between absence and presence.

Rolando Vázquez
is photographer and assistant professor of Sociology at the Roosevelt Academy of Utrecht University in The Netherlands. His research circles around three interdisciplinary topics: visual social experience, postcolonial thinking and the critique of modern time.

TIVAL
(US)
Direkt
et.se

2 JUNI
tom

3. THE CITY'S PERIPHERIES

Klas Rönnbäck

THE FRENCH BLOCK AND THE SWEDISH HUNT FOR COLONIES

In central Gothenburg today, there is still a neighbourhood called Franska tomten (the French block). Behind the name lies a history that is more than 200 years old and forgotten by nearly everyone. In the City Museum's large exhibit about the history of the city centre, there is only a short sentence about how, at the end of the 18th century, there was a particular warehouse here for French goods.[1] The French warehouse has an even older history, which is related to Europe's colonisation of America.

1. Gudrun Lönnroth (2003) *Hus för hus i Göteborgs stadskärna* (*Building by building in Gothenburg city centre*). Göteborg: Göteborgs stadsmuseum.

SWEDEN'S FRUITLESS HUNT FOR COLONIES

When America was "discovered", Spain and Portugal established extensive colonies in the "New World", and other European states soon followed suit. The Swedish government also tried to establish colonies on other continents: the 17th century colonies Nya Sverige (New Sweden, in Delaware in what is now the US) and Cabo Corso (in what is today Ghana) were short-lived. After that, the Swedish state made a number of failed colonisation attempts (for example, Tobago, Madagascar and Guyana's coast) during the second half of the 18th century.[2] When Gustav III came to power, Sweden was completely lacking in colonies on other continents, a loss of prestige that the king could not accept (also see Mikela Lundahl's chapter in this book).

During the American War of Independence, France provided military for the British colonies against their arch enemy Great Britain. Along with the peace negotiations in 1783, France came to receive two islands in the Caribbean – Tobago and St. Lucia. The Swedish king saw his chance. The Swedes had tried to colonise Tobago previously – so now how could the French king deny Sweden this island? At the same time, Gustav was not so picky. In a letter to the Swedish ambassador in Paris, Gustav Creutz, he wrote that he would be happy with any old island in the West Indies – why, if the situation demanded it, even just a place to store Swedish goods (without having to pay customs on them).[3] The Swedish king also hoped that Louis XVI's foreign minister Vergennes himself would realise "the advantage France would have, if during a future war the Royal Majesty had a colony in that part of the world."[4] But small-mindedly enough, as King Gustav himself put it, the French did not see what advantage they would have from this – but rather demanded compensation in the form of trading benefits. Also involved in this event was the fact that the Swedish king had had diplomatic conversations with Catherine II of Russia, which the French foreign minister learned about. There was a risk that the historical Swedish-French alliance would dissolve, which the French wanted to prevent.[5]

The negotiations would drag out for almost a year, and Gustav Creutz was replaced by a new ambassador, Eric Magnus Staël von Holstein. It was finally in July 1784 that the parties had an agreement. Sweden had not agreed to any of the concessions other than supplying a storage place for French goods in Gothenburg. The French king, in turn, did not want to lose Tobago. But he could offer the Caribbean island St. Barthélemy to the Swedish king. In the tractate from 1 July 1784, which the regents signed, it says:

2. Carl Sprinchorn (1923) "Sjuttonhundratalets planer och förslag till svensk kolonisation i främmande världsdelar" ("18th century plans and proposals for the Swedish colonisation of foreign places"), *Historisk tidskrift* (*Historical magazine*), pp. 109–162; Aleksander Loit (1984) "Sveriges kolonilotter" ("Sweden's colonies") in Ronny Ambjörnsson & David Gaunt (eds) *Den dolda historien – 27 uppsatser om vårt okända förflutna* (*Hidden history – 27 essays about our unknown past*). Malmö: Författarförlaget.

3. Ingegerd Hildebrand (1951) *Den svenska kolonin S:t Barthélemy och Västindiska kompaniet fram till 1796* (*The Swedish colony St. Barthélemy and the West India Company up until 1796*). Lund: Ph. Lindstedts.

4. Quoted in Åke Essén (1928) *Johan Liljencrantz som handelspolitiker. Studier i Sveriges yttre handelspolitik 1773–1786* (*Johan Liljencrantz as a commerce politician. Studies in Sweden's foreign trade policies 1773–1786*). Lund: Gleerups, p. 231.

5. Ingegerd Hildebrand (1951), p. 27f.

Article 4. His Majesty's subjects shall always have the right, to store in Gothenburg's harbour, in the place, and with the provisos that will be decided upon, all necessities, products and trade goods, either from France or its colonies in America, which are transported on French ships.

...

Article 8. In trade for and as compensation for those benefits, which French trade and sea-faring, through the implementation of this freedom of storage in Gothenburg, receives, his Majesty gives for ever to the King and Crown of Sweden, complete ownership and control of the island St. Barthélemy in the West Indies.[6]

6. Reproduced in *Utdrag utur alla utkomne Publique Handlingar, Placater, Förordningar, Resolutioner och Publicationer* (*Excerpts from all published Public Documents, Placards, Regulations, Resolutions and Publications*) (1802), part 13.

St Barthélemy, Gustavia harbour. Litography ca 1800, artist unknown. © Sjöhistoriska museet.

THE SWEDISH SLAVE TRADE ON ST. BARTHÉLEMY

At that time, the Swedish state did not have the best finances, and many had probably hoped that the negotiations with France would be significantly more successful than they were in the end. The King himself personally needed a success in negotiation, if for nothing else than as propaganda after his long journeys abroad with the goal of getting colonies or financial subsidies for the Swedish state. The now former Swedish ambassador Gustav Creutz commented on the somewhat slender results of the negotiations in a letter to the king: "C'est toujours quelque chose à presenter aux yeux de la nation" ("It is always something to show the nation").[7] He does not seem to be particularly overwhelmed, which is not a surprise. The reason why the French chose to offer St. Barthélemy is because it was the least valuable of all their colonies in the West Indies, and the island was geographically distant from the others.[8]

The island that Sweden thereby came to control was small and stony, just 24 square kilometres. Back at the time of the early expeditions, it was realised that it would never serve plantation purposes, the way other countries' colonial possessions did. Nor did the small population form a significant market for Swedish products. The solution was to call St. Barthélemy, and its capital Gustavia, an international free port. Ships from various nations could trade here, paying a smaller customs fee. For a short time, St. Barthélemy became an important transit harbour for American tradesmen. An important commodity was slaves. The Swedish West India company got the king's blessing to trade slaves, with the king retaining a quarter of the profits.[9] But soon other countries decided to forbid slave trade – Denmark in 1792 and Great Britain in 1807. During the Vienna Congress in 1815, Sweden too signed a declaration forbidding slave trading. And yet boats with slaves continued to come to St. Barthélemy. It would take until the 1830s before slave ships stopped calling at Gustavia – around the same time that Great Britain decided to get rid of slavery completely.[10]

7. Essén (1928), p. 235.

8. Ingegerd Hildebrand (1951), p. 39.

9. Göran Skytte (1985) *Kungliga svenska slaveriet* (*Royal Swedish slavery*). Stockholm: Askelin & Hägglund.

10. Ibid, p. 106ff.

No one seems to have tried to count how many slaves passed through the Swedish colony. At its height, in 1812, there were around 2 400 slaves on the island itself.[11] But most of the slave trade in Gustavia was transit trade that left the island, including to the American south. In sum, the trade was probably very small compared to the many millions of slaves that made up the transatlantic trade in total.

11. Hannes Hyrenius (1977) *Royal Swedish slaves*. Göteborg: Demographic research institute, Göteborgs universitet.

EXACTLY WHERE WAS FRANSKA TOMTEN?

In exchange for the little Caribbean island, Gustav III offered Louis XVI a storage place in Gothenburg. It was this place that came to be called Franska tomten (the French block) – the first map in the Gothenburg City Museum collection that explicitly uses this name is from 1802. Paradoxically, there was some confusion about where Franska tomten actually was. What is now Packhusplatsen was at that time a dockyard, called Masthamnen harbour, which was part of Stora Hamnen, or the Large Harbour (now Stora Hamnkanalen, or Large Harbour Canal). There is no doubt that Franska tomten was near Masthamnen. As already mentioned, today there is a block called Franska tomten, near Packhusplatsen (area 20 in Nordstaden). In the Gothenburg City Museum history, the name Franska tomten is given in the description of this area.

The idea that the historical Franska tomten was here is most likely incorrect. In the Gothenburg City Museum archive there are three contemporary maps (from 1802, 1809 and 1817) that use the name Franska tomten. They all point to one of the properties in a neighbouring block – the area on the corner of Norra Hamngatan and Packhusplatsen, where the Court of Appeals now is, in the block that is now called Stora Tullen (area 13 in Nordstaden).[12] In the Gothenburg City Museum's history of Gothenburg's city centre, the area is said to have had two brick buildings there in 1850 – no buildings before then are mentioned.[13] In the Gothenburg City Museum archive, it

12. See "Plankarta över Franska tomten" ("Map of Franska tomten") by C W Carlberg 1802, Gothenburg City Museum archive, capsule 11; "Plan Charta no. 1 som utvisar alla i Giötheborg varande Kronans tillhörige byggnader och lägenheter" ("Map no. 1 that shows all of the Crown's buildings and spaces in Gothenburg") by V. Arborelli, 1817, capsule 8; "Karta öfver Masthamnen" ("Map of Masthamnen") by L W Brandenburg, 1846, based on an original from 1809, capsule 11.

13. Gudrun Lönnroth (2003), p. 485.

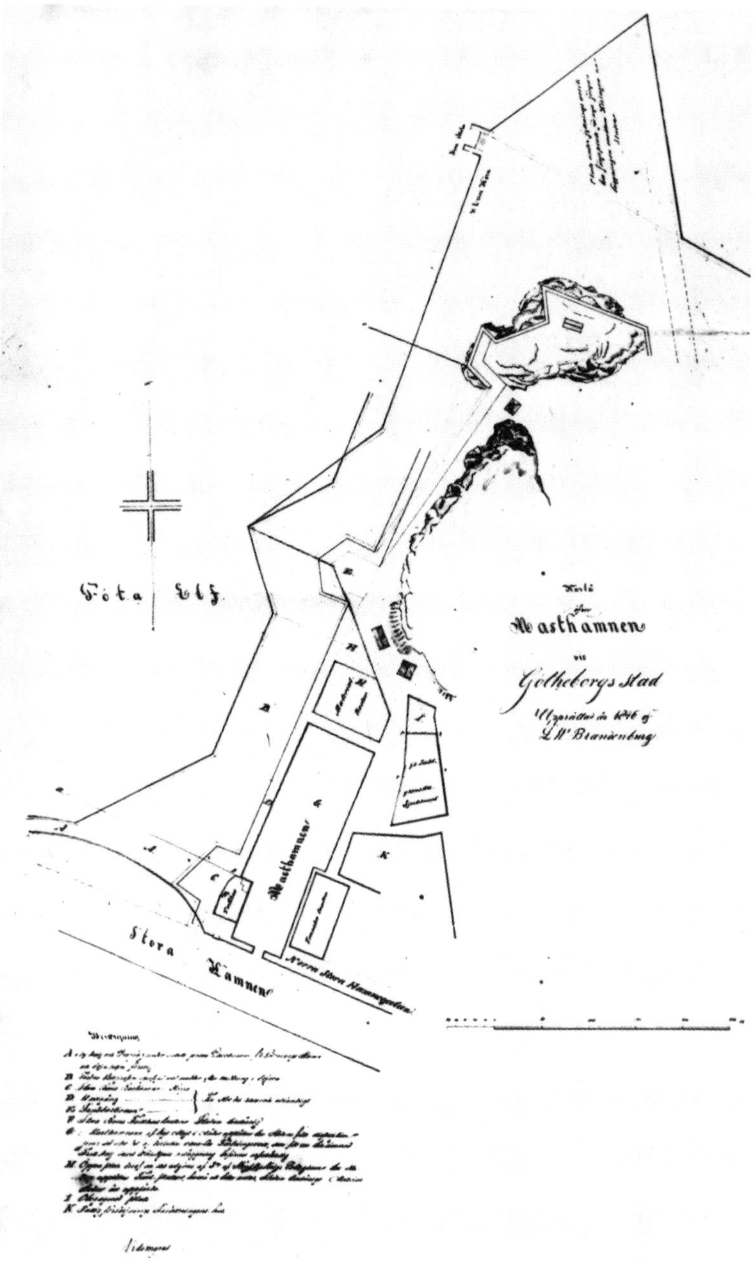

Map of Masthamnen. Drawn by LW Brandenburg 1846, following an original from 1809. © Göteborgs stadsmuseum.

seems as though no contemporary map suggests that the historical Franska tomten was located in the area that today bears the name. The author has not managed to find out where this most likely incorrect information came from, but it was probably when the current area-division was carried out in 1920, which is seen for example in the large map of Gothenburg that was prepared for the jubilee exhibit in 1923.[14]

14. See "Kartverk över Göteborg med omnejd" ("Map of Gothenburg and environs") by A Södergren, 1923.

FRANSKA TOMTEN LOSES ITS IMPORTANCE

According to the tractate from 1784, the French subjects would have the right "for all time" to a storage place in Gothenburg. In exchange, the king would get St. Barthélemy "for ever". But the Swedish colony in the Caribbean was never the financial success for Swedish trade that Gustav III probably hoped for. Perhaps there was cold comfort in knowing that Franska tomten never brought much financial profit for French traders either. At the beginning of the 19th century, it is unclear exactly when, they seem to have stopped using the storage place.

In 1815, the General Customs Office of the king requested to establish a victual scale (a provisions scale) in Franska tomten.[15] The proposal does not seem to have been approved, but the request suggests that by that time, French traders did not use the area anymore. Later during the 19th century, Masthamnen harbour was also closed, and the muddy and reedy land around it was drained.[16] The foundation was laid for today's Packhusplats.

In 1878, the Swedish crown sold St. Barthélemy back to France. There is nothing left today of the historic buildings in Franska tomten. All that is left is a name from a long-gone time.

15. See "Ang. plats för viktualievåg i Göteborg" ("Regarding a location for a victual scale in Gothenburg"), correspondence from Fortifikationsdepartementet (the Fortification Department), Gothenburg City Museum archive, capsule 221:1.

16. Gudrun Lönnroth (2003), p. 530.

Klas Rönnbäck has a Ph.D. in Economic History and works at the University of Gothenburg. He studies European colonialism and trade in colonial goods during the early modern period.

Ingrid Martins Holmberg

SITES OF AMNESIA
Politics of remembrance and forgetfulness concerning Romany camps in the Gothenburg city centre

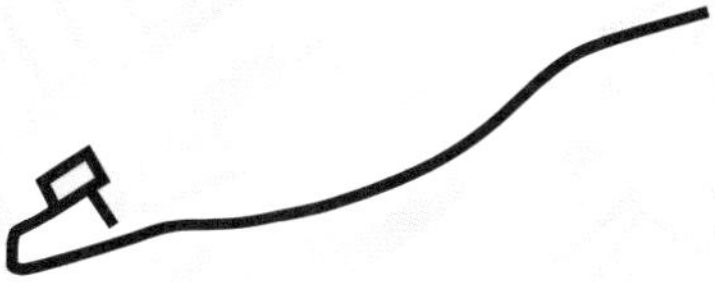

A pair of photos in the internet-based archive of the image company Kamerareportage show a group of Romany who have set up their tents in the little park by Bergslagsbanans railway station building at the beginning of March 1953.[1] The pictures show wagons, long tables laid out and laughing people having relaxed conversation. With these views, the pictures effectively focus on the celebratory side of life, exactly as we expect it in Romany-style: beautiful festive clothes, camaraderie and freedom. A couple of pictures dated a few days later show the predictable police visit – the other side of Romany life. The local ordinances do not allow camping, fires or dogs off the lead in the city area, and every camp of tents must have permission in order to stay more than one night. In these pictures too, some smiling people can be seen, but the expressions of others show the tense atmosphere.

1. Kamerareportage owns the negatives from, among others, the newspapers *Göteborgs-Tidningen*, *Göteborgs Handels- och Sjöfartstidning* and *Göteborgs-Posten* and is western Sweden's largest picture company.

This Romany camp was located in one of Gothenburg's most lively places, where people journeying in and out, city residents and new arrivals all met, and where many goods were re-loaded. Today this place is next to Gothenburg's new travel centre, Nils

Ericson terminal. The place's historical importance is reflected in the fact that in 2008, Bergslagsbanans railway station building was "listed", which means being named a historic building by the county administration board. This essay looks at apparently non-related phenomena that were co-existent in time and space – a Romany camp and Bergslagsbanans station building – and discusses the conditions for how they are incorporated into the city's self-image and memory.

Photo 1. A group of Romany who have set up their tents in the little park by Bergslagsbanans railway station building at the beginning of March 1953. The picture shows long tables laid out and people having relaxed conversation. The Photo effectively focuses on the celebratory side of life, exactly as we expect it in Romany-style: beautiful festive clothes, camaraderie and freedom.

ROMANY IN THE CITY'S SELF-IMAGE

The city's self-image is intimately connected to who and what is allowed to take place in the collective memory. The right to the past in the form of memory is decided by unequal power relations that give precedence to certain individuals, groups or occurrences, and such precedence tends to be naturalised over long periods of time. Therefore, one can agree with Leonie Sandercock that there is both cumulative and consolidating power in social memory: "Stories about the past have power, and bestow power."[2] It is therefore not the past itself, but the *shapes* and *content* of the past's performance as memory/history that are important to analyse. (See Abby Peterson's chapter in this book.)

It has been documented that Romany camps have been part of the European landscape since the Middle Ages. The first Romany came temporarily to Sweden in 1512, and since the late 19th century Romany camps are a relatively reoccurring and well-known phenomenon both in the Swedish countryside and on the edges of cities. The border between the claimed cultural landscape and the planned city, with its vaguer place definition, allows a freer and more unplanned usage. The Romany camps have left their imprint, primarily in the government archive, and the information there to a great extent shows a number of reactions considering the camps to be a sort of nuisance. Traces of the Romany camps – regardless of where they are situated

2. Leonie Sandercock (1998) *Making the invisible visible*. Berkeley & Los Angeles: University of California Press, p. 1.

– are mainly found in the border between what is allowed or sanctioned and what is not allowed, the transgression.[3]

3. Cf. the discussion about travellers in Birgitta Svensson (1993) *Bortom all ära och redlighet. Tattarnas spel med rättvisan* (*Beyond honour and honesty. The Gypsies' play with justice*). Stockholm: Nordiska museet.

The official writing of history is traditionally based on the authorities established within the national state. The Romany (seen as a group) often seem to have avoided societal control. This sets the conditions in many ways for the position of Romany camps in collective memory. The camps have meanwhile left some impressions in the cultural historical collections, such as at the Nordic museum, where surveys of the Swedish Romany took place over several years during the 1940s and 1950s, by Carl-Herman Tillhagen, among others.[4] Despite this, it is very hard to get detailed knowledge of the Romany camps' placement, extent, shape, length, context and so on.

4. www.nordiskamuseet.se/Publication.asp?publicationid=3507&topmenu=144 (2009-03-04).

Judging by the pictures in the named press archive, Romany camps seem to have been continually existent in Gothenburg during large portions of the 20th century. Every picture comes with a precise summary. Photos from the outskirts of the city show "Gypsy children at a camp in Mölnlycke" in 1921; "Gypsy camp in Billdal" in 1927; "Gypsy school in Hindås" in 1946; and "Gothenburg 1 September 1959, performing at Stora Teatern (The Big Theatre), The Gypsy Baron and ensemble, including Berit Bohm and Ruth Kjerrman, visiting a Gypsy camp outside Gothenburg." Photos from the city's edges, like those from inside the city, show "Gypsies living in a caravan by Kruthusgatan" in 1944; "Gypsy camp by Levgren meadow" in 1949; "Gypsy wedding" in Gothenburg in 1957; "Gypsy funeral" around 1960; and "Gypsies in the city in 1951, Östra Hamngatan – Spannmålsgatan". The latter picture illustrates the unbelievable contrast created by the Romany people's very presence in the city's public space in the 1950s: the meeting between the strictly clothed "modern" male Gothenburger and the "premodern" Romany woman with her long skirt and jewellery.

Foto 2.
A photo dated a few days later shows the predictable police visit – the other side of Romany life. The local ordinances do not allow camping, fires or dogs off the lead in the city area, and every camp of tents must have permission in order to stay more than one night.

THE CITY'S MATERIALITY AS A MEMORY AND SELF-IMAGE

The architecture of the Romany camps (layout and organization of tents and caravans, places for formal or informal social intercourse and places for intimacy and privacy etc.) is variable. Although the organisation of the camps (as with city plans and architecture) follows specific social and cultural patterns, their logic is far from the rules of property planning, national registration and city planning. In direct contrast to the camps, are regular buildings. Since buildings can be "listed" as landmarks, they can also gain legitimacy in collective memory . In this case, the current railway station building the historical information presented concerns the circumstances of the way the building was developed (the architect/builder, function), as well as later function-related physical changes. That is, the Bergslagsbanan station building is discursively linked and connected to a national history of the railway-system; the information mentions only the building's most obvious function (as an arrival hall for trains and a waiting area for travellers), but nothing else beyond it.

Any temporary or undesired uses of the place, such as the Romany camp in 1953, remain unknown. However, this exclusion is not a specific treatment that would require revision or a correctional measure were it pointed out. Instead, it is the case that buildings are generally and in most contexts understood as representatives only of their functions as they were originally defined. Cultural heritage authorities are, in this respect, no exception. But this example sheds light on a general complication that affects the basis for how the collective memory of city space is constructed.

But the building's materiality *per se* also dictates the ways through which the city creates the memory of itself. This is the most concrete and thorough form of memory-construction, and at the same time the least analysed.[5] The city's materiality entices us as second nature at the same time that it legitimises and naturalises amnesia regarding the Romany camps.

5. Michael Landzelius (1999) *Dis[re]membering Spaces. Swedish Modernism in Law Courts Controversy*. Diss. Göteborg: Institutionen för kulturvård, Göteborgs universitet; Ingrid Martins Holmberg (2006) *På Stadens yta. Om historiseringen av Haga* (*On the surface of the city. On the historicisation of Haga*). Diss. Göteborg: Makadam förlag.

The city itself leaves the camps outside its memory, and this can be said to happen in two related ways. First, the building of a city is a consequence of land's legal-financial division into units, the usage and shape of which is regulated in plans. In this way, the building of a city is permanently bound to historically specific forms of ownership and democracy, and the city's building can be seen as a sort of materialised collective memory – permanent presentations of power relationships, ideals and social negotiations. The Romany camps, with their ephemeral character and variable architecture, are never testimonials to heritage, status and rights. Second, the city's morphological shape affects the separation and meeting of people. One can see this in the fact that there has always been room set aside for things such as shops and markets, parks and playgrounds, private and public transportation, workplaces and homes, while at the same time there has never been room set aside for Romany camps. No matter where the Romany camps have been, they have been in illicit places. Modern city development, based on modernist ideas about the separation of unrelated things, has always and consistently rejected those who do not use the city the way it was planned.

Information about the camp by Bergslagsbanans park in 1953 cannot be found in the national register, area statistics or building permission archive, where information is based on regulation. Camps are too variable to equal a city building; they create neither an architecture nor a morphology that lasts, and that can later be analysed with regard to its users' self-image, visions, conflicts or power relationships. For the same reasons, one can only find scattered information about Gothenburg's Romany camps in the contexts that bear institutional responsibility for the collective memory that is created and protected; that is, within the framework of museums and archives. Of course, the "next to" position of the Romany lifestyle complicates the possibilities of reconstruction, but it is the very shape of memory politics that gives amnesia its legitimacy.

CONCLUSION

The temporary character of the Romany camps, society's forms of control of ownership and use, together with the fact that the forms for creating memory to a large extent reflect these forms of control, mean that the Romany camps are cut off straight away from the city's collective memory – even if, and when, they have been in the city's symbolic centre. Those without property and address are doomed to remain outside the city's materialised self-image and memory, and this is a general fact that goes far beyond Romany camps (see Helena Holgersson's chapter in this book). When the tents have been taken down, the chairs and pots packed away and the dogs put in the caravans, there is nothing left that can testify to this usage of space.

Creating a fairer memory must be a goal, but it must occur on different grounds than simply adding certain ethnically, culturally or socially defined groups. What is needed is a diversified, reflective and contradictory memory than can serve as a resource for establishing alternative worlds and new pictures: "Memory makes us human. Without it people are turned into a formless mass that can be shaped into anything the controllers of the past desire."[6] This is about establishing a memory that can handle and exceed historical conditions through which social patterns of the existence of property, of being without property, of laws and transgressions, and of power and oppositional power have developed. A memory that also observes the cultural expressions that, in a *carnivalesque* way, deviate from prevailing norms. If such a collective memory were possible, imaginable and understandable, current times would be full of many more possibilities.

6. Aleksandr Nekrich, Mikhail Heller (1986) *Utopia in power. The history of the Soviet Union from 1917 to the present.* New York: Summit Books, p. 9.

Ingrid Martins Holmberg
Ph.D., works as a lecturer in Integrated Conservation at University of Gothenburg. Her research concerns the material and imaginary constructions of places, particularly in relation to cultural heritage processes.

Minoo Alinia

WHERE I BECAME AN IM/MIGRANT

One of my friends in Gothenburg reminded me that Gothenburg has been the longest stop in the journey that has comprised my entire adult life. Oddly enough, I had never reflected on it. How can I explain this? Is it the place I am indifferent to or is it the passing of time? What counts in the experience of a place or time? Isn't it our memories and relationships that give the places and times we have passed through meaning and content? Isn't it these experiences that make them important points in our lives, that we hold on to so we don't get lost, or that on the contrary we separate ourselves from, in order to go further? I happened to first meet Sweden in Gothenburg, and as an immigrant, it was the cold, bureaucratic side of Sweden that I came into contact with. Perhaps it was this that explains my ambivalent relationship with the city. But it moves me. For me, Gothenburg means familiar faces, friends, relationships and circles where I feel at home, but also many bitter memories. Although I now live in Stockholm, a large part of me is still there.

As a child, one of my wishes and dreams for the future, if a very diffuse one, was to have a life of constant movement, never to stop. The thought of remaining in one place seemed very boring and gave me feelings I could not name, but that I now understand as anxiety or claustrophobia. It isn't often that one of my wishes comes true, but this one did. However, the movement, the journey, became a migration with the prefixes *im* and *em*, and so was far from my childhood dreams, far from an adventure of the privileged, far from the hypocritical romanticisation of mobility and migration. It was a migration whose direction and content I could not foresee. I had no control over it and had not chosen it. But at the same time, it was a consequence of my decisions and of the life I had chosen to live, with all that implied. I was very aware of this.

Yes, it was in Gothenburg that I met Sweden and it was in Gothenburg that I, 29 years old, was transformed into an immigrant. The years I had behind me suddenly did not count. This transformation meant that to other people, I was now a history-less being, one of many in the faceless mass called "immigrants", whose unwelcome presence had to be dealt with.

The year was 1990, in the middle of a economic recession. In Sweden, this was the year when the right wing entered Parliament, in the body of New Democracy, a party that came to influence Swedish immigration policy for a long time. The world was confused amidst capitalism's dizzying conquest, and racism made inroads into Europe's streets and city squares. "The laser man" scared all of Sweden. Driven by racism, he used a laser weapon to shoot 11 immigrant men over the course of a few months, before he was arrested. In August 1990, I applied for asylum in Sweden. After a short interview at the police office in Gothenburg, I was send to the Swedish Migration Board office in Sagåsen, which is in Kållered, outside Gothenburg. During my time as an asylum-seeker, I was sloughed off to another station, then another, and yet another. In Sagåsen, I shared a room with a woman I already knew. Her background was like mine and she had come to Sweden at almost the same time. After about a week, we were sent to a boat near Lundbyhamnen harbour in Hisingen.

On the boat, we followed a female official, who gave us bedclothes and showed us the room where we were to stay. We walked down many stairs. There were so many people, mostly Africans. We came to the room where we were to stay. The room was very small, perhaps twenty square metres, cold, rectangular and worn out, with a small round window with iron bars on it, right near the ceiling. It was right above the water level in this old, worn out boat that had been removed from traffic and was now being used as refugee camp. (See Ulla Björnberg's chapter in this book.) In the room, there was a bunk bed with torn and dirty pillows and mattresses, a very small sink and a wardrobe. We put our suitcases on the floor, looked at one another in confusion and suddenly, without saying anything, tears began running from our eyes. The female official continued, unmoved, to explain the practical details. After a few seconds, we interrupted her and said that we were not going to accept this inhumane situation, that it was undignified and that we were not going to stay. We went back to Sagåsen with our suitcases. We found the person responsible, a young woman, and told her in our broken English what it was like on the boat. She coldly said that "if you are not satisfied, go back to where you came from" and she left without waiting for a response.

We decided not to give up but instead to try to defend our value as human beings, so we sat outside the official building to hunger strike. Many other asylum-seekers came to express their sympathy. They could not do anything other than to give us moral support, since we were all in a weak position, a relationship of complete dependence. It was around 11 when we got back to Sagåsen and we sat there until the officials began to leave for the day. They walked past without even looking at us. We had nowhere to spend the night and we realised quite soon that this was not going to lead anywhere. We understood that we did not have the right to question or demand anything, but instead should just ask nicely and be grateful. Since Sweden was a democratic country, we had trouble understanding it, but later we came to understand that this democracy did not apply to us. (See Helena Holgersson's chapter in this book.)

The denigration and humiliation had only just begun. We went back to the boat and registered, but had no plans to stay there. Instead, we forced ourselves upon various friends and acquaintances at night. We never went back to that room but just returned to the boat every day, registered, ate our lunch, sat outside for a few hours and talked, cried and laughed at our misery, sang, dreamt and then left in the afternoon. After awhile, a doctor's note was a blessing for us and we were moved to another location. This time it was the hotel Tre kronor near the tram station in Svingeln in eastern Gothenburg. Most of the people at the hotel were Iranians and Arabs, some were eastern Europeans and Russians, and there were almost no Africans at all. The living conditions here were much better.

In 1996, I returned to the refugee camp in Sagåsen because of my work on an essay in sociology at Gothenburg University. It was about the "recall project" within what was then the Swedish Migration Board. It was, just as it sounds, about recalling residence permits and throwing out people who were seen as having "lied" about their identity, no matter how many years they had lived in Sweden. This project also recalled lives. A young man committed suicide because, having lived in Sweden for many years and having created a life here, he was going to be thrown out. I wanted to interview people who worked with refugee cases about their view of the situation. I was well-received by two handling officers. The first was rather nervous and even said, when he saw my tape recorder, that "here we are quite scared of such machines". It felt like a small triumph. I had not forgotten how I had been treated in Sagåsen just six years before, not by this particular person, but that was not what was important. I had not stopped being an immigrant. Thanks to my tape recorder and the university that now stood behind me and that gave me an identity and legitimacy, they were now "scared" of me.

It is said that sociology demystifies society and various social processes, but I have also been disillusioned. I am no longer naive about my place in Sweden. This both frees and inhibits.

My university studies in Gothenburg, the Gothenburgian intellectual milieu and the people and circles I came in contact with on the way were the start of another journey, a sort of homecoming. Perhaps they were also what saved me from drowning. They paved the way for an intellectual migration where I could reunite my life and my history and get insight about what this migration – with its prefix – meant.

Minoo Alinia
has a Ph.D. in Sociology and is a Research Fellow at the Department of Social Work at Mid-Sweden University. Her research concerns globalisation, migration, the Diaspora, racism and gender.

Ulla Björnberg

IMMIGRANTS AND THE GROWTH OF THE CITY
History and present (1958–2008)

My first assignment as a sociologist in the middle of the '60s was to carry out a study of the housing and work situation for the foreign work force that came to Gothenburg at the end of the '50s. This was a very expansive period in the city's history that lasted up until the oil crisis in the '70s. Between 1962–1969, the number of foreign residents in Gothenburg doubled from 15 000 to 30 000. The largest group by far were the Finns (around 40 % in 1967), but there were also many from southern Europe, Yugoslavia and other parts of Europe.[1] Among other companies, Volvo, SKF (producer of rolling bearings) and the shipyards needed workers.

Most of the foreigners (as they were then called) got housing in old, worn-down wooden buildings in the inner city. These were houses that were to be torn down and they were not really maintained. Many people were offered housing in barracks and houseboats, which were owned by the workplaces; they were outside the city near the companies, particularly along Norra Älvstranden, where the shipyards were located and where today there are entirely new buildings (see Minoo Alinia's chapter in

1. Utlänningar i Göteborg (Foreigners in Gothenburg): U 1970:12. Göteborg: Göteborgs Stads statistiska kontor.

this book). The housing offered to the young men was, in other words, mostly temporary. This created an extreme category of housing with poor access to recreational centres and service, which increased the immigrants' feeling of rootlessness, isolation and anonymity. Not unexpectedly, the research showed that a clear majority of those who lived in barracks and houseboats were displeased with their housing in comparison with those who lived in flats, even if the flat was in a worn-down, inner city building. Those who got temporary housing only remained for a short time and many changed homes several times to improve their situation before they left the city.[2]

2. Ulla Björnberg, Gunilla Fürst (1968) *Utländsk arbetskrafts anpassning på en expanderande arbetsmarknad* (*Foreign workers' adapatation to an expanding job market*). Göteborg: Sociologiska Institutionen, Göteborgs universitet.

Using this answer key, one can claim that immigrants at this time were discriminated against because they were sent to housing that was geographically separate and unattractive. This was an existence that had nothing much to offer other than the opportunity to earn money. Gothenburg still receives many immigrants. How has the situation for them changed since the housing crisis at the end of the '50s?

IMPROVEMENTS AND EXPANSION

At the beginning of the '60s, local politicians judged it as absolutely necessary to expand the city. The municipality silently decided to buy as much land as possible in nearby small municipalities with the goal of building a satellite city north of Gothenburg – a "Brasilia". At the same time, the old buildings in the inner city would be torn down. In general, all the demolition and building work was given to non-profit municipal housing companies (see Tiiu Soidre's chapter in this book).[3] Despite the financial crisis that hit in the middle of the 1960s, the project retained its impressive vision. But housing was prioritised at the cost of services, recreational centres and other things that could contribute to a pleasant living environment. The social administration in Gothenburg was concerned about the development, and in a statement regarding the general plan for the

3. Lennart Zintchenko (1993) *Nybyggarstadsdelen Hammarkullen i ett föränderligt Sverige* (*The newly built neighbourhood Hammarkullen in a changing Sweden*). Solna: Byggforskningsrådet, p. 2.

planned satellite city wrote that the method of building would contribute to housing segregation and "modern slums". The neighbourhoods would be unattractive, the residents would have nothing to do and they would feel no responsibility for the area or a sense of belonging to it. This would contribute to social problems, crime, destructive urges and drug abuse.[4]

The predictions came true, at least in the parts of the newly built areas that were the least attractive. It took a while until services and tram lines were built. In the meantime, it was easy to get housing since there was an overproduction of flats, particularly in 1972-73. Initially, the new housing was attractive, even if the living environment was poor. They were modern flats built to high standards and many of those who moved in appreciated that; there were also green landscapes nearby – forests, streams and attractive areas.[5] On the other hand, people found it difficult to deal with the media's black picture of the newly produced neighbourhoods. The residents felt that they had to defend their reasons for moving to these areas. Ethnological studies showed that those who spoke negatively about the areas were in part representatives of the media who had not been there, and in part people who worked in schools or at the housing administration who wanted more resources for their work.[6]

But turnover of residents was also high. The lack of things to do in the area was particularly marked among young people. They had nowhere to go but just hung out in open places. The lack of resources contributed to them spending their time with the gang and harassing other residents.[7] After a period of ten years, the situation stabilised, in part through active efforts to create cultural activities in the area. However, those who could chose to move to other parts of the city. In the middle of the '70s, a new programme for housing construction started. This was very attractive to families with children. The building of small houses for private ownership gathered pace after all the criticism of the million dwellings programme's areas of mass

4. Gothenburg's social administration statement 10/1 1969 Dnr/100.

5. Eric De Geer (1981) "Göteborgs finländare. Några uppgifter om Göteborgs största invandrargrupp" ("Gothenburg's Finns. Information on Gothenburg's largest immigrant group"), Göteborg: Göteborgs Historiska Museum, annual report.

6. Sven B Ek, Magnus Bergquist & Kerstin Lökken (eds) (2002) *Stadens janusansikten: göteborgare tycker om Göteborg* (*The city's Janus face: Gothenburgers on Gothenburg*). Göteborg: Etnologiska föreningen i Västsverige.

7. Lennart Zintchenko (1993).

produced blocks of flats. This was another type of suburb, on a small scale, with private ownership and proximity to natural landscapes.

THE DRIVING FORCES OF POLARISATION

As a result of the oil crises in the 1970s, labour immigration basically stopped. Instead, various groups of refugees began to come to Sweden and Gothenburg. During 1990–2006, the entire population growth of 51 000 people in Gothenburg was composed of people with foreign backgrounds.[8] Many refugees were given housing in the satellite suburbs and today the areas are populated by people from different parts of the world – Latin America, the Middle East, the former Yugoslavia, Somalia, Iran, Iraq, Syria and Afghanistan. Like many other cities, Gothenburg is polarised in terms of class and ethnicity. Certain neighbourhoods on the edges of the city have become "Swede-sparse", which can be viewed as a result of the past decades' transformation of the inner city.[9] In statistics showing the percentage of the population dependent on welfare, the northern neighbourhoods are over-represented in comparison to the western and central ones. A large majority of welfare recipients have a foreign background and many have no other source of income.[10] Since welfare is designed as a temporary solution, long-term dependence on social assistance implies poverty.

The polarisation is connected to the collusion between housing policies and market powers. Policies have paved the way for the market to play the decisive role in divisions and forms of tenancy – rentals, cooperative dwelling in multiple-family homes, and ownership of small homes. The city's politicians are well aware of this situation, and people have tried to influence the composition of forms of tenancy by transforming rentals to cooperatives. The building of new areas has basically ceased in the city, which given the fact that the rate of immigration to the city has not slowed down at the same pace, has caused a new

8. Roger Andersson, Åsa Bråmå & Jon Hogdal (2009) "Fattiga och rika – segregationen ökar. Flyttningsmönster och boendesegregation i Göteborg 1990–2006" ("Poor and rich – segregation is increasing. Patterns of movement and housing segregation in Gothenburg 1990–2006.") Göteborg: Göteborgs Stad, Stadskansliet.

9. For more on the development of Swede-sparse areas, see Roger Andersson (2001) "Skapandet av svenskglesa områden" ("The creation of Swede-sparse areas"), in Lena Magnusson (ed.) *Den delade staden* (*The divided city*). Umeå: Boréa. Se även Irene Molina (1997) *Stadens rasifiering. Etnisk boendesegregation i Folkhemmet* (*Racialisation of the city. Ethnic residential segregation in the Swedish Folkhem*). Uppsala: Institutionen för Ekonomisk Historia, Uppsala Universitet.

10. "Göteborgssamhällets utveckling" ("The development of Gothenburg society"), (2008), Göteborg: Göteborgs Stad, Stadskansliet.

housing crisis. Housing policy has been changed, and instead of special housing units and rentals, policy makers have chosen to prioritise cooperatives, full market prices and high mortgages for those who invest in cooperatives. Even the non-profit municipal housing has been transformed to cooperatives, which has meant that there is a shortage of rentals. Municipal housing has also been put on sale (which is illegal).

The distribution of housing in the new housing regime contributes to increased segregation. This is emphasised in a new study of patterns of moving in the "population-wise most expansive areas" in Gothenburg, which shows that there is a clear tendency for newly arrived immigrants, people with low incomes, high unemployment and non-European backgrounds to move to certain areas on the northern periphery. The study also shows that those who move from these same areas have jobs and have lived in Sweden for a longer time than those who stay. The polarisation is mostly driven by people with high incomes and many choices, a process enhanced by the fact that nearby municipalities outside Gothenburg have built housing with the focus on well-to-do households with children. Another driving force behind the patterns of settlement for immigrants is that asylum-seekers are mostly advised to live with relatives or acquaintances – this is called "arranging their own housing" – because the refugee authority has very little access to housing. In addition, property-owners, including parts of the non-profit municipal housing companies, can choose tenants. As a result of these selection mechanisms, ethnic housing segregation in Gothenburg increased rather than decreased in 2006 and 2007. The central and western areas have the highest percentage of well-educated people and the highest incomes, while the north-eastern areas have the lowest percentage of well-educated people and the lowest incomes.[11]

11. Ibid.

The population distribution across housing areas in Gothenburg has come about because of the actions of the involved actors – everything from the purchase of land, the ownership of properties, the allocation of areas for various types of housing and activities, and finally the residents' preferences and opportunities. From after the Second World War up to the middle of the 1970s, a merging of municipalities created conditions for planning how the land was to be used for various purposes. According to the plans, housing would be separated from workplaces in the centre of the city and in other peripheral areas. The demolition of the inner city's housing areas meant above all that properties for offices, shops and administration were built instead. As a result, the city came to be dominated by work activities while the suburbs' population increased. Property-owners in the inner city encourage this development since business and office locales are more profitable than houses. In order to satisfy housing needs for single people, couples without children and people with low incomes, areas were planned for different categories of housing. The result was that the suburbs with small houses were populated by families with children and good incomes and the areas with blocks of flats were populated by households with lower incomes, single people with or without children, and households with social problems. Immigrants who had neither been on a waiting list nor had the capital to buy more attractive housing also moved to these areas.[12] The less attractive housing on the city's periphery became a thoroughfare with a lot of movement in and out, which created social concerns.

The structure put in place during the '60s has therefore been reinforced and deepened over the past 50 years. Because the buildings have at least 60 years' write-off, the structure will remain for the foreseeable future. My current research is on refugee families, with a focus on children and wellbeing. It has been almost 50 years since my first study, but for the newly arrived from other countries, the housing crisis, and the discrimination, remains.

12. Hans Fog & Ann-Mari Westerlind (1979) "Göteborg stadskärna. Region. Framväxt. Framtid" ("Gothenburg city centre. Region. Growth. Future"), Stockholm: Byggforskningsrådet.

Ulla Björnberg
is Professor of Sociology at the University of Gothenburg and her research focuses on issues of family, sex and welfare.

Mats Widigson

THE BARRIERS OF THE KNOWLEDGE CITY

The city is a place not just for developmental possibilities but also a place where societal problems are concentrated and strengthened. Globalisation is creating an ever more knowledge-intense society, *at the same time* as ethnic and socioeconomic segregation is increasing in big cities. A growing number of children, therefore, are starting their geographically short but socially long journey towards eventual citizenship in the knowledge city from areas characterised by ethnic diversity and relative poverty.[1]

1. Integrationsverket (2006) *Rapport integration* (*Report on integration*). Norrköping: Integrationsverket.

GOTHENBURG AND THE ISSUE OF INCREASED PARTICIPATION IN HIGHER EDUCATION

Gothenburg presents itself, with some justification, as "Gothenburg the Knowledge City". With 60 000 students at Chalmers University of Technology and Gothenburg University, Gothenburg is one of the Nordic region's largest and most popular university cities in terms of the number of students applying. Also in the Gothenburg region are some of Sweden's most research-intense companies. Development and modernity are linear concepts that spatially are connected to the growth of the city, as in Hisingen's southern area, where IT clusters, telecommunications industries and educational centres have been established on the shipyard ruins. A structural change has taken place from production and occupations based on the shipping and manufacturing industries to a growing service sector and a more knowledge-intense work situation. Since these jobs require other qualifications, post-secondary education has received more importance in the distribution of welfare.

In the Middle Ages, the city and a life within the city walls was connected with freedom. Serfs could be freed from feudal serfdom in the city, hence the legally and emotionally resounding expression "Stadtluft macht frei" (City air makes you free).[2] Today, however, the knowledge city is surrounded by educational barriers. The change from industrial city to knowledge city is rather different, depending on which part of Gothenburg one is referring to, and the issue of broadened university recruitment is intimately connected to a larger discussion of equality. An individual's choice to study further is a question of lifestyle, identity and one's vision of the future; of freedom of choice and independence, the opportunity to take advantage of one's rights and resources and of diversity being valued. From a societal perspective, the profits are financial and democratic. At first glance, the educational system can seem to be strictly meritocratic: diligence and talent get good grades, which gives access to higher education, which in turn is decisive for one's career destination. However, unequal conditions make the issue of recruitment complicated and open it to a discussion on fair and ethical equality regarding degrees of freedom of choice. Where local differences are large and swiftly increasing, the job of the educational system to compensate for this becomes more important and measures must respond to a partially new situation. When the city changes, the paths to university also change.

2. Robert E Park, Ernest W Burgess, Robert D McKenzie (1925/1984) *The city. Suggestions for investigation of human behaviour in the urban environment.* Chicago: The University of Chicago Press, p. 12.

GOTHENBURG THE KNOWLEDGE CITY AND A SCHOOL FOR EVERYONE

In general in Sweden, the educational level is high. In total, four-fiths of the working-age population have a secondary school education and 30 percent of those aged 25–64 have higher education.[3] A historical look back at the skewed recruitment to the educational system shows two factors that contribute to skewed recruitment: at every point when students are to make choices, students from higher social groups consistently choose alternatives that lead to higher studies; and students from higher social groups on average get higher marks than others at all levels of education.[4] In terms of gender, nowadays more women than men go on to higher education (the percentage of men at Gothenburg University is 36 percent, as compared to 44 percent in the country). According to the school laws and the teaching plans, the school system, which includes infant school, primary school and secondary school, has to guarantee equal education for all.[5] In Gothenburg's school plan, it says that today Gothenburg is an education and knowledge city with the ambition of gaining a leading position in an international perspective.[6] This elitist thought, however, is combined with a thought of equality. The school plan also claims that everyone in Gothenburg the knowledge city has the right to the knowledge they require for their future life, that Gothenburg is working towards sustainable social development and that the school has a particular responsibility towards those pupils who, for various reasons, have trouble reaching the goals of education.

One way to illustrate social differences is to use comparative figures, where the number 1.0 means perfect representation and shows how high the percentage would have been if social background did not make a difference to the likelihood of beginning studies. The comparative figure 0.5 shows that the percentage is half as large as it would have been if people with a certain social background had been represented in relation to their percentage of the population. If one compares those starting university

3. Onni Tengner, Ingeborg Amnéus (2008) *Universitet & Högskolor. Högskoleverkets årsrapport 2008* (*Universities and colleges. Swedish National Agency for Higher Education annual report 2008*). Stockholm: Högskoleverket.

4. Robert Erikson, Jan O Jonsson (1993) *Ursprung och utbildning. Social snedrekrytering till högre studier* (*Origin and education. Skewed social recruitment to higher studies*). SOU 1993:85. Stockholm: Fritze.

5. Skolöverstyrelsen (1985:1100) *Skollag och skolförordning* (*School laws and regulations*). Stockholm: Utbildningsförlaget; Utbildningsdepartementet (1994) *Läroplan för det obligatoriska skolväsendet och de frivilliga skolformerna* (*Teaching plan for the obligatory school system and voluntary school forms*). Lpo 94:Lpf 94. Stockholm: Fritze.

6. *Skolplan för Göteborg 2007–2008* (*School plan for Göteborg 2007–2008*). www.goteborg.se (search for "skolplan," 2009-04-03).

at Gothenburg University and the equivalent number for the country, students with a working-class background have a comparative figure of 0.63 (0.73 for the nation), students with foreign background have 0.94 (1.0 for the nation) and those with university-educated parents have 1.68 (1.46 for the nation).[7] The educational level of parents is more decisive than national origin in terms of the likelihood of getting a university education. Even if the Swedish National Agency for Higher Education judged Gothenburg University to be a model in its work towards equality, it ought to be pointed out that in fact, only 30 percent of the students grew up in Gothenburg.[8] Behind the more general information about recruitment to Gothenburg University, there remains a picture of inequality at the neighbourhood level in the transition frequency from different areas of the city.

A KNOWLEDGE CITY WITH CITY WALLS

In Gothenburg, class and place coincide to a great degree.[9] The city has geographical areas where people with post-secondary education comprise just one-third of the population in comparison with the areas where they are the highest, where the students who leave primary school have lower marks and where those who leave without finishing are double as high as the average.[10] The situation is further complicated by high unemployment and high rates of ill health in these areas. Even how the area is considered probably affects this negatively via discursive stigmatisation. (See Nils Hammarén's chapter in this book.) In 2006, the National Board of Health and Welfare described a situation where the number of poor people was greatly increasing, more in Malmö and Gothenburg than in Stockholm, and segregation was having even deeper effects.[11] The situation is even more serious since the same areas also have a strikingly high percentage of young people. In a report from the National Board for Youth Affairs, the area of Gothenburg called Hjällbo

7. Thomas Furusten, Anna Lundh (2007) *Utvärdering av arbetet med breddad rekrytering till universitet och högskolor: en samlad bild* (*Evaluation for work on broadened recruitement to universities and colleges: a summary*). Stockholm: Högskoleverket, p. 20; Onni Tengner, Ingegerd Amnéus (2008), p. 121.

8. Högskoleverkets utvärdering av arbetet med breddad rekrytering 2007 (the Swedish National Agency for Higher Education's evaluation of work on broadened recruitment 2007). www.hsv.se (search for "breddad rekrytering," report per school, 2009-04-03).

9. Johan Fritzell, Roger Andersson (2000) *Välfärdens förutsättningar. Arbetsmarknad, demografi och segregation* (*The conditions of welfare. The job market, demographics and segregation*), SOU 2000:37. Stockholm: Fritze; Integrationsverket (2006) *Rapport integration* (*Report on integration*). Norrköping: Integrationsverket.

10. Statistisk årsbok Göteborg/utbildning (Annual statistics on Gothenburg/education). http://www4.goteborg.se/prod/sk/statistik/statistikR5.nsf (2009-04-03).

11. Socialstyrelsen (2006) *Social rapport* (*Social report*). Stockholm: Socialstyrelsen.

is mentioned; 35 percent of the youths between the ages of 20 and 25 neither studied nor worked during 2006.[12] These local variations in conditions are important to consider when the vision of an open university is to be realised.[13]

12. Ungdomsstyrelsen (2008) *Fokus 08 – en analys av ungas utanförskap* (*Focus 08 – an analysis of young people's outsiderness*). Stockholm: Ungdomsstyrelsen.

13. Regeringen (2001) *Den öppna högskolan. Regeringens proposition 2001/02:15* (*The open university. The government's proposition 2001/02:15*). Stockholm: Regeringskansliet.

It is hard to get an exact picture of the percentages of the population of different neighbourhoods in the city that go on to higher education. Still, the tendency is clear. If one looks at the population in the neighbourhood and compares it to the number accepted to Gothenburg University, Angered and Gunnared in northeast Gothenburg ought to have twice as many accepted students as they have. If one also takes into consideration the fact that the population in these neighbourhoods is young (comparative figure around 1.5), the percentage of those who study further ought to be significantly higher than that. Even if there are no neighbourhood-level statistics that can shed light on the frequency of transition to higher studies, one can most likely claim that there are socially underprivileged geographical areas with a large concentration of students with multiply disadvantageous backgrounds, which leads to low participation in higher education. With this background, it is strange that the issue of local differences in the transition to university is not emphasised as a prioritised goal, whether at Gothenburg University or at Gothenburg city's Centre for School Development.

In Gothenburg, with its high concentration of educational possibilities, this paradoxical relationship is obvious. The opportunities for higher education and the freedom of choice that this gives are near; socially, however, the path to university is nevertheless long for many youths. Today there are no physical city walls that keep people out, but instead there are social barriers that are just as hard for the individual to get past and that make demands on the educational system's compensatory role. The barriers are large, multi-faceted and mutually reinforcing; the problems are not just on side of the assortment of possibilities but also in terms of to what extent students from different backgrounds develop an identity that allows space for higher education to be sought after and admired as worth the effort. One difficulty in discussing the issue about the effects of neighbourhoods is in admitting the existence of the walls that limit the space for action without letting them contribute to the stigmatisation of the areas and groups. It is important to point out that there are unbelievably great strengths in these areas. They are places that also symbolise potential, home districts, security, pride and solidarity, and it is important for all of society that more youths study further not *despite* their background, but *with* it.

Mats Widigson
is a teacher at Angeredsgymnasiet and a postgraduate student in Social Sciences with educational orientation at the Centre for Education Science and Teacher Research, University of Gothenburg.

Nils Hammarén

"SEE YOU IN THE SUBURBS – IF YOU DARE!"

When I was little, I lived in Borås, a medium-sized city in south-west Sweden, seventy kilometres east of Gothenburg. I grew up in a green and relatively idyllic villa area called Sörmarken. Here there were no neglected rental flats and no poverty and most people belonged to a well-established middle-class. Some kilometres from Sörmarken was the neighbourhood of Hulta. I spent many years there in school. As a child, I often heard people talk about Hulta. I was told that there were social problems, poverty, criminality and many "immigrants" there. I learned that Hulta was not like Sörmarken – that the place made a difference, not least between the people. The stories I was told made me feel nervous about Hulta, despite or perhaps because I spent several hours there every day.

When I was a little older, I took part in a so-called spruce war. Different neighbourhoods – including Sörmarken and Hulta – competed against each other to see who could make the largest Easter fire. In the spruce war, we spied on each other at night time, trying to discover where our resistance hid their spruces and, in the best case scenario, found some. But the spruce war was also a word war, a way of measuring status and strength and, not least, a war of representations and identities. The picture I had of Hulta was not unimportant to the spruce war's results. The boys from Hulta sometimes came to Sörmarken and many of us got over-excited and shaken. We had heard so much, so often. Sometimes we got scared, capitulated and told them where our well-hidden spruces were.

THE SUBURBS IN THE FUN-HOUSE MIRROR

Twenty-five years later, when I was writing a dissertation about young men's identity processes in Gothenburg's "multicultural" suburbs, I was struck by similar representations. The suburbs were described as exotic and exciting, but also problematic, dangerous and "immigrant-dense". During the 1960s – at the time of the million dwellings programme's birth – the suburb symbolised modern society's utopian visions and the new art of social engineering. Here was the promise of modernity.[1] A decade later, that description began to change. The suburbs lost status and came to be seen as social dump populated by the underprivileged. It was in the 1980s that the picture we see today was established. Now the suburbs symbolise "the immigrant" and "the stranger". The suburbs are viewed as threatening and foreign places populated by uncivilised and socially degenerate individuals.[2]

In 2006, when Gothenburg's north-eastern areas were hit with a two-hour long power failure, this picture took both frightening and comic overtones. On the basis of incorrect police information, several media announced that there was chaos and violent rioting in Gothenburg. There were reports of large gangs of youths going crazy in the northeast, and of large-scale vandalism. Shopping centres and schools were described as more or less ruined. The message was that the suburbs were burning and that the developments in the suburbs of Paris were now a problem here too. But the information was wrong. The day after

1. Per-Markku Ristilammi (1994) *Rosengård och den svarta poesin. En studie av modern annorlundahet* (*Rosengård and black poetry. A study of modern difference*). Stockholm/Stehag: Symposium.

2. Ibid.

the "riots", it was obvious to most editors that they had made a mistake. The "vandalism" was not much worse than what takes place over the course of a normal weekend. In the Hjällbo neighbourhood, someone had smashed a window in a tram and at the offices of the Handelsbanken. Admittedly, youths had thrown stones at the police. But that all the shopping centres and the schools in north-eastern Gothenburg were more or less ruined was completely wrong. Schools, neighbourhood administrations, housing companies and other authorities criticised the reports and some newspapers and the police had to "put their tails between their legs" and apologise.[3] A relevant question to ask, of course, is how this awful description was possible.

3. *Göteborgs-Posten* 2006-10-10.

Gothenburg is one of Europe's most segregated cities and the differences between people create a sort of soil where myths, stereotypes and inequalities can develop. To be included or excluded is a circumstance that Gothenburgers, and not least the young men I have interviewed, have to relate to in some way. It is undeniable that every era has its own difference-creating conditions, but identity as a Gothenburger was perhaps more unproblematic and taken for granted a couple of decades ago than it is today. Today, varying living conditions are expressed in such different lifestyles that previously common reference frameworks are no longer obvious.[4]

4. Ove Sernhede (2004) "Göteborg och den sociala ojämlikhetens geografi" ("Gothenburg and the geography of social inequality"), in Andersson et al (eds) *Goda projekt och sega strukturer. Rapport i utvärderingen av storstadssatsningen i Göteborg* (*Good projects and weak structures. Report on the evaluation of the Big city effort in Gothenburg*). Göteborg: Göteborgs Stad, Stadskansliet.

SPATIAL IDENTITY STRATEGIES

There are many different ways of understanding a city. A common method of interpretation is the socioeconomic one, where one can relatively quickly see how things divide into "poor" versus "rich" areas. Another way of understanding the city is to give its various areas and residents different characteristics and values. These divisions and pictures of segregation can lead to different interpretations and be used in different ways. Based on how the individual understands the city and what picture she or he develops, it is possible to work out different strategies for resistance.

This resistance can be important to illuminate since it situates and brings attention to different kinds of power relationships. That is, we can understand what creates power relationships by looking at the powers that try to destabilise them.

In several of my interviewees' stories, the sociogeographically divided city is a recurring subject. As a "suburban bloke", one is highly aware of the ideas people have of one's own neighbourhood and the young men who live there. Different identity strategies are developed. Often, young men aim their indignation at the media's depictions of "the suburbs" and "the immigrant bloke", and they try to develop contrasting pictures in relation to the presupposed stereotype. In certain contexts, they distance themselves from Swedes, who they describe as wimpy or promiscuous. The young men might develop images of how people in certain (rich and Swede-dense) neighbourhoods have looser sexual behaviour, while people in other (poor and Swede-sparse) neighbourhoods are more careful to protect their reputations and try to maintain a certain respectability. What is most common, however, is that they try to avoid the stereotype by "relinquishing" their "immigrantness" or "suburban blokeness". In this case, they make common cause with the majority view of "suburban blokes" as a problem, distance themselves from the stereotype ("other" immigrants and suburbs), and signal that "I am not one of those" or "I do not want to be seen as inferior". In these cases, Swedishness is put on a pedestal, and they portray themselves as Swedish, equal and included. The picture of the "suburban bloke" and the suburb becomes a contrasting picture.

In other words, young men use space to create divides. They can also use their sense of ethnic and locational belonging to create tension, or to create respect with a threatening tone. The conception that usually occurs in the media of the suburbs being "dangerous" and populated by "ghettofied" (male) residents is then a point of departure in identity work. For example, two young men, Toni and Fabian, talk about how they play with and use the "bad reputation" to seem tough and cool when they meet racist youths from other, richer and more "Swede-dense" neighbourhoods in Gothenburg.[5] In this way, they feel that they gain status and respect, which compensates for the stigma they feel they receive. They answer and stage and confirm the stereotype for those who expect it: "If you expect a dangerous guy, you're sure as hell going to get it." In this way, they can work on their assigned position and create space for action beyond the image that they were not part of formulating.

RESISTANCE

The Gothenburg-based historian of ideas Michael Azar writes in a foreword to Frantz Fanon's *Black skin, white masks* that all types of resistance are bound to the oppression that the resistance is supposed to undermine.[6] The remedy for the poison must be found in the poison itself. Either one can choose to use the weapons of the opponents (categorisations, language, values, etc.), to be like the opponent and reverse the power relationship, or else one can use one's own weapons, but in a way that confirms to one's opponent that one is "different". This also indirectly verifies the opponent's way of legitimising their position of power: "they" have different values; "they" are not like "us".

A central part of the young men's identity work seems to be that they use stereotypes and oppose how they are constructed by using this construction themselves. Identity becomes a starting point from which they gather to protest oppression.[7] In this way they become actors, by participating in the power relationships they are opposing. This is like the way that some groups sometimes protest by using the negative designations through which they are stigmatised.[8] For example, think of how insults such as "nigger", "queer/gay" or "svartskalle" (literally, "blackskull" and used in Sweden to denigrate foreigners) are used by blacks, homosexuals and immigrants in an attempt to destabilise the power of these names and to make them ineffective.[9]

The consequences of structural changes and "closed" geo-

5. Out of consideration for Toni and Fabian and the other boys' integrity, I have given them pseudonyms.

6. Michael Azar (1995) "Fanon, Hegel och motståndets problematik" ("Fanon, Hegel and the problematics of resistance"), (foreword) in Frantz Fanon *Svart hud, vita masker* (*Black skin, white masks,* translated by Stefan Jordebrandt). Göteborg: Daidalos.

7. Tiina Rosenberg (2005) "Inledning" ("Introduction") to *Könet brinner!* (*Gender is burning!,* translated by Karin Lindeqvist) Judith Butler. A selection of texts chosen by Tiina Rosenberg. Stockholm: Natur och Kultur.

8. Beverley Skeggs (1999) *Att bli respektabel* (*Formation of class and gender. Becoming respectable,* translated by Annika Persson). Göteborg: Daidalos; Paul Willis (1977) *Fostran till lönearbete* (*Learning to labour*). Göteborg: Röda Bokförlaget.

9. See for example Fanny Ambjörnsson (2003a) "'Kom nu hora så går vi!' Om svar på tal, ut-

graphical borders in Gothenburg are identity constructions that in different ways explore the possibilities of creating resistance and upgrading status. The socioeconomic "map" of the city is reflected in attitudes, ideas, understandings and stereotypes. In the same way that clothes, hairstyles, jewellery or other accessories comprise an important part of one's self-representation, urban belonging, ethnicity and sexuality can also be used to mark a position. In this way, one's identity is something to "play with", to load and to use to strengthen certain impressions, to practice resistance, to offer contrasting images and to (re)define the content of representations.

manande beteenden och andra skamstrategier" ("'Come on, whore, we're going!' On responding to speech, challenging behaviours and other shame strategies"), in Thomas Johansson & Philip Lalander (eds) *Sexualitetens omvandlingar. Politisk lesbiskhet, unga kristna och machokulturer* (*Transforming sexualities. Political lesbianism, young Christians and macho cultures*). Göteborg: Daidalos; Fanny Ambjörnsson (2003b) *I en klass för sig. Genus, klass och sexualitet bland gymnasietjejer* (*In a class by oneself. Gender, class and sexuality among secondary school girls*). Stockholm: Ordfront.

MEETING WITH JOHNNY

One afternoon, I am sitting and talking to Johnny on the phone. He is 17 years old and lives in one of Gothenburg's northeastern "Swede-sparse" neighbourhoods. I know Johnny from before and he had promised to ask two friends if they wanted to participate in my study. This afternoon, I sense some doubt and worry in Johnny's tone of voice. Carefully and ramblingly, he searches for words and says, "How are you going to portray them [his friends]? I don't know if they're right for your study. They're not, like, bad. Not ghetto." I laugh but soon become serious again when I try to explain that I am not looking for a certain type of bloke, just that they should live in a certain area and be of a certain age. It is obvious that Johnny, with his background of negative experiences regarding how his neighbourhood and those who live there are portrayed, has certain expectations about the kind of people I want to meet, as well as about how I (the Swedish middle-class researcher) will portray his friends. Johnny's doubt is reasonable, but soon he buys my explanations and we decide on a time and place for the interview. The conversation comes to an end but before we hang up, he says ironically, "Yeah, so come next week, if you dare!"

Nils Hammarén has a Ph.D. in Social Work and works as a lecturer at the Department of Social Work, University of Gothenburg. His research concerns questions of youth, ethnicity and exclusion.

Ove Sernhede

WORDSILAH AND THE CRITIQUE OF NEOLIBERAL URBAN POLICY

A spectre is stalking Europe – the ghost of the suburban revolts. In recent years, we've seen battle-like pictures on TV from Paris, Lyon, Rotterdam, Copenhagen and a number of other cities where suburban youths confront police forces equipped like the military. During Christmas and New Year's in 2008, Rosengård in Malmö and Tensta in Stockholm also became part of this news story. In the late summer of 2009, added to the list were Biskopsgården, Angered and Backa in Gothenburg, Gottsunda in Uppsala and some other "million dwellings programme suburbs" around Sweden.[1] Confrontations between youths and the police are not part of daily life in Swedish suburbs, but they do occur, even if they rarely develop into riots and vandalism. It is possible that the events of the late summer of 2009 were the beginning of a pattern of development that many believed the Scandinavian welfare states would be spared.

1. The term "million dwellings programme" is used to describe the suburban mass housing built in Sweden during the period 1965–1974, these housing projects are now the home of large groups of immigrants and the contemporary poverty in the metropolitan areas of Sweden.

Gothenburg is a city characterised by tensions between the structures of the industrial era and the dynamics of the growing post-industrial information age. The new-liberal urban developmental patterns of branding, gentrification and territorial stigmatisation, which we see in many other cities, also is a prominent feature in Gothenburg, a city which, according to national reports, is the country's most segregated. As in territorially stigmatised urban areas all around the world, in Gothenburg's north-eastern "immigrant-dominated" suburbs there is a hip-hop culture that comments on and relates to the development of the city. The Gothenburg group Wordsilah ("silah" means "weapon" in Arabic, so the group's name means "the word as weapon") is composed of three rappers, two men and a woman. In their YouTube hit, "I skuggan av den blågula flaggan", ("In the shadow of the blue and yellow flag") they insightfully and distinctly deconstruct the post-industrial urban policy that has stigmatised the million dwellings programme's "Swede-sparse" suburbs and at the same time gentrified and made the inner city "cool". The song is a sharp critique of the myths and mantras of new liberalism and reveals how the new forms of comradery are growing in the hybridised suburbs. With the help of effective symbolic language and quotes from Olof Palme, the video develops a subtle critique of modern Sweden, which distances itself ever more from the visions of the welfare state.

> What can one say about this welfare society?
> Collectivity is now a forgotten word
> Replaced by the individual
>
> The People's Home – it became cooperative housing in the centre of the city
> Everyone wants to be in the midst of things
> So you have to deal with the devil
>
> What our parents bled for is now just stuff, class divisions are decoded through
> Blue-yellow senses
> Memories from before are appealing but time is running out

***

Throughout the entire European continent, there is currently a development that is segregating and separating the immigrant-dense housing areas in big cities from the rest of society. Sweden is no different. These areas are engaged in what the sociologist Loïc Wacquant calls a process of territorial stigmatisation. In his newly published book *Urban Outcasts. A comparative sociology of advanced marginality*, Wacquant discusses similarities and differences between developmental patterns in the American ghetto and French suburbs.[2] The territorial stigmatisation has a decisive influence on the development of both the political system's strategies and the expressions of the vulnerable and marginalised groups. Wacquant thinks it is also the spatial, or one can also call it the place-political, consequences of what he calls "advanced marginality" that create the basis of the fury that causes the suburbs to rise up, such as in France in 2005, when 300 cities were set on fire. In his study *Badlands of the Republic*, the cultural geographer Mustafa Dikeç shows how this French suburban revolt must be viewed as one link in a long historical chain of urban insurrections.[3] Dikeç sets the starting place for this in 1981, when British youths in poor and run-down neighbourhoods such as Brixton (London), Toxteth (Liverpool) and Moss Side (Manchester) rose up against the Thatcher regime's disassembly of the welfare state and the militarised British police's racist provocations. In the same year, French authorities began to worry about a "Brixton en France". National investigations into the situation in French banlieues were carried out at the same time as marginalised and frustrated young people in these areas began openly to show their displeasure with poverty, unemployment and the second-class citizenship they were given. Etymologically, "banlieue" comes from "banned", that is to say that the word refers to a place that is condemned or left out of the rest of society.

The events in France in 2005 were much discussed in the Swedish media, but the youths, social workers and researchers who were interviewed did not give a clear-cut answer to the question of whether such a development would be possible

2. Loïc Wacquant (2008) *Urban outcasts. A comparative sociology of advanced marginality*. Cambridge: Polity Press.

3. Mustafa Dikec (2008) *Badlands of the republic. Space, politics and urban policy*. Oxford: John Wiley & Sons Ltd.

here. The social polarisation that became more and more obvious in the 1980s and that Dikeç says is a consequence of the growing new liberalisation of Europe's cities is also apparent in Gothenburg. In the urban space here, there is the development of splintering processes that place some areas on the margins while at the same time a new societal climate is created. Zero tolerance, strict control and the systematic surveillance of certain groups and places are some of the more central aspects in a city that is more and more characterised by people living in different worlds. It creates a basis for the development of stereotyped concepts about those who are other. In the fear of the Other, the Other's spatial placement in the city also plays a significant role. To have one's home in a "badland", or in a "reservation" as some of the young people call their neighbourhoods, means in the long-run that one is a "bad person" and that one is an object for internment.

Even if the situation for youths in French cities cannot be compared with the situation in Sweden, there are parallels. In the autumn of 2008, the National Board for Youth Affairs published a report, "Focus 08", about conditions for youths in the suburbs. It shows that 35–40 percent of all young people between the ages of 20 and 25 in neighbourhoods such as Hjällbo (Gothenburg) and Rosengård (Malmö) neither study nor work. Save the Children's regular studies of child poverty in these areas show that almost 65 percent of the children here grow up in families that live on the edge of poverty. A report on housing segregation in Gothenburg between 1990–2006, ordered by Gothenburg's city office and published in the spring of 2009, shows that both segregation and the divides between rich and poor are increasing.[4]

The suburbs' political actions and the expressions of youth culture have long been dominated by young men, but there are signs that suggest that women are coming forward and becoming more visible. Even if those who confront the police are mostly young men, in the hip-hop culture there is a clear tendency towards increased female participation, in rap music

4. Roger Andersson, Åsa Bråmå, Jon Hogdal (2009) "Fattiga och rika – segregationen ökar. Flyttningsmönster och boendesegregation i Göteborg 1990–2006" ("Poor and rich – segregation is increasing. Patterns of movement and housing segregation in Gothenburg 1990–2006"), Göteborg: Göteborgs Stad, Stadskansliet.

and break-dance. The connection between Molotov cocktail-throwing youths and hip-hop must be problematised. In various contexts, hip-hop veterans have pointed out that it is counter-productive to burn cars and fight with the police. In recent times, both internationally and here, there has been a discussion about new tendencies in the locally anchored but globally connected hip-hop culture's relationship to education and local, grass-roots democracy. In a similar way as the workers' movement early on used culture and education as strategic tools to give the working-class self-awareness, the young hip-hoppers are now working in some of the million dwellings programme's stigmatised suburbs to organise and coordinate marginalised groups outside of the political arena. It is devastating when this sometimes provocative culture is viewed as a threat.

In reality, these suburban young people often have knowledge that is valuable for all of society, since in their cultural expressions they comment on and give form to social problems and oppositions. By refusing to listen to and to consider the insights and criticisms that are articulated, we miss out on useful contributions to the discussion about how society's development can be understood and handled. What had happened if French society had been capable of considering and being more open to the invitations to dialogue that exist in French suburban rap? The scenes that were played out in the autumn of 2005 would of course have taken place anyhow, but there would perhaps have been an opening that could have led to a better understanding of the situation for the people in the suburbs of the big cities, and that might have been significant. Even if it is now starting to smoulder in million dwellings programme suburbs in Sweden and Gothenburg, the situation is not as tense and explosive as it is in France. The official institutions, like the police and schools, still have the chance to start a dialogue that might bring about a change. There are voices from the margin that are seeking contact – search for "Wordsilah" on YouTube, click on "I skuggan av den blågula flaggan" and let the exchange begin.

Ove Sernhede
is the director of Centre for Urban Studies, Hammarkullen. His research deals mainly with questions of modernity, identity and youth culture.

4. THE CITY AS STAGE AND PUBLIC SPACE

Mattias Wahlström

"THE GOTHENBURG EVENTS" 2001
The city as counter-space

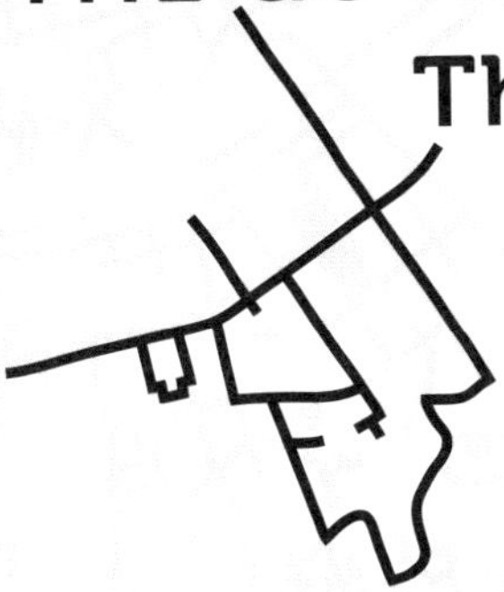

I

In June 2001, an EU summit meeting was arranged at the Swedish Exhibition and Congress Centre in Gothenburg. Tens of thousands of people were on the city's streets, demonstrating against both the EU and the president of the US, George Bush, Jr., who was visiting. Many also took part in discussions at the open forum that had been built along the canal. Perhaps the demonstrations and the public debates would have made a greater impression had it not been for the rioting, reported internationally, that took place over the course of these days.

II

How did it turn out this way? Knowing that not even the starting point for an explanation can be neutral, I choose to begin the narrative at Hvitfeldtska secondary school.[1] In consultation with the network of political/social movements, the municipality had decided to use a number of centrally located schools as housing for demonstrators who had travelled to Gothenburg.

1. This essay is based on my own observations, interviews and various secondary sources; see Micael Björk & Abby Peterson, (eds) (2002) *Vid politikens yttersta gräns. Perspektiv på EU-toppmötet i Göteborg 2001* (*At the outer limits of politics. Perspectives on the EU summit meeting in Gothenburg*). Eslöv: Brutus Östlings bokförlag Symposion; Göteborgskommittén (2002) *Göteborg 2001: Betänkande* (*Gothenburg 2001: Reflections*). Stockholm: Fritzes offentliga publikationer; Erik Wijk (2002) *Göteborgskravallerna och processerna* (*Gothenburg's riots and processes*). Stockholm: Manifest.

On Thursday 14 June – the day before the summit meeting was due to start and the same day that the President of the United States arrived in the city – it turned out that the police suspected that terrorists had hidden weapons inside Hvitfeldtska. The school was surrounded by police officers and by containers that were lifted in. There were then long drawn-out negotiations about how the 500 people who were locked in the school area would be able to leave. The discussions between the police and the movement representatives broke off just as they were nearing a solution, and orders came from those in charge that everyone in the area was to be apprehended. Unaware of this decision, the majority of those locked-in gathered to proceed out of the area. The police defined this as a riot and started a violent attack in which people were indiscriminately hit with truncheons and attacked by dogs. Militant groups responded by throwing stones. 459 people were arrested.

A symbolic break-in to the summit meeting had been planned for the following day. The police in effect crushed the organisation of this event by arresting considerable numbers of members of the local branch of the non-violent network Ya Basta during the school event on Thursday. A common interpretation is that this, in combination with the dammed-up frustration created by the Hvitfeldtska event, caused the violent riots. These began when the police interfered with Friday's "anti-capitalist march" from Götaplatsen down towards the area of the summit meeting. Only a couple of hundred activists participated in the riot, but when it spread to Gothenburg's main street – Kungsportsavenyn – it had such power and violence that the police had to retreat. The rioters were then free to burn chairs and break windows in banks and fast food restaurants.

The same evening, a Reclaim the Streets party in Vasaparken was attacked by rightwing extremists, who were let in and out by the police cordon. The confrontations between the police and the partymakers that followed culminated in a policeman being injured by a stone and his colleagues opening fire and injuring three people. One young man was shot in the back and barely survived.

On Saturday evening, the police's National Task Force searched for weapons at Schillerska secondary school and in particular for an "armed German activist with bright yellow hair". All of the youths staying at the school were forced to lie in the cold on the asphalt outside, enduring taunts and threats from police officers. The Task Force found neither weapons nor a yellow-haired German.

Despite the conflicts, three peaceful demonstrations with tens of thousands of participants took place during the summit meeting, with the slogans of "Bush not Welcome", "Sweden out of the EU" and "For a Different Europe".

III

Both demonstrations and regular confrontations can be seen not only as a purely physical fight for Gothenburg's space but also about the meaning of Gothenburg, and particular places in the city, as well as how this meaning can be used to make various normative and political points.[2] As the sociologist Henri Lefebvre has pointed out, space is not given – it is always produced in the tensions between various forces.[3] For the Marxist Lefebvre, the main conflict is between capital's *abstract space*, whose *exchange value* is central, and people's *lived spaces*, which are formed around their *use value*. With Lefebvre's words, one can see a demonstration as the creation of a "counter-space", when the street is taken over in opposition against transformations of the city governed by market forces.

With this starting point, one can claim that a counter-space was created in Gothenburg in June 2001, in both the free discussion forum along the canal and during the various political actions and demonstrations. Afterwards, radical commentators wanted to see the violent confrontations as a direct spatial expression for the antagonism and the gap between the people

2. Cf. Mattias Wahlström (Forthcoming) "Producing spaces for representation. Racist marches, counter-demonstrations, and public-order policing." *Environment and Planning D: Society and Space*.

3. Henri Lefebvre (1991 [1974]) *The production of space*. Oxford: Basil Blackwell (transl. Donald Nicholson-Smith).

on one side and the EU powers and capital on the other. To a certain extent, there is something in this. When an international institution like the EU temporarily "takes over" a specific location, its power structures and oppositions are temporarily expressed in the city space. Power structures that are normally dispersed and impersonal become symbolically concretised and located at a certain place. This makes it easier for political opposition to be concentrated at a certain time and place.

However, it would be wrong to reduce spatial conflicts in Gothenburg to a mechanical consequence of power structures. One can just as well say that various groups of demonstrators, *with the help* of the police and EU powers, actively *produce* a model of international conflict. In this way, Gothenburg becomes what the sociologist Thomas Gieryn would call a "truth-spot" – a place that, through the way it is shaped and talked about, is made into an example of something universal, "proof" that certain assumptions about the world are true.[4] A place in the city and what happens there can, under certain conditions, be used to make more general sociological or political claims. In this case, one can say that a temporary EU summit meeting gave the citizens a new position from which to represent their civil will.

In light of this, it ought to be pointed out that a political demonstration can be seen as a demonstration in both meanings of the word. The word refers both to a collection of people who express an opinion in a public space, and at the same time to an illustration of a certain fact (or a function of a certain technology) in front of an audience.[5]

One could say that a political demonstration has political *content* in the form of slogans, speeches, etc., but that it also tries to show something through its *form* – which events take place, by whom and where. That thousands of people were motivated to travel from all around Europe to participate in demonstrations aimed at criticising President Bush and the EU, demonstrated both the presence of strong popular engagement

4. Thomas F Gieryn (2002) "Three truth-spots" *Journal of the History of the Behavioral Sciences*, 38(2), pp. 113–132; Gieryn (2006) "City as truth-spot. Laboratories and field-sites in urban studies", *Social Studies of Science*, 36(1), pp. 5–38.

5. Andrew Barry (1999) "Demonstrations: sites and sights of direct action", *Economy & Society* 28(1), p. 75.

as well as distance from the political leaders participating in the meetings being held behind police lines. On the other hand, after the events, a large part of the leftwing movement, especially Attac Sweden, suffered a crisis of confidence. In many people's opinion, they had not distanced themselves enough from the violence. They had demonstrated in the same place, which was thought to show collaboration. The participants in the riots revealed a conflict, but their protest came to be understood (not least thanks to the news media) as more aimed at Gothenburg the city than at the EU delegates. The material attack on the city's main street was so symbolically loaded that while the injured demonstrator hung between life and death in hospital, the media focused almost solely on the cost of the Avenyn's broken windows. This is how strongly exchange value can dominate.

Among the police and local politicians, the original idea was to demonstrate the Gothenburgian spirit of understanding (see Gunnar Falkemark's chapter in this book), something that ought to have been in line with EU politicians' desire to show closeness to the citizens by having a moving summit meeting. The plan was that only a few police without protective gear would need to be visible to the demonstrators. Gothenburg would demonstrate how open Swedish society works. After the Friday riots on the Avenyn, these ambitions got mixed up with something else. The police actions seemed primarily aimed at demonstrating that they had control of the city space, now that it had become possible to doubt that. Seated festival participants in a park were apprehended and those who had chosen to sleep in the "wrong" school were hauled out onto the pavement and insulted by the police's anti-terrorist force. Vasaplatsen and Schillerska secondary schools became symbols for the police's power over the city territory. But even far from these places, one had the unpleasant experience, in central Gothenburg, of being at the mercy of the police; of being critically studied by suspecting police officers at one of their roadblocks; of being

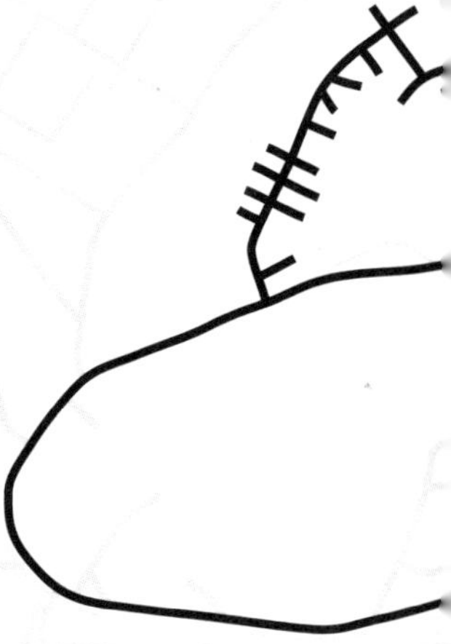

forced to move out of the way of police officers in riot gear, running towards an unknown destination with hard expressions; and during a concert, of receiving a message that the police had begun to open fire.

The demonstration of state power still did not stop after the exhausted, frustrated and scared police officers had gone home to tend their wounds. The demonstration sites became "truth-spots" in a way that the activists had not intended. In the following years, people's presence in "wrong" locations in the city while the summit meeting was being held contributed to them being given unprecedentedly hard sentences, in some cases on surprisingly weak grounds.[6] The clearest example is perhaps the eight people who, during a police attack, were in a flat in which the so-called liasion centre was located. Since they were in a place from where a number of text messages were sent out, of which a couple encouraged people to rescue demonstrators thought to be under attack by police, they were in effect sentenced for having collectively controlled the riots. Place proves guilt.

IV

The political demonstrations in Gothenburg were an attempt to turn the city a place where social conflicts could be expressed spatially, and to attract attention of international media – a "truth-spot" where a number of social problems could be demonstrated, primarily the democracy deficit in the EU and George W. Bush's foreign policies. As this text is being written, just under a decade later, it seems that in June 2001 Gothenburg primarily symbolised the violence of demonstrators critical of globalisation and the police's lack of organisation and methods of working. Hardly what either of these actors would have wished for.

6. Erik Wijk (2003) *Orätt. Rättsrötan efter Göteborgshändelserna* (*Wrong. Corrupt legal practices after the Gothenburg events*). Stockholm: Ordfront; Eric Östberg (2002) *Göteborgskravallerna och rätten. Några iakttagelser ur ett människorättsperspektiv* (*The Gothenburg riots and the law. Some observations from a human rights perspective*). Stockholm: Svenska Helsingforskommittén för mänskliga rättigheter.

Mattias Wahlström works at the Department of Sociology, University of Gothenburg, and his research concerns policing and social movements.

Olle Hagman

THE REVOLT OF THE ASPHALT INDIANS

I

During the late summer of 2007, there was a new sort of protest against automobile traffic in Gothenburg. The night of 28–29 August, three people sneaked out and let the air out of the tyres of around 30 "city jeeps".[1] They left notes on the windshields, encouraging the owners to "take responsibility for the environment and begin taking public transport". The headline read: "Your city jeep kills." The activists called themselves the Indians of the Asphalt Jungle. Similar actions had taken place previously in Stockholm and Sundsvall. The goal was to "make it uncomfortable to own a city jeep". Some newspapers reported that the activists had cut the tyres, but the Indians claimed that they had not damaged any cars. On their website,[2] there were instructions that described how one could unscrew the cover of the valve and place some gravel there. When the cover was screwed on again, the air would slowly leak out of the tyre. Two weeks later, the action was repeated. Over the course of a couple of nights, the air was let out of 120 city jeeps in the centre and some other neighbourhoods.

1. "Stadsjeep" ("city jeep") is a Swedish term for a tall, often four-wheel-drive car. The term got popular after the type of car became common in Sweden and it comprises both what the car industry officially calls SUVs (Sport Utility Vehicles) and so-called Crossovers.

2. http://asfaltsdjungelnsindianer.wordpress.com (2008-01-20).

II

Every city is characterised by the dominant method of transportation of its time. Once, Gothenburg was characterised by sea traffic, with harbour cranes rising towards the sky, canals that crossed the city and riveting hammers at the shipyard whose blows echoed over the river. What affects the city picture most today is cars. The streets are filled with cars that are being driven or are parked. The sound of motor traffic drowns out all other sounds. Even the air's chemical composition is for the most part influenced by cars. Gothenburg smells of cars.

Gothenburg is a car city in two ways. First, two of the country's largest car-producers have their plants here. Volvo Cars makes cars for individuals while Volvo AB makes lorries and buses. Also, there are many suppliers in the region, as well as a lot of development and research. To this, one can add the large oil harbour, where most of the oil is used as fuel for cars. Around 10–15 % of the population make their living directly from car-related work (see Bengt Furåker's chapter in this book).

Second, Gothenburg is a car city because the car dominates over other kinds of transportation. Most day trips, both locally and regionally, take place in a car.[3] The dominance of cars is in part because public transportation – compared with, for example, Stockholm – is poorly built up. This is usually explained by saying that the city is more spread out. Gothenburg is a large city in terms of space, but the densely-populated centre is small. In this way, the city is more like American cities than traditional European ones. Besides the local and regional traffic, Gothenburg also experiences a lot of through-traffic, with two European roads cutting through the city. The traffic on both E6 and E20 is combined with local traffic.

Maybe Gothenburg could also be called a car city in the cultural sense. Many claim that the policies have been more car-friendly than in other places in the country and that the city was planned for cars rather than for people. Car traffic takes precedence over other kinds of traffic.

3. In Gothenburg municipality, half of all trips take place by car, one-fourth by public transportation. Even in the centre, the car dominates. 38 % of trips in the centre take place by car, 26 % by public transportation, 22 % by foot and 13 % by bicycle. If one considers the length of the trip, the dominance is even larger. Commuting to the city from outer areas and neighbouring municipalities is extensive and more than 80 % takes place by car. Göteborgs Stad (2007), "Resvanor i Göteborgsregionen 2005" ("Travel habits in the Gothenburg region 2005").

III

In Gothenburg, there is also a long history of protest against cars. One of the first and most drawn-out was the occupation of Kungstorget in 1976. People were protesting against the building of an underground carpark. According to the protestors, this would attract more cars to the city. The action succeeded – there is still no garage there. This was followed by sit-in demonstrations in Gothenburg and other cities at the end of the 1970s and beginning of the 1980s, also in protest against the power of cars over the planning of the city. Then, for a few years, the protests moved outside the city. Many Gothenburgers took part in "tree-hugging actions" in Bohuslän, against the building of a motorway between Gothenburg and Oslo, "Scan Link", which Volvo's then-CEO Pehr Gyllenhammar had walked at the head of. Opposition was the strongest to the section between Gothenburg and Uddevalla. Volvo demanded that its plant be located in Uddevalla, which had been hard hit by the shipyard crisis.

At the end of the 1980s, the protests moved into the city again. They were driven by the environmental movement, which demonstrated more or less regularly once a month for around two years. Several times, traffic was blocked at a strategically chosen location. During the first actions, the police watched without getting involved. The first seems to have taken place without any conflicts. A reporter from the *Göteborgs-Posten* newspaper was there and interviewed some drivers. Several sympathised with the protestors. As the actions began to be repeated, the atmosphere became more tense. On one occasion several drivers lost patience and began to drag protestors away. One protestor was run over and broke an arm. Several editorials demanded that the police react to the protestors. Soon they intervened more and the environmental movement stopped its protests.

Two years later, in May 1994, a last blockade was carried out, when around 40 people sat down on the crossing between Sprängkullsgatan and Vasagatan streets, next to Gothenburg

University's social science faculty. The initiative came from students at the social science departments, but many belonged to the environmental movement and had been involved in previous protests. No cars were stopped. The students had applied for permission but not recived it. The police were prepared and they diverted traffic. Around half of the protestors were apprehended and fined.

The baton was then taken by a group with international connections that called itself Kritiska Massor (Critical Masses), who took a softer line. They gathered once a month for about a year, riding their bicycles through the city. They were careful not to break any traffic laws, waving in a friendly manner to drivers and ringing their bells. At the same time, they handed out pamphlets that demanded that car traffic be limited for the benefit of other kinds of transportation.

IV

Over time, there has been a change in how the protests have been shaped. During several of the first actions, particularly the occupation of Kungstorget and the protests against the motorway in Bohuslän, drivers were not involved at all. The demonstrators focused on the politicians and their plans to build up infrastructure for cars. The sit-in demonstrations that came later affected drivers as well. The demonstrators turned to them and questioned their choice to use cars rather than public transportation or bicycles, even if they also focused on the politicians. They were the ones who allowed a majority of drivers to "run over" minorities on the issue of traffic planning. In the sit-in demonstrations on Sprängkullsgatan in May 1994, they referred to the fact that five years earlier, the street had been judged to be a "private nuisance", but nothing had been done about it.

The actions of the Indians of the Asphalt Jungle in the autumn of 2007 affected drivers, but more selectively. The target was not drivers in general but drivers of a certain kind of car. The Indians questioned their personal choice of car. While the sit-in demonstrations in 1994 were aimed at the social order that defends and is defended by the majority, it was now a minority that was the focus. The affected jeep-owners could not claim that they acted "like everyone else". The protest was about their individual choices and responsibilities. It allowed them, on the other hand, to act like victims.

The type of car that the Indians targetted was already being questioned, among others by the Green Party, which had proposed a so-called "jeep tax", by the Swedish Road Administration and by the organisation the Swedish Association of Green Motorists. But this type of car also had its defenders, who claimed that it was necessary for car producers who wanted to survive, not least on the American market. When Volvo's first "real" city jeep, XC90, was presented in 2001, in the middle of an economic recession, it was considered by many to be Volvo's saviour.

One reason why city jeeps became the target is that in recent years the environmental question has "shrunk", so that the issue of global warming forced aside other issues (see Martin Letell's chapter in this book), and city jeeps were already considered "carbon dioxide pigs". Another reason is that – viewed with a social scientist's spectacles – are particularly appropriate as symbols. First, they are easy to recognise. Their design makes them easy to differentiate from other cars. Second, many of the functions that their owners paid extra for, such as four-wheel drive and extra-high clearance, are seen as poorly suited to a city environment. Third, since many of these functions can be seen as unnecessary, and since many city jeeps are relatively expensive, they can be seen as an expression of luxury consumption. Fourth, with their size, which makes them both fuel-devouring and dangerous to other drivers, and with their often consciously aggressive design, they can be seen to express an egotistical way of relating to the rest of the world.

V

The sit-in demonstrations of 1994 followed the model for what the anthropologist Victor Turner called a "social drama".[4] Such a drama is comprised of four phases. It starts with some people consciously committing a crime; they also accept responsibility and are prepared to take the punishment. The demonstrators admitted that they had broken the law, but they claimed they did it to stop a "larger" crime. They said they were speaking for "others" who could not speak – that is, they were not acting in their own interests. Participants differed about who these "others" were. For some, they were those who lived and worked in the area, for others it was the car-less travellers, and for others still it was "nature". The action took place over a limited time period with four distinct phases. It started with a "breach", when the demonstrators sat on the crossing. It was followed by a "crisis", when the police encouraged them to get up and leave the street. After the blockade itself, there was a long phase of "redressive action", when some were put on trial and given sentences, which finally led to "reintegration". Although no traffic was stopped, they were sentenced for "hindering traffic". The fine was 1 200 SEK, about the same as driving through a red light. The explanation for why the sentence was so hard, I think, is that they questioned the current social order, which emphasises the car's "usefulness" over its negative consequences, and they thereby were viewed as a threat to the order.

4. Victor Turner (1983) *Dramas, fields, and metaphors. Symbolic action in human society*. Ithaca: Cornell University Press.

The protests in 1997 by the Indians of the Asphalt Jungle were different. There was no one who stepped forward and took responsibility, and therefore there was no one who took the punishment. Protesters avoided direct confrontation. The opponent was not involved in the action. By avoiding the punishment, there was no chance of reintegration. The protest had no clear timeframe, but instead took place via occasional efforts that continued until they took a one-sided decision at the end of the year to have a "ceasefire".

VI

Protests against cars will continue. The question is which form they will take in the future. Will they return to being aimed at the politicians or will they continue to be more individually focused? It is clear that many people in Gothenburg depend on cars and that the percentage of people who take public transport, ride bikes or walk is only increasing slowly. The car industry is in the midst of a crisis, but cars continue to roll. When things improve, people will buy new cars, whether Volvo has survived the crisis or not. The polarisation of the population that cars create will remain for the foreseeable future.

Olle Hagman
has a Ph.D. in Social Anthropology and is currently working at the Section for Science and Technology Studies, Department of Sociology, University of Gothenburg. His research deals with motoring and the journeys of everyday life.

Daniel Enstedt

A DIVIDED BODY
Christian faith and sexuality in Gothenburg

When, on 27 October 2005, the Church of Sweden decided to allow blessings for same-sex unions, the reactions were swift in coming. During the weeks that followed, more than 800 priests made their displeasure known by signing a protest that was published on the internet. The "priest declaration", as it came to be called, was initiated by assistant vicar Yngve Kalin, who, along with a number of the other priests who signed it, worked in the Gothenburg diocese. This is how Kalin justified the priest declaration:

> We, priests in this church, who have signed this declaration feel that this decision contradicts the order for relationships and marriage, as God through His word has revealed it to us and as it is defined as a relationship between one man and one woman. God's word does not allow us to bless any other types of couples.[1]

1. http://deklaration.kalin.nu (2005-11-10).

Not long after the priest declaration aroused media attention, another list came, this one on the homepage of the Institute for Contextual Theology. There they wrote that the general synod's decision about blessings for same-sex unions "is completely in line with how we understand God's continual revelations throughout history".[2] Judging by the protest, in the Church of Sweden there were two widely differing views of the issue regarding blessings for same-sex unions.

2. http://www.iktsverige.org/iktuppro.pdf (2009-01-20).

The picture of Christianity in Gothenburg's city and diocese sometimes is portrayed as rather narrow-minded. For a long time, Gothenburg appears to have housed major opposition to female priests, which has then paved the way for the protests against blessings for same-sex unions. That almost one-third of the priests who signed the priest declaration work in the diocese of Gothenburg, while advocates for the blessing were only 12 percent, seemed to confirm this picture of Gothenburg. The question is how well this actually fits.

More than a year after the debate regarding the general synod's decision, I began a series of interviews with priests who had signed the priest declaration and with members of EKHO (Ecumenical groups for Christian homosexual, bisexual and transgender people). In my interviews with EKHO members, another picture of Gothenburg developed. The interviewees described Gothenburg as a place where Christian homosexual, bisexual and transgender issues were on the agenda, where a serious effort was made to fight homophobia and change Christianity from the inside. How can Gothenburg appear as a reactionary outpost within the Church of Sweden at the same time housing Sweden's perhaps most active EKHO group?

MAPPING GOTHENBURG

The parishes in Gothenburg can be divided according to the positions taken by the priests on the issue of blessings for same-sex unions. Since parish members' opinions can completely or in part deviate from what the priests think, it is important to emphasise that no immediate conclusions can be made based on this categorisation regarding how entire congregations view the issue. Also, not all priests in Gothenburg have made their opinion about the issue known.

Out of Gothenburg's 37 parishes, 6 did not officially take a position for or against the decision to bless same-sex unions. In 14 parishes, the priests agreed with the decision, while 10 parishes were characterised by opposition to the decision. 7 parishes had both advocates and opponents, even if the majority was positive towards the decision (see Picture 1).

Regarding how men and women viewed the issue, there is a relatively clear picture. Of the 31 priests who opposed the

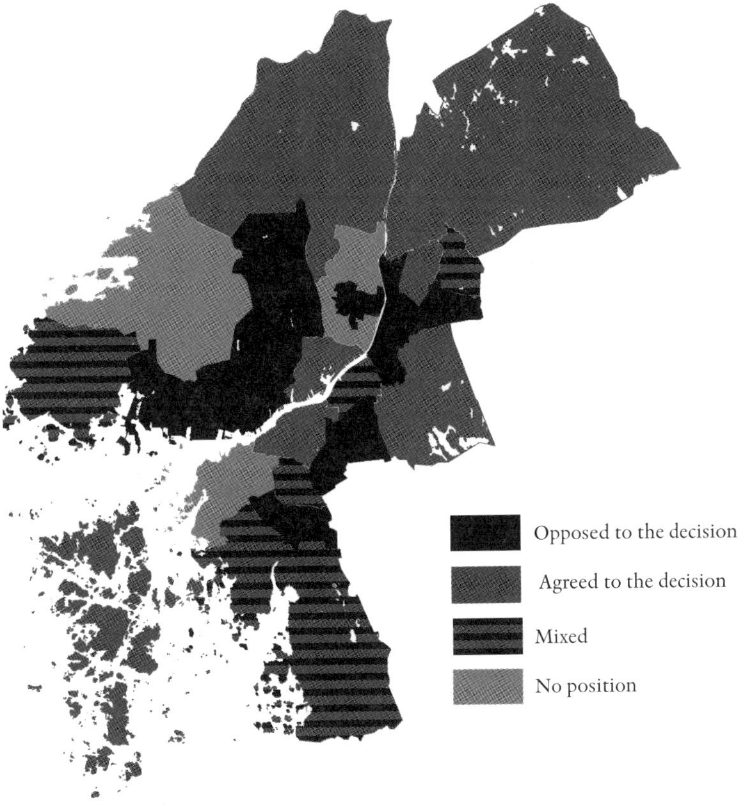

Picture 1. Gothenburg city regarding positions on the issue ofblessings for same-sex unions.

proposal in Gothenburg city, all were men. Of the 52 who had the opposite opinion, 30 were women (58 %). The advocates of the decision were in other words overwhelmingly women, while all of the opposition within Gothenburg city's parishes were men.

In regard to the relationship between Gothenburg city and diocese, another relevant aspect appears. In the diocese, 244 priests signed the priest declaration, of which 3 were women (1 %). Gothenburg city therefore houses 13 % of those who are against blessings for same-sex unions within the diocese. In regard to advocates of the decision, the opposite is the case. Gothenburg city houses 60 % who are for blessings for same-sex unions within the diocese.

The opposition to blessings for same-sex unions is noticeable within Gothenburg diocese, but not to the same extent in Gothenburg city, even if opposition is also represented there. Those who advocate blessings for same-sex unions are predominantly women who work in Gothenburg city, while the opponents are almost all men in Gothenburg diocese.

OPPOSITION

It is no coincidence that it is in Gothenburg diocese that the opposition is the strongest, nor that it was Yngve Kalin who was behind the priest declaration. The decision in 1958 to allow the ordination of women in the Church of Sweden aroused a number of reactions. The bishop of Gothenburg, Bo Giertz, was one of the people who defended the protests. Giertz helped start the *Church gathering around the Bible and revelation*, an association that is critical towards the decision to make the priesthood open to women. Bo Giertz's current successor as the chair of the *Church gathering* is Yngve Kalin. As a follow-on to Giertz's protests against female priests, the priest declaration won some legitimacy and aroused enthusiasm amongst the church-goers within the Church of Sweden who have a so-called "classic Christian belief". Another phalanx among the west Swedish devout that connects to Giertz's influence and uses Gothenburg as its display window is the Mission Province. The Mission Province, which only accepts male priests, spreads the rumour of Gothenburg being unfriendly to female priests. That Bishop Giertz was placed in central Gothenburg in 1958 and assistant vicar Kalin is located in one of the diocese's parishes in the provinces 50 years later is almost symptomatic of the displacement that has taken place in the Gothenburg diocese.

GOTHENBURG AS A CHRISTIAN LGBT CITY

Elisabeth Ohlson Wallin's photo exhibition *Ecce Homo* caused much debate within the Church of Sweden in the 1990s. The exhibit comprised twelve photographs in which LGBT people portray biblical events. When it became known that the photographs were going to be shown in Annedal church on 21 November 1998, for awhile a bitter discussion took place in the west Church of Sweden. Rural dean Bengt Inghammar, who conducted a church service in connection with the exhibition, was reported to the cathedral chapter because of his involvement. What became clear during the time that the exhibition was at Annedal church was that Gothenburg was a divided city in regard to the relationship between Christian belief and sexuality. When the general synod made its decision to bless same-sex pairs seven years later, this opposition was again accentuated in Gothenburg.

The department for diversity in Gothenburg city stated in 2006 that it is harder to be LGBT in Gothenburg than in Stockholm or Malmö. The report named "a strong conservative religiosity" as a cause for this situation. But in the same year, in an inspection of municipalities conducted by the National Swedish Association for Sexual Information in regard to LGBT people's situations around the country, Gothenburg obtained a pass and was ranked in second place after Borås. This shows a somewhat better situation than what is usually thought (see Arne Nilsson and Cathrin Wasshede's chapters in this book).

The relationship between Christian faith and sexuality has a difficult history. In particular, the "classic Christian faith" has had a hard time accepting and including LGBT people. John Fortunato has called this situation the *Gay Predicament*, which gives Christian LGBT people three possible strategies. The first alternative is to distance oneself from Christianity, the second to distance oneself from LGBT sexuality. The third alternative is that the opposition between sexuality and "classic Christian faith" remains, but Christianity is reformulated based on an LGBT perspective. Such a reformulation occurs in many LGBT Christian circles, including EKHO in Gothenburg. In their mission statement, EKHO writes that the organisation works for "freedom and justice for homosexual and bisexual as well as transpeople in Christian churches and associations".[3] In the quote, EKHO's liberation theology is revealed. But this does not mean that a synthesis between an LGBT perspective and "classic Christian faith" has occurred, nor that the "classic Christian faith" has been given up completely. Rather, the sort of Christianity that Kalin represents plays the role of EKHO's antithesis. EKHO's objectives are formulated in relationship to an articulated opposition, which is called "classic Christian faith". The situation that the *Gay Predicament* describes is itself the driving force behind LGBT Christianity, or as the sociologist Jodi O'Brien writes, this situation has given birth to a specific queer Christian identity.[4] It is not about ending the situation but rather about living it.

3. http://www.ekho.se/mal.html (2008-08-15).

4. Jodi O'Brien (2004) "Wrestling the angel of contradiction. Queer Christian identities." Culture and Religion, 5(2), pp. 179–202.

OPPOSITION AND POSSIBILITIES

In Stockholm, where the opposition is more marginalised than in Gothenburg, EKHO is not as active. The opposition that still exists against the blessing of same-sex unions in Gothenburg city is is a precondition for an active EKHO group. Also, few other cities in Sweden are big enough to make an active Christian LGBT group possible. The combination of a limited and outspoken opposition and a large enough recruitment base has contributed to the EKHO group in Gothenburg being strong. The question is what will happen if the conditions for this opposition change. Since EKHO's current goals are mainly about fighting the opposition that "classic Christian faith", among others, creates, it is reasonable to assume that the EKHO group's activities will decrease or be thoroughly reformulated if the opposition ends. The priest declaration does not just create situations and opposition, but also contributes to the conditions for social and religious change.

Christian groups, both those behind the priest declaration and its antagonists, are constituted by and organised around different understandings of Christian faith and sexuality. As long as the opposition expressed by the priest declaration continues, conditions will exist for the change EKHO is fighting for. Different understandings of the question of Christian faith and sexuality are important for how Christian religious and social life is organised in a city like Gothenburg.

Daniel Enstedt works at the Department of Literature, History of Ideas and Religion at the University of Gothenburg, and does research on Christian faith and sexuality.

Cathrin Wasshede

BEARD AND SKIRT
Gender bending in public space

A person with a long flower-patterned skirt walks down Avenyn in central Gothenburg. As you get closer, you see that the person has a beard. It is a man. He looks happy and pleased. He is heterosexual. Another person wakes up in a flat in one of Gothenburg's suburbs[1] and looks out the window. Something sticky is running down the window. On the rug in the hall below the mailbox there is also the same sort of mess. It is egg. This person sometimes wears brightly coloured trousers with flowers on them; skirts only in private. He is a man, has a beard and is scared of harassment. He is bisexual. Another person wears skirts in the winter. It is more comfortable to have long Johns underneath a skirt than underneath trousers. The fear of being attacked lives parallel with the pleasure of resistance. This is also a man. He is gay.

Gothenburg is often portrayed as one of Sweden's most anti-homosexual cities. The basis of this designation is that in the 1990s the city was head of the list of statistics in terms of threats, violence and harassment against homo- bi- and transsexuals.[2] At the same time, the city is described as homosexual-friend-

1. See note 1 in the Introduction.

2. Eva Tiby (1999) *Hatbrott? Homosexuella kvinnors och mäns berättelser om utsatthet för brott* (*Hate crime? Homosexual women's and men's stories about being victims of crime*). Stockholm: Kriminologiska institutionen, Stockholms universitet.

ly, with a large array of gay clubs and a well-attended annual LGBT festival. Newspaper headlines refer to Gothenburg as the "rainbow city" (see Daniel Enstedt's chapter).[3]

Regardless, there are clear norms regarding gender-bending, as shown in the descriptions above. They are based on three young political activists' reflections regarding their usage of skirts.[4] The situations are different for the three men. Why? One possible factor is what I have chosen to call heteroprotection; that is, how much protection one has against homophobic reactions.[5] The degree of heteroprotection is affected by how one makes gender, how one positions oneself regarding hetero-, homo- and bisexuality and how much "safety" one has for one's experience in gender-bending. How much heteroprotection one counts on having also plays a role. This protection is situational and varies depending on where in the city one is; it is a difference between walking dressed in a skirt on Avenyn, where there is anonymity, and doing it in one's own neighbourhood, where neighbours can find norm-breakers more provocative or threatening (see Sara Uhnoo's chapter). Maybe the neighbours know that the bisexual man has relationships with other men, while the heterosexual man on Avenyn is relatively anonymous. This probably affects people's reactions to their gender-bending. The more heteroprotection one has, the more room one has for gender-bending. This is the opposite of what people usually think, since people assume that gay men are significantly more gender-bending than heterosexual men (see Arne Nilsson's chapter). If people understand you as gay, you risk being harassed. If you are understood as hetero, your gender-bending can pass. To belong to the dominant norming category in the (hetero)normative gender order brings with it a feeling of naturalness and superiority. It gives a feeling of security. This "heterosexual safety" can be compared to the sort of safety with which middle- and upper-class people move in society.

The heterosexual man says that he saw a man in town with a

3. *Göteborgs-Posten, Två dagar* (*Two days*), 2008-11-29, pp. 4–11.

4. The activists work in the so-called outside-parliament left in Gothenburg.

5. Cathrin Wasshede (2010) *Passionerad politik. Om motstånd mot heteronormativ könsmakt (Passionate politics. Resistance to heteronormative gender power)*. Malmö: Bokbox Förlag.

skirt on and that he thought the man was "terribly sexy". After that, he began, both in private and public contexts, to strategically wear a skirt, "to break gender roles". However, there are strong limits to consider: "I am, despite everything, manly. You shouldn't be this sissy who... I don't know if there is still a fear of appearing unmanly." An example of how he maintains this balance is to not choose clothes that are "too obviously women's clothes". Sometimes he thinks an item of clothing in a shop window is nice, but he does not buy it because he then would risk being seen as a man who wants to dress like a woman. With his skirt, he wears a relatively masculine shirt and he also has a beard. The strategy is effective. He has a high degree of heteroprotection. The limit for his gender-bending is at the point where he risks being viewed as homosexual; I interpret his talk about sissies and unmanliness as directly related to homosexual men. As long as he is understood to be heterosexually manly, gender-bending is not only imaginable but in his political context also desirable. The gender researcher Marie Nordberg formulates this as the "gay man" functioning as a sort of border control, with the goal of retaining gender polarisation and thereby heterosexuality. Even if a man challenges gender limits, he must look like a heterosexual man, have the right tone of voice and not act like a sissy, she writes. An "overcommunication of femininity" threatens men's heterosexual positioning.[6] The question is to what extent his choice of shirt is really gender-bending? What is he bending? Clothing norms for heterosexual men. But is that the same as being gender-bending?

At home in the suburbs, the bisexual man shows me his skirts and dresses. He says that he avoids wearing them in public places because he is scared of having to deal with homophobic reactions. It has been provocative enough for those around him that he has worn trousers in the "wrong" colours and patterns. On a number of occasions, people in his neighbourhood have called him a "fucking fag" and thrown stones at him. And at his

6. Marie Nordberg (2004a) "'Kvinnlig maskulinitet' och 'manlig femininitet.' En möjlighet att överskrida könsdikotomin?" ("'Womanly masculinity' and 'manly feminity.' A possibility to bend the gender dichotomy?"), *Kvinnovetenskaplig Tidskrift* 1–2, pp. 47–65, and Marie Nordberg (2005) *Jämställdhetens spjutspets? Manliga arbetstagare i kvinnoyrken, jämställdhet, maskulinitet, femininitet och heteronormativitet* (*The tip of the equality spear? Male employees in female jobs, equality, masculinity, feminity, and heteronormativity*). Göteborg: Arkipelag.

work at a school, he has been the victim of homophobic harassment, from colleagues, students and parents. He wants to work against traditional masculinity, but his limit is also at the point of overcommunication of femininity. When I mention that he has a beard, he says that this facilitates his choice of clothing: "Then I at least have one manly attribute. I feel like the reaction from those around me will be less powerful. Because they see the beard and think, 'Yeah, yeah, he hasn't completely given up his correct gender identity.' And then it's not as threatening." In comparison to the heterosexual man, his strategy is not successful – despite his beard, he has been harassed. This can be because of the place's character – the neighbourhood in the suburbs – and it can be because of the lack of safety that his bisexuality and working-class background offer. He does not expect any real heteroprotection. I would like to claim that what he experiences is a violent attempt to restore the gender and sexuality order.[7]

The gay man, who also lives in the suburbs, says that he wears skirts for reasons of comfort. When, in the leftwing political circles in which he used to move, this was interpreted as a "sexual-political statement" and as an expression of a genuine gay identity, he stopped wearing a skirt out in the city. He felt that his skirt-wearing was simplified, even if he also saw it as a way of showing his non-heterosexuality. However, this was not unproblematic because of his unsafety and a certain fear of coming out as gay. When he discusses this fear and the awareness of risk he had when he was dressed in a skirt in public space, he points out that despite everything, it was a fear he could handle: "When there is a clear negative danger [...] one can also muster a sort of desire to oppose: you know what the problem is and you just have to be strong." Now he only wears a skirt at home and in drag-activist contexts. In practice, he opposes heteroprotection itself – by openly defining himself as gay and by using a skirt without combining it with something specifically manly. He does not try to avoid the stigmatisation

7. Judith Butler (2006) *Genus ogjort. Kropp, begär och möjlig existens* (*Undoing gender.*). Stockholm: Norstedts Akademiska Förlag.

that his total lack of heteroprotection entails. Instead, he turns it into a sort of resistance strategy; in the same way that queer activists oppose the assimilation of homosexuals into heterosexual society, instead demanding an existence on their own terms. The long experience of outsiderness that he has in regard to expected masculinity and heterosexuality can be part of what I interpret as resistance to heterosexuality. He does not want to come inside the walls of protection.

In sum, one can see how the three men have different degrees of heteroprotection and different ways of relating to it. The heterosexual man takes it for given. When I ask him if he is scared of being attacked in town, I get a negative response. There is nothing that clearly threatens his high level of heteroprotection. Along with this, Nordberg points out how heterosexual men's usage of skirts can be described with the concept of metrosexual, which according to her is a tool to "differentiate heterosexual men who recognise aesthetic and femininely coded activities from homosexual men".[8] The bisexual man has limited heteroprotection, but longs for it because of his experiences of harassment. The gay man has no major heteroprotection, but he is not interested in having any either. He uses his outsider position as a basis for his resistance.

Men's strategic employment of skirts and/or dresses can be seen as a continuation of the political struggle in the 1970s, when the Gothenburg Socialist group Red Gays advocated the usage of dresses with the goal of political freedom.[9] But how emancipating is men's usage of skirts? On the one hand, it has emancipating potential because of its displacement of gender and sexual meanings. At the same time, there is a risk of reproducing "us" (heterosexuals) versus "them" (homosexuals, bisexuals, transsexuals), which becomes clear when the gay man has to act as border control for what it is possible to do as a man. Nordberg also takes note of the risk when she writes that men's idealisation and affirmation of femininity can be interpreted as an updating of hegemonic masculinity. According to

8. Marie Nordberg (2004b) "Det hänger på håret – maskulinitet, femininitet, makt, mode och konsumtion" ("Because of the hair – masculinity, feminity, power, style and consumption"). Paper given at *Den gode, den onde, den normale – nordisk mansforskningskonferens 2004* conference. http://www.kvinfo.su.se/lankar/mansforskn%20konf%20-%20Nordberg.pdf.

9. Greger Eman (2000) "Klänningens betydelse för mänsklighetens frigörelse. Om den socialistiska gruppen Röda bögar i Göteborg 1976–78" ("The dress's significance for the liberation of humanity. On the Socialist group Red Gays in Gothenburg 1976–78"), in Martin Andreasson (ed.) *Homo i folkhemmet. Homo- och bisexuella i Sverige 1950–2000* (*Homo in the Folkhemmet. Homosexuals and bisexuals in Sweden 1950–2000*). Göteborg: Anamma.

gender equality rhetoric, "the new man" is softer and less authoritarian and is positioned in opposition to "the traditional man". At the same time, men as a group still have a superior position in society.[10] So – is the man in a skirt just a new version of hegemonic masculinity? Perhaps the heterosexual man on anonymous Avenyn. But definitely not the bisexual man or the gay man out in their neighbourhoods in the suburbs.

10. Marie Nordberg (2004a).

Cathrin Wasshede has a Ph.D. and works at the Department of Sociology, University of Gothenburg, and studies resistance to heteronormativity and gendered structures of power.

Arne Nilsson

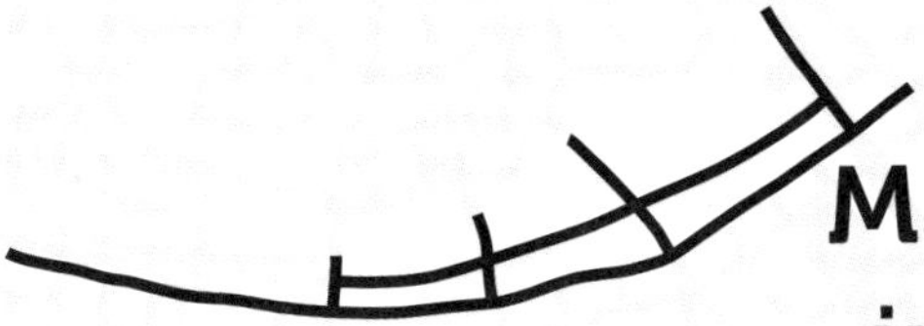

FROM RUNDAN TO BÖGBERGET
Male homosexual life in "the city of parks"

Gothenburg is a city of parks. In the middle of the city, there is the Kungsparken, between the moat to the north and Vasastaden to the south. Every day, thousands of people pass through the park on their way to and from work, shopping and entertainment in the city within the moat. On beautiful summer days, its lawns are filled with sun-bathing and picnicking city residents.

I wonder how many of these people know that not long ago this park and the surrounding area were places for a blooming male homosexual life. For decades around the middle of the 20th century, in and near "the Park", as participants in homosexual life called it, there was a landscape of meeting places along paths, on benches, in bushes and in public toilets. The meeting places were connected by Rundan (the Round), a promenade walk that stretched from Heden in the east to Pustervik in the west.[1]

Homosexual life in this environment generally was of two types: socialising with friends and acquaintances and sexual

1. What I say here about male homosexual life 1930–1980 I have previously presented in the books *Såna och riktiga karlar* (*Men like that and real men*) and (with Margareta Lindholm) *En annan stad* (*Another city*). Similar patterns have been shown in other studies in the west partially during the same period, as in Gert Hekma (1992) *De roze rand van donker Amsterdam*, George Chauncey (1995) *Gay New York. The making of the gay male world, 1890–1940*, Hans Kristiansen (2008) *Masker og motstand. Diskré homoliv i Norge 1920–1970* and Matt Houlbrook (2005) *Queer London*.

activity with strangers. Those who took part in the former were mainly men "like that", men who were seen as homo. They could go on walks along Rundan with friends or walk alone and meet friends and acquaintances on the way. Here and there, gangs hung out together and in some cases developed a camp culture, with shouts, jokes and quick-wittedness, along with the usage of female names.

Sexual life was typically comprised of hasty meetings in bushes or urinals. Men "like that" did not generally have sex with one another; they usually thought of each other as too unmanly for that. They often wanted to have a "real man". And there were "real men", who were seen as manly and not as homo. Not infrequently, the sexual meetings were connected with implicit prostitution; the "real man" afterwards might get some coins, a cigarette, or maybe a little alcohol.

At this time in Gothenburg, it was to a large degree in these forms and in this environment that male homosexual life took place. One reason was that there was a housing shortage and cramped housing conditions, so many single men lived with other people. To get together at a locale was unusual, because there was little money. Homosexual life at homes and at locales would arouse attention; on the contrary, it needed to be hidden. There were no particular locales for homosexual life. Out in the city, it was seen as natural for men to go around in the evenings and at night. In the protection provided by the park's darkness and bushes, as well as behind the walls of the urinals, it was possible to live out one's homosexuality. Up until 1944, homosexual intercourse was criminalised. And there was moral legislation.

One reason why homosexual life took place out in the city was that it was where "real men" were. Those who belonged to this category more than others, "ordinary" working-class men, not least young ones, were to a large extent out in the city in the evenings. They lived in cramped conditions and men were not expected to be home at night.

But to be out in the city is one thing and to have sexual relations with men is another. One reason why "real men" were prominent in homosexual life was probably that heterosexuality, in regard to sexual behaviour, was not so important for status and identity amongst working-class men. Maybe it was, as George Chauncey puts it in the book *Gay New York*, more important what pleasure one's sexual partner could give than the partner's physical gender.[2] To take a superior position in sexual intercourse, to be "serviced", seems to have been common – perhaps often it was a matter of seeing the intercourse as a sort of heterosexual intercourse between a "real" man and a "womanly" man. It does not seem to be the case that they made a big deal out of these meetings; they seem to have been a part of daily life. For example, one could make a stop in the urinal on the way home from work. Silence and anonymity contributed to shielding them from other parts of life and from emotional involvement.

2. George Chauncey (1995) *Gay New York. The making of the gay male world, 1890–1940*. London: Flamingo.

Economic inequality and poverty contributed to the involvement of "real men" in homosexual life, particularly during the period before the Second World War. Many could not afford to get married and start a family. Not only did material scarcity contribute to overcrowding, it could also be used as a pretext for participating. This could be a reason for refraining from marital sex and instead having sex with men, men from whom one could also get paid. Besides, young women were expected to wait and an unwelcome pregnancy could be catastrophic.

This pattern of relationships, participants and places for male homosexual life slowly disappeared during these decades. In the park, the possibilities for having sexual meetings were impeded because bushes were cut down and facilities were removed (see Ingrid Sahlin's chapter). This was in part an expression of the "hunt for homophiles" that took place after the war, including by the police. Also, the child-welfare authorities were involved; the hunt was legitimised by saying it had to do with the prostitution of boys. Here, it ought to be noted that the minimum age for same-sex sexual intercourse between consenting adults was 18 years after de-criminalisation in 1944, and not 15 as was the case for heterosexual intercourse.

"Real men" slowly disappeared from the Park. They got better financial circumstances and it became harder to legitimise participating in homosexual life because of a lack of money. More had enough money to get married and start a family, something that was supported by the state's population and family policies, through child subsidies and the building of housing. Many moved from cramped and unmodern flats in the centre of the city to new suburbs. It was no longer so easy to walk past the meeting places. Married men became more tied to families and homes, supported by the new ideal of equal marriages and and later also by increased living in small houses and increased paid work among married women. Time outside of work was employed in "recreational activities". It was less common for men to be out in the city without a particular goal and the growing ideal of orderliness also contributed to this.

Through the complication of sexual meetings and because of "real men" gradually disappearing, the Park became less attractive for men "like that". Other changes contributed to this as well. A heterosexual pleasure culture for youths, such as dance halls, developed. Young women and men got closer. The city in the evening became less of a place for men of all ages but more of a place for youths of both genders.

There were also changes amongst men "like that" which made the Park less important as a meeting place. The hetero dance halls created a longing for such places of their own. Homosexual organisations and clubs developed, also as a result of the identity, fellowship and culture that had flourished in the Park. The housing situation was improved, so more people got their own home. Homosexual life at home became more possible. As with clubs and organisations, homes invited intimacy, and this hindered participation amongst men who did not view themselves as homo.

Some decades after the Second World War, there were only traces left of homosexual life in the Park. This did not mean, however, that this kind of male homosexual life no longer existed. Many continued to enjoy it, including those growing numbers who were couples or lived together. And in heteronormative society some people still needed to hide their homosexuality, and hesitated to participate in clubs and organisations. During the 1960s and '70s, a new place developed for a kind of life similar to that in the Park: Bögberget (Queer Hill) in Slottsskogen. It was more peripheral and to a large extent wooded, so homosexual life was easier to hide there. It was near a parking lot, which was advantageous, since many participants now travelled in cars.

Homosexual life at Bögberget was not at all as large as that which had existed in the Park. It later came to shrink, too. The opportunities for homosexual life have worsened over time because of increased competition for the park's space. It has become harder to hide. The most noticeable expression of competition is the laying out of a frisbee-golf course near and partly on Bögberget. The increased competition probably relates to gentrification, densification and demographic changes in the nearby inner city, a change that expresses increased acceptance of city life.

The deterioration of Bögberget as a place for male homosexual life has occurred at the same time as the need for it might have increased due to social exclusion within the homosexual world. Researchers talk about the commercialisation and aesthetisation of homosexual life in clubs and bars, with increased demands to appear in particular ways, with specific bodies, specific hairstyles and specific clothes.[3] There is a new homonormativity that excludes unwanted types of sexual expression, such as by reducing the public homosexual sphere to consumption spheres and gentrified neighbourhoods.[4] Men who either cannot or do not want to live up to the demands might increasingly be referred to places such as Bögberget.

3. Alison Rooke (2007) "Navigating embodied lesbian space. Toward a lesbian habitus", *Space and culture* 10(2), pp. 231–252.

4. Diane Richardson (2004) "Locating sexualities. From here to normality", *Sexualities* 7(4), pp. 391–411.

Homosexual marriage falls in line with the new homonormativity, the fight for which has been and is central to the gay movements' political fight for citizenship (see Daniel Enstedt's chapter). In the book *The Trouble with Normal*, the queer theorist Michael Warner says that every argument for homosexual marriage demands intensified consideration of what is thrown in its shadow. It has been my aim to contribute to this here.

Arne Nilsson
is Associate Professor in sociology, he has done historical-sociological studies of (homo) sexuality and gender in Gothenburg and on the Swedish transatlantic liners around the middle of the 20th century.

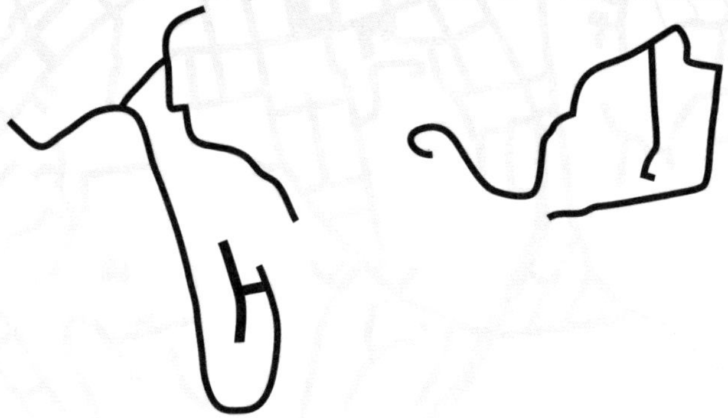

Sten O Karlsson

THE EPOCH OF THE PROLETARIAT Gothenburg 1919–1934

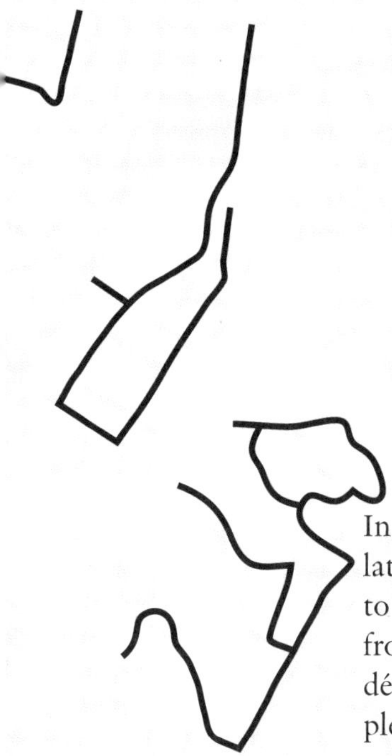

In the autumn of 1918, the Social Democratic ideologue and later finance minister Ernst Wigforss arrived in Gothenburg to work as a lecturer at the Latin School. In a letter to a friend from his student days (and future fellow minister) Östen Undén, he described the housing market: "Lots of homeless people or people who have to live together any which way in order to avoiding walking the streets."[1] On the other hand, there were single "old widows and bachelors" who had 5–12 rooms in their entire house. The cold academic felt "almost like a Bolshevik" when he saw these injustices.

1. Ernst Wigforss (1951) *Minnen II* (*Memories II*). Stockholm: Tiden, pp. 93–94.

The background to this housing crunch was in part a lot of immigration (the new industrial company SKF had expanded greatly and needed workers), and in part because the building of houses had basically stopped during the war. The social gaps that had always been large in Gothenburg had widened even further during the war years. At the time, the city was one of the country's most class-segregated.

From a cultural perspective, during the wars, Gothenburg was two cities. In the centre, there was the middle-class brick-building city with old Gothenburg, Vasastaden, Lorensberg and lower Masthugget. Around this middle-class core, the working-class city was arranged. It was comprised of the wooden-house neighbourhoods in the oldest parts of Haga, Majorna and Landala, and above all the governor's houses (landshövdingehus, see Mats Franzén's chapter) with its three floors (the bottom made of brick, the others of wood). The neighbourhoods that were built after 1880 were almost entirely composed of this type of building: Annedal, upper Masthugget, Olskroken, Gamlestaden, and also the newer parts of Majorna and Landala. In all of these neighbourhoods, working-class families were numerically and "culturally" the dominant majority.

During the 1930s, more than two-thirds of Gothenburg's workers lived in governor's houses. This unique housing environment came to have a big influence on the everyday life and mentality of working-class families. Where the working-class city and the middle-class city bordered each other, the residents were reminded on a daily basis of the sharp class differences. Vasastaden's students were viewed by the working-class youths from the neighbouring area of Landala as "sissies", worthy of a thrashing or at least a dose of appropriate taunts. Taimi Grehn, who grew up between the wars in Gamlestaden, has aptly described the mentality of the time: "Ten of God's commandments ought to be held holy to a certain extent except for the eleventh: 'You shall always be in solidarity with the working-class.' God's commandments were flexible."[2]

According to Grehn, the women's project was to maintain respectability and morals on their own terms without forgoing class solidarity. The project also had a less sympathetic downside: the strict condemnation of women and men who, for various reasons, did not live up to the moral standards of working-class culture. Amongst those who were socially frozen out were married women who were gainfully employed. In a typical orderly working-class family, the man was the only breadwinner, while the wife was responsible for the children,

2. Message from the Department of Ethnology, Gothenburg University, no. 8:1987.

home and household. "The women in our house thought that it was manly to get involved in politics and that it was unwomanly to get involved with union things."[3]

3. Archive for dialects, area names and folklore in Gothenburg, IFGH 6298 (Grehn, Gamlestaden).

This "gender contract" meant that all local politics were completely dominated by male values. According to Grehn, in Gamlestaden it was quite common that men went to prison for lèse majesté or other political sins. The condemned was carried out in a golden chair to the police car by comrades who sang political songs.

Housing segregation and the class divisions in Gothenburg contributed to the development of a radical anti-authoritarian proletarian segment. The city's working-class movement became known for its stubbornness and unwillingness to fall into line in terms of political leadership, LO (Landsorganisationen), tenants' or union organisations. Even a normally calm person like Per Albin Hansson (the party leader of the Social Democrats from 1925 to 1946) could lose patience with the local stubborn-headedness. During a party committee meeting, chairman Hansson is said to have exclaimed: "It's hell, what goes on in Gothenburg!"

From its creation in 1890 to the large strike in 1909, the Arbetarekommunen (Workers' Group) had been a reliable supporter of then-party chairman Hjalmar Branting's reform line. But during the years around the large strike in 1909,[4] the tensions between the generations in the Gothenburg workers' movement grew. During the First World War, the conflict between youth clubs with pacifist views and the Workers' Group's older leadership increased. The splitting of the party in 1917 (see Håkan Thörn's chapter) led to the creation of a new Branting-critical break-out organisation: Gothenburg's Nya Arbetarekommun (New Workers' Group). The new left-Socialist group had a firm foundation in Gamlestaden and Olskroken's youth clubs and also in the metal workers' union (particularly amongst SKF workers). Two young men – Martin Andersson and Albin Ström – would soon become known as the promi-

4. A failed attempt from the Social Democratic union LO to start a general strike in Sweden. When the strike was cancelled in advance, due to insufficient strike funds, this led to massive defections from LO.

nent figures in the "young left". Above all, Ström would play a key role for how the local proletarian segment developed during the period between the wars – but this is another story that demands its own telling.[5]

Besides a political and union radicalisation, the workers in Gothenburg also took the initiative on the housing issue. The passivity of the privately owned building contractors and the mass unemployment in the early 1920s had driven builders to start their own companies based on things other than speculation and profits. The young people running the building cooperatives were driven by high socialist ideals and a strong belief in a better future for the people in working-class neighbourhoods. Ideological oppositions soon caused the worker-cooperative movement to split into two companies with different views of equitable salaries and building on speculation. However, both companies became known for building modernised governor's houses that were of a very good quality.

In 1932, the modernist and architect Uno Åhrén – known from the Stockholm exhibit two years earlier – was hired as the city engineer in Gothenburg (see Michael Landzelius' chapter in this book). That same year, together with political economist and Social Democrat Gunnar Myrdal, later co-author of *An American Dilemma*, he carried out a local housing study that came to be the basis of both the Myrdal couple's pamphlet *Kris i befolkningsfrågan* (Crisis in the housing issue) and the epoch-making housing-social study that received funding from the Social Democratic government in 1934. The goal of the new housing policies was to get rid of class-segregated housing though state subventions and rationally produced "healthy houses". This was in line with the classless Folkhem that Per Albin Hansson had been championing since 1928 but which the followers of the party dissident Albin Ström viewed as gross blasphemy against the "eleventh commandment". The governor's houses in Gothenburg was viewed by Åhrén and Myrdal as frightening examples of housing environments that

5. See Sten O Karlsson (1993) *Arbetarfamiljen och det nya hemmet. Om bostadshygienism och klasskultur i mellankrigstidens Göteborg* (*The working-class family and the new home. On housing hygenism and class culture in Gothenburg between the wars*). Stockholm/Stehag: Symposion.

reproduced the old-fashioned class spirit and a "socially hygienic" unhealthy family culture. The time was over for governor's houses and closed neighbourhoods. Åhrén and Myrdal thougt that they ought to be replaced by industrially built narrow houses with exposure to the light and in park environments. Sandarna in the west and upper Johanneberg were to be Åhrén's housing-ideological gifts to Gothenburgers. In 1942, he left the city, disappointed by the hard-nosed local opposition to the housing revolution he had tried to carry out.

Nevertheless, after 1945, the implementation of the recommendations of the housing-social study would result in revolutionary changes to the everyday lives of Gothenburg's working-class families. For most of them, this meant moving out to the new "class-neutral" post-war suburbs, such as Guldheden, Högsbo and Kortedala and, after 1965, to even more peripheral neighbourhoods like Backa, Bergsjön and Angered. During this period, most of the old buildings in classic governor's house neighbourhoods such as Annedal, Landala and Olskroken were demolished. This development can be seen in the development of local football. It was no coincidence that the fall of previously successful neighbourhood clubs such as Gårda BK, Krokslätts FF and Landala IF coincided with the evacuation of the central working-class areas, which undermined both recruitment and public support. The opposite connection is found between the success of upstart clubs in the 1990s, such as BK Häcken, Västra Frölunda IF and Gunnilse IS, and their location in million-programme areas with residents of low average ages.

In the new Gothenburg of the post-war period, working-class families no longer risked being affected by unemployment or emergency employment that forced the man to live in work camps in sparsely populated areas. The kitchens of homes, which had once been public arenas for social interactions and (male) political debates, now got more practical functions in the age of washing machines, hoovers, televisions, child subsidies, health insurance and supplementary pension. The various neighbourhood solidarity rituals women had developed had become superfluous. Even if most people found the modernisation of everyday life to be the realisation of the Swedish translation of the Internationale's promise "from the dark we rise towards the light", during the 1970s various neighbourhood organisations began to publish nostalgic writings about a vanished world. Workers who had grown up in the 1920s and 30s in Gothenburg claimed that amidst the poverty, there had been a sort of pride and solidarity, social qualities that had gotten lost and left emptiness behind them.

Nowadays it is no longer only nostalgic pensioners in Gamla Majpojkar (literally, the Old Boys of Majorna) and their brother and sister organisations that are concerned about the once genuine proletariat culture. Since the 1970s, neighbourhoods that were built by the worker cooperatives of the 1920s – Kungsladugård and Bagaregården – have also been populated by the middle-class. Places such as Älvsborgsgatan and Mariaplan now have cult status as the spiritual centre of the "Majornas", even if they actually are in the area of Kungsladugård. Even Haga and the "real" Majorna have partially avoided the excavators, but at the price of gentrification, which has socially transformed the neighbourhoods so they are now unrecognisable (see Håkan Thörn's chapter in this book). In the middle of "Linnéstaden", the area of middle-class chic restaurants, there is now an Ernst Jungen Square. Jungen was a Social Democratic bigwig who is known by few today. But in the struggle between "the eleventh commandment" and the followers of the classless folkhem, he was amongst the winners who wrote history. Since the advocates for the eleventh commandment during the period between the wars were predestined to lose the fight for the city's soul, those who in the future will search in vain for a Martin Andersson Street or an Albin Ström Square.

Sten O Karlsson
is Associate Professor in Technology and Social Change, working as a lecturer in Cultural Studies at the University of Gävle.

Michael Landzelius

WOMEN'S CORSETS, ELECTRIC RAZORS AND MALE ARCHITECTS' SPIRITUAL MASTURBATION

In the autumn of 1935, the scaffolding was taken down from the first modernist building on Kungsportsavenyen. The Avenyen, as it is called, was then a calm street of blocks of flats populated by Gothenburg's wealthy, far from commercialism and attention-grabbing window displays. While all other buildings had semi-private gardens between façade and street, Kungsportsavenyen 29 sported a paved area in front of gigantic shop windows. But there was more to it than that. It wasn't just any old goods in the windows that caught attention. Here, we will see how the building in a peculiar way was part of the time's linking of women's bodies and architecture.

The liberal *Göteborgs-Tidningen* newspaper reported: "Modernist Gothenburg is appearing here and there. Wherever a hole appears in a row of buildings, it is soon filled in with a building with the modern clean lines. . . . The filling of the hole on Avenyen in the row of buildings between Engelbrektsgatan and Kristinelundsgatan is now completed. The contrast between old and new is striking."[1] The conservative *Göteborgs Morgonpost* described the building as "of the most modern design" where

1. *Göteborgs-Tidningen* (GT) 1935-12-03.

"the impression of a patched up old cloth probably will remain" because "no harmony between them is possible".[2] The building was made possible only after Head of City Planning, architect Uno Åhrén (see Sten O Karlsson's chapter), initiated a revision of the entire city plan for Avenyen in connection with building contractor J Alfred Olsson's first application for building permit. The revised plan provided for recasting the whole street in the same way with another 50 buildings!

2. *Göteborgs Morgonpost* (GMP) 1935-11-07.

When the new building, designed by architect Nils Olsson, *de facto* was there, the row of old buildings could not but appear as "old cloth", or as a row of unbrushed brown teeth. In an attempt to capture this process, the newspapers described the building in the same terms as human bodies, with words borrowed from odontology, tailoring and the hygienism of the time. But this doubled idea of human bodies and architecture was also characterised by gender.

The business housed in the building was the Spirellasalongen – a corset shop. What is fascinating is how the modern design of the building and the modern shape of the ladies' underwear sold in it blended together and tainted one another.

In the gigantic display-windows of both shop floors, sparsely dressed women in corsets were exposed.[3] And in the press, Spirellasalongen published advertisements of smiling, scantily clad women. The texts were linked to the ideas of the time about modernity: "Dashing, lively and hearty – that is the impression one gets of the modern woman."[4] Another advert underlines the corset's shaping features: "It is sewn for your figure – *emphasises* its beautiful lines – and *hides* its flaws."[5] A third states that "the ingenious construction allows ... the muscles full freedom ... the condition for making dancing, sports and long walks completely enjoyable."[6]

3. See the blurred front-page photo in GT 1935-12-03.

4. Spirellasalongen advert in *Göteborgs Handels- och Sjöfartstidning* (GHT) 1935-12-07.

5. Spirellasalongen advert in GMP 1935-11-28.

6. Spirellasalongen advert in GT 1935-11-24.

But the combination of the naked modernist filling and the corset-dummies were upsetting. The municipal City Council member, Liberal Party member and doctor Siri Wikander-Brunander objected to a number of things "as signs that public activities must be tightened up", including "a modernist building with a corset exhibition on Avenyen".[7] She also stated that "the modernist building on Avenyen stands there shrieking with its display-windows amongst the old patrician buildings!"[8]

7. GHT 1936-10-30.

8. *Morgon-Tidningen* (MT) 1936-10-30.

Two Conservative politicians also expressed their opinions. The architect and building contractor Sven Steen defended the house against his party colleague, the senior school teacher Ture Hulthén. Their discussion included the most revealing remarks with regard to the conflation of modern architecture and modern women's corsets. "Mr. Steen", the liberal *Morgontidningen* newspaper wrote, "returned to the so-called scandal building on Avenyen and assumed that Mr Hulthén's contempt was less related to the building itself than to what there was to be seen inside."[9] Though he did not agree with Hulthén that the building was "the worst example of what can happen", Steen's uncertainty about what Hulthén was actually referring to shows that he must have found Hulthén's contempt for Avenyen 29 just as applicable to the building as to the semi-naked dummies.

9. MT 1936-11-20.

Under pressure from intensive urban restructuring there had earlier been a proposal to establish a City Beauty Council in Gothenburg. The City Council decided upon this proposal soon after "the corset building" was completed, and these two issues became intertwined in the debate. The motion for a City Beauty Council was rejected, but the debate fused aesthetic and moral positions and shows how urban restructuring and development rights came in conflict with matters of opinion and taste, propriety and morals, as well as with a sexualised understanding also of built space. The criticism from Wikander-Brunander and Hulthén were aimed at both the building and the content in its huge windows. To them, the naked façade in itself yelled for attention, but the corset-dummies sprinkled salt into the wound by a similar exhibitionism foreign to the propriety of the upper-class surroundings.

Spirellasalongen was not the only business to offer ways of shaping female beauty in the 1930s of Gothenburg. Advertisements in the press show the contemporary modernist discourse on architecture being linked to a wider male discourse on hygienism and "bodies without flaws". The Stockholm Exhibition in 1930 manifested the idea about a new architecture and design. Several years later, Erik Wettergren, chairman of the Swedish Arts and Crafts Society (which played a central role in the exhibition) wrote about the shift in Swedish design that he had contributed to: "And then, when functionalism arrived with its stern and zealous beliefs and its electric razor, how wonderfully exciting was it not to provoke the traditionalists and other philistines with anything that was glossy and cold."[10] The metaphor "electric razor" was not arbitrarily chosen. During the 1930s, thousands of older buildings all across Europe were clean-shaven from various decorative elements seen as "disfiguring" and "excessive", while new designs were shaved already at the drawing board.

10. Erik Wettergren in *Form* 1938: 2.

Women were to be similarly shaped. During the last week of the Stockholm Exhibition, in the autumn of 1930, the beauty salon Paraffineum in Gothenburg advertised: "New lines are required in modern times – not only in furniture styles and architecture – no, even the human body is remodelled. The ideal of our time is the sound, hardened and slim body – the body of young lines. Thanks to modern technology and scientific methods in beauty care, it is today indeed possible for each and everyone to become slimmer and thereby healthier."[11] Here, building construction is linked to the shaping of women, and just as modern architecture and the corsets offered by the Spirellasalongen, Paraffineum's bathing technology was based on "scientific methods".

11. Paraffineum advert in GT 1930-10-05.

In another advertisement, there was a picture of a smiling, corseted woman in high-heeled shoes, hidden only by text placed over her waist and hips. Under the headline "Nothing to hide!" the graphic form teased the desire of the male gaze. "Wearing a décolleté dress or a swimming suit, a woman of today ought to be able to display a flawless body", the advert says, and therefore she must "remove all disfiguring hair growth". The advert offers "a modern method … liquid Taky," which works "quickly and thoroughly" and makes the skin "white and smooth as alabaster".[12] Successful in achieving such skin, women could become replicas – living forgeries – of the sculptures that at the same time were being shaved off from old buildings. While one type of female ornament was removed from masculinist culture, real women were (re)formed into another.

12. AB R. Barlach advert in GHT 1936-08-15.

Male architects at this time agreed that buildings were gendered female. The Stockholm architect Karl Martin Westerberg, a conservative classicist, wrote about modernism: "It is as artistic product that she should be looked upon and judged, and it is in this quality of hers that she is justified in certain areas of building."[13] The Gothenburg architect Erik Holmdal, a modernist, agreed with regard to the gender of architecture. In an interview under the headline "The façade of a building is like a woman," he said: "In the past, architects could work under other conditions; which resulted in more decorations. I am thinking of the façade, which before enticed their creators to splendour. But it is no doubt with a building as with a woman. If beauty is not there from the beginning, one can never add it on with artificial means. Our buildings and façades are … conceived from the inside out. The beauty lies in the utility of the building."[14]

13. *Byggnadsvärlden* 1930: 27A.

14. MT 1935-08-10.

In this gendered discourse, men are active shapers while women are passive, shaped. As Holmdal says, the architect should not expend his creative powers on "artificial means". All sorts of "excessive ornaments" were by modernism seen as both ugly and morally objectionable. In a peculiar article by the Stockholm architect Hakon Ahlberg, such ideas are connected to the modern culture of the body. Entitled "Sports and form", the article notes that "sports forms the musculature, the body", yet also emphasises that "it influences the understanding of form in general". For Ahlberg, there "exists an intimate and often stated relationship between modern sports and the strivings for modern form in especially architecture and the applied arts". What some in the debate about the "corset building" view as aesthetic immorality, Ahlberg looks upon as positive: "The naked form, the poetry of steel and machinery, is no apathetic product of industrialism – it is a child of the will of the modern spirit, and in this will, sports have a decisive share."[15]

But this will and this spirit have to be channelled. "Lost in spiritual masturbation" and "isolated in aesthetic regard" – with these words, the Stockholm architect and editor-in-chief of *Byggmästaren* (the Swedish journal of architecture), Sune Lindström, criticised much of modern architecture.[16] The almost eugenic discourse continued with further sexual metaphors: "The architect needs, from the beginning of his career, to understand his position as one part of an act of creation, which will not bear good fruit if he seeks only to satisfy himself – alone." The other part was "the public, the people, the nation." For Lindström, architecture was a gendered and sexual business, but not for pleasure. The architect was the inseminating male party and what he sowed should not be wasted on spiritual masturbation but should be functional and useful. When the building was finished, it was "with a building as with a woman," beauty was an issue of a corseted skeletal physiognomy that gave both buildings and female bodies beautiful "utility".

What I have sought to show here is five things. First, that in the 1930s, buildings were actually seen as a specific kind of female bodies, both by architects and laymen. Second, that neither women nor buildings were only terms in discourse, but indeed actual objects that were shaped according to patriarchal rules: "the will of the modern spirit" was male and realised through technologies of power rooted in the "electric razor", hair-removal methods, and "the poetry of steel and machinery". Third, that the way in which function and aesthetics, skeleton

15. Hakon Ahlberg in *Form* 1932: 7.

16. Sune Lindström in *Byggmästaren* 1937: 1.

and appearance, construction and façade, are blended display an impossible and logically contradictory understanding of essence as the visual presence of the inside on the outside. Fourth, that the power to make visible and to have the unequal right to shape that which is forced to appear in a controlled field of vision confronts the impotence that relates to being exposed as a passive object to be consumed by the gaze. Finally, that this power is nonetheless fragile since male desire itself threatens to undermine the efficiency of patriarchal control when architects and other men lapse into unproductive "spiritual masturbation".

The male gaze and the aesthetics of skeletal physiognomy are hence sensitive as well as deeply political issues relating to the gendering and sexualising of everyday discourses, practices and built spaces. These issues thus point far beyond the amusing aspects of a fight over a corset shop with scantily-clad corset-dummies.

Michael Landzelius
is Associate Professor and Research Coordinator at the Department of Sociology, University of Gothenburg, working on issues of spatial jurisdiction and urban safety and security.

Anne-Lie Steen

FROM MUTUAL SEX TO RAPE
Heterosexual negotiation practices in the city's social venues

From an international perspective, Sweden has a very high reporting frequency of rapes and other sexual crimes. In 2008, more than 5 379 rapes were reported, which comes to 59 crimes per 100 000 residents. This is more than a doubling in the most recent decade. The majority of these reports take place in the three big city regions: Stockholm, Gothenburg and Malmö. The largest increase of reported rapes involves cases where the parties are acquainted with one another. This has been explained by increased entertainment offerings, changed alcohol habits and new meeting places for temporary sexual contacts.[1]

1. BRÅ (2005:7) *Våldtäkt. En kartläggning av polisanmälda våldtäkter* (*National study of rapes reported to the police*). Stockholm: Brottsförebyggande rådet, Information och förlag.

In Gothenburg, a number of measures have been taken in order to create safety. Via work between various actors within the project "Safer and more humane Gothenburg", security measures in the form of, for example, better lighting, can be seen as part of the fight against sexual crime (see Ingrid Sahlin's chapter). If one looks at the number of reported sex crimes in Gothenburg, these measures can be said to have had the effect of decreasing the number of reported crimes committed by strangers that take place outdoors. At the same time, the number of reported rapes that take place in private locations has dramatically increased. The downside of these social safety measures, which have been concentrated in public places, is that they create the idea that public space is dangerous while private space, ironically enough, is seen as safer and more secure.

Rapes in social venues

Social venues cannot be seen only as an arena for positive contacts between people. They are also an arena where meetings that later result in rapes and other sex crimes take place.[2] Research shows that rape is a type of crime where the victim does not necessarily receive legitimate status and thereby does not seem equally worthy of protection as victims of other crimes.[3] Rapes that go to trial, and that take place in connection to social venues, are, from an empirical perspective, a big urban problem, which can be partially understood based on more general conditions, such as the city's anonymity. In order to understand what makes this possible, the city's contextual conditions also need to be analysed, based on its specific terms. This means, besides the appearance, content and access of social venues, analysing who, and to what extent, different cities are experienced as dangerous, and examing access to and people's view of public transport.

Social venues in Gothenburg are primarily situated around the main street Avenyn, where there are many restaurants, pubs, dance spots and clubs. That these meeting places comprise part of the city's public entertainment activities does not mean that anyone has access to them. One limitation is age – many of these social establishments have a minimum age of at least eighteen years. Another more accessible public space in Gothenburg is Nordstan, the city's and Sweden's largest shopping centre. It is a meeting place for many young people, often in their early teens, where initiative is taken to another, more private form of social life in the shape of parties in someone's home.

2. The essay builds on empirical material comprising all the verdicts classified as rape that have gone to trial and received convictions in the Gothenburg Court 1984–2000. Of these, around one-third took place in connection to various types of entertainment activities.

3. See Ulrika Andersson (2004) *Hans (ord) eller hennes? En könsteoretisk analys av straffrättsligt skydd mot sexuella övergrepp* (*His (word) or Hers? A gender theoretical analysis of criminal legal protection against sexual abuse*). Lund: Bokbox förlag; Jeffner, Stina. (1998) *Liksom våldtäkt typ… Om ungdomars förståelse av våldtäkt* (*Like, you know – rape… On the importance of gender and heterosexuality to young people's perceptions of rape*). Stockholm: Utbildningsförlaget Brevskolan; Martin, Patricia Yancey (2005) *Rape work. Victims, gender, and emotions in organization and community context.* New York & London: Routledge.

When one studies cases of rape that have led to convictions, one sees that, besides the ones in public venues, these also take place in a private social arena that can partly be understood as an effect of the age limit of public social life. Rapes that take place in connection to social venues are often referred to as a form of initial voluntary sexual meetings, as in pick-ups or dating, that then result in rape.

In these convictions, where the perpetrator often denies rape and instead claims it was voluntary and mutual sexual activity, one can see how the victims thought about and handled different risks connected to dangerous places. In court material, which can be said to constitute examples of how women's strategies for handling risk have failed, one finds culturally anchored ideas about women's sexual exposure, which is important for understanding their actions.

HER HISTORY – A RAPE STORY

It is clear from the victims' stories that there is a high degree of consciousness regarding the risks of facing sexual attacks or unwanted sexual activities. In the stories, one can see how the situation, relationship and place receive importance. The various risks experienced have a clear connection to ideas about private and public, where both the meeting place and the place where the crime occurs are important components for understanding how the women reason.

The transportation scenario

> She looked around to try to get a ride with someone and then saw him in his car. She had met him previously. His friend had lived with one of her friends. She asked if he could drive her and how much he wanted for the ride. (Verdict from Gothenburg Court)

The city's anonymity creates fear and worry, and thereby a need of security and safety (see Sara Uhnoo's chapter). As people move around in the city's social venues, this creates situations where trust in and fear of other people become decisive. One of these situations is the trip home after a night out and the concomitant risk and fear of being the victim of a sexual attack when one is on the way home.

Women's worry or fear is aimed at strangers and unknown men and is handled by them trusting other men with whom they are more or less acquainted. These men can be very superficial acquaintances – a neighbour, a friend of a friend, an acquaintance of the family. But fear of the unknown also can mean that a woman places her trust in a man she met that evening and who seems trustworthy. The transportation scenario also has a local touch in that in Gothenburg there are few methods of publication transportation available when the pubs and dance restaurants close, and there is usually a major lack of taxis. Many choose to share a taxi with someone they "know", or to take an unlicensed taxi. A very large number of nightlife-related rapes take place when a woman uses an unlicensed taxi.

The dating scenario

> At Femman, she had told him that she was not going with him to have sex with him. She even said this to his friend. He said that X was not 'like that'. (Verdict from Gothenburg Court)

The dating scenario can be said to take place in both the private and public nightlife arenas, even if the meeting place is more often in some sort of public social venue. Here, one can see how women handle what they experience as risks in order to be part of a heterosexual love and sex arena without being exposed to unwanted sexual activities. At the same time that women express their right to sexual integrity and sexual self-determination, they also use various security strategies where, before they go out with a man, they try to clearly communicate their intentions. Confidence and trust in individual men here is about women's judgements of men's communicative ability, and about them appearing to be nice men on the surface.

In these cases, it is clear how women find themselves in an ambivalent position where they expect that their sexual integrity and self-determination will be respected by these men. In order to be on the safe side, they still try, at a very early stage, to make it clear that they are not interested in having sex. Women describe how men, who first seemed to be nice, suddenly transform and appear threatening. Confidence in the men makes them describe the attack as unreal, like a joke, or like in a bad film. They wait, for what seems like too long, to call for help, or to try to escape, and they do not think that a rape will be carried out, but that the men will accept that they do not want to have sex. However, the contract that was agreed upon in the public arena no longer applies.

The party scenario

> When one of the girls asked if she wanted to go to an after-party in Västra Frölunda, she did. If it had just been boys in the car, she would not have gone. (Verdict from Gothenburg Court)

The party scenario often takes place when people have met up at Nordstan and together gone to someone's house to have a party. It is not surprising that many of the victims are teenage girls, if one considers the high age-limits at many of the public establishments in Gothenburg. In the party scenario, one can see how girls/women discuss how they can participate in a desirable social life without risking being the victim of a sexual crime. Here, security is about avoiding being the only girl/woman in the company of boys/men. Another of the party scenario's security strategies is that the girl/woman makes sure she already knows some of the boys/men in the group. So here it is the male strangers who are viewed as a risk. When rape then occurs at a private party, the girls place much of the responsibility on themselves. They judge their actions as not good enough, and think that they should have understood better, or they should have put up more resistance.

SAFE PLACES AND SAFE MEN

The high reporting frequency of sexual crimes cannot only be understood in regard to an increased selection of entertainment activities, changed social habits and increased consumption of alcohol. Instead, the analysis above shows that ideas about and fear of unknown men and dark places leads to women's risk evaluations and security strategies, which themselves can be counterproductive. Media attention, juridical evaluations and society's security-enhancing measures create ideas about what a real rape is and who a real rapist is.[4] In Gothenburg, there has been disporportional media attention paid to rapes by strangers in dark public places. The analysis of fear and security strategies can also be understood in terms of equality and democracy. Images of dangerous places and dangerous men work as limitations restricting women's access to public spaces.[5] As long as women's bodies are seen as sexually accessible in the absent of an explicit expressed no, a non-agreement, we cannot view men and women as sexually equal.

4. Anne-Lie Steen (2010, forthcoming) *Offentliga föreställningar om kön och sexualitet. Rättssystemets granskning och bedömning av våldtäktsfall* (*Public opinions about gender and sexuality. Assessment, classification and judgement in rape court cases*). Göteborg: Göteborgs universitet, thesis. Sociologiska institutionen.

5. See Amnesty International. (2008) *Case closed. Rape and human rights in the nordic countries. The Danish, Swedish, Finnish and Norwegian sections of Amnesty International*; Carina Listerbom (2002) *Trygg stad. Diskurser om kvinnors rädsla i forskning, policyutveckling och lokal praktik* (*Safe City. Discourses on women's fear in research, policy development and local practice*). Göteborg: Chalmers tekniska högskola, thesis, Tema Stadsbyggnad, Sektionen för arkitektur; Maria Wendt Höjer (2002) *Rädslans politik. Våld och sexualitet i den svenska demokratin* (*The politics of fear. Violence and sexuality in Swedish democracy*). Lund: Liber.

Anne-Lie Steen
works at the Department of Sociology, University of Gothenburg. Her research focuses on the discursive production of sex, sexuality, shame and respectability in rape court cases.

Sara Uhnoo

YOUNG AND (UN)SAFE
The geography of fear, social darkness and spatial confidence

We live not in places, but in the description of places.[1]

The city of Gothenburg is working to be a "safe" city for its residents and visitors. Safety walks are organised in neighbourhoods and the physical character of places are changed through rebuilding, clipping bushes and putting up lights. All this is to increase the experience of safety. The goal is for all Gothenburgers to feel safe in public space (see Ingrid Sahlin's chapter). So how do the city's young people talk about safe and unsafe places? I have interviewed around 40 secondary school students from various areas in and close to Gothenburg. Their discussions about places of fear draw detailed maps of the city, a *geography of fear*, where certain places or entire neighbourhoods are categorised as creating fear or being dangerous.[2] The unsafety of places is thought to vary according to *who* one is. Dimensions such as gender, class and ethnicity are given meaning, but so is a person's social connection to a place. A place's experienced danger is also time-related. Fear is said to come with the dark, often later in the evening or at night. Rather than natural dark-

1. Wallace Stevens (1955) *The collected poems of Wallace Stevens*. London: Faber.

2. Gill Valentine (1989) "The geography of women's fear", *Area* 21(4), pp. 385–390.

ness, when the sun sets at a certain time, they describe a *social darkness*. The fear is connected to the character of social life, social activities and the categories of people who are thought to be in a place. The logic is that the social life of places changes with the onset of darkness; the non-dangerous people disappear while dangerous, evil types ("strange people", "impudent youths", "gangs", "mafias") take them over and make them unsafe. The conceptions of unsafe places connect in this way to assumptions about individuals or groups who are thought to live or just be there temporarily. In the young people's discussions about (un)safe places, the socially dark Slottsskogen, the shopping centre Nordstan/Femman and the (non)dangerous suburbs recur.

Through mass media, urban myths, rumours and their own experiences, young people build up their conceptions of places. When they give a picture of unsafe places, the anonymous urban city environment as a whole is contrasted with the friendly and safe countryside, where they spend free days. Sometimes, specific geographic places in the centre are named. A typically unsafe place that is named is the centrally located Nordstan shopping centre, which at the time of the interviews was open at night. Nordstan is pictured as characterised by a crackled social life and unsafe anonymity – "anyone can do anything to anyone". One girl defines safety as a feeling trust, not paying attention to the social surroundings and sitting down and closing one's eyes. In Nordstan, she would "never" do that because then she would "think that someone would come and, like, kick you in the back". A young man says that "anyone can come and stick a knife in your back". Others talk about youths who do "whatever and people walking past have never seen you before and don't care either". Instead of avoiding places that feel unsafe, young people can fight against the fear and occupy the city space. One man expressed the idea of having "spatial confidence"[3]: "I won't let anyone stand there and think he's cool and prevent me from walking there." One's own autono-

3. Kristen Day, Daisy Carreon & Cheryl Stump (2003) "Confrontation and loss of control. Masculinity and men's fear in public space", *Journal of environmental psychology* 23(3), pp. 311–322.

my, being able to use city space, is seen as more important than considering any possible concerns. Nordstan is therefore not experienced as an unsafe place for everyone, not for those who dare to defy fear and not for the young people who feel they own the place. Someone who works at the city's victim support centre for young people illustrates the importance of place to an individual's feeling of security by talking about a group of "real, real criminals" who "don't walk to Avenyn because they don't feel safe, because it is another type of people there, but down in Femman, they are like kings".

On a structural level, the places that are felt to be unsafe are clearly gendered. Unsafe places for young men are thought to be open and busy public places, such as squares or larger bus or tram stops. They are connected with the fear of young people in groups, "gangs". Meanwhile, young women describe deserted and dark places and connect it to the fear of sexual assault and of "the man in the bush" (see Anne-Lie Steen's chapter). One young woman talks about when some female friends walked on a "really, really dark" path through the centrally located Slottskogen park and how they overcame their fear – "the girliness" – by pretending that they were a group of loud men: "If we are a group of guys who are walking here, no one will jump us. So we ended up walking like this and: 'Oh, ray, ray...' [singing with a deep man's voice], singing and ... we didn't feel threatened." When they were no longer women, the place stopped feeling threatening.

It is not just centrally located anonymous places that are used by the general public, such as Nordstan and Slottsskogen, that are experienced as unsafe, but rather entire neighbourhoods. A young man who lives in a central area says that in the evening he avoids certain areas since "most of the criminals live there". The division of the city into dangerous and less dangerous areas reflects how the mass media portrays Gothenburg as a socially, ethnically and housing-wise segregated city, where certain areas are stamped as problem areas. Approximately the same areas are pointed out as dangerous by young people. These are a handful of neighbourhoods in north-eastern Gothenburg, the so-called immigrant-dense suburbs. Still, the young people in the named areas, and even youths from other neighbourhoods, show a united front against the stereotypes spread by the mass media about "immigrants" being violent. Ignorance is mentioned as the basis of these stereotypes – they ought to come here "if they dare" (see Nils Hammarén's chapter). At the same time, they are also influenced by dominant images and they participate in reproducing them to a certain extent. A hierarchy of status makes it possible for certain ethnic groups to be stereotyped, described as more violent and depicted as the scapegoats for a certain area. One young woman, who points out that she is not racist ("this will sound extremely racist but...") divides the area's ethnic groups into "integrated" versus "violent". Another young person, who identifies as an immigrant, makes stereotypical descriptions and talks about the "newly imported" in the area who "play mafia". Here, there is a separation between *us* (the majority of the immigrants) and *them* (the minority of the immigrants). Insofar as the group that is identified as the least established in an area's social camaraderie is described as a threat to the area's safety, a picture is produced of a threat that comes partially from the outside. But marginalised groups can be both feared and afraid. Certain youths who position themselves as immigrants express a fear of racist attacks, of drunk "skinheads" who are thought to move around in the city's central areas during the weekend evenings.

Even a socially vulnerable working-class area, Tynnered, is described as a suburb by youths who talk in terms of social class rather than ethnicity. A young woman who lived there said that the most frightened young people in Gothenburg are snobs, blonde men with hair slicked back and pointy shoes. With a lot of laughter, a socially privileged group – young, rich, Swedish men from nearby upper-class areas – are depicted as vulnerable, afraid and naked after being robbed of everything they own:

"If a snobby type went to Tynnered, he would be robbed right away." They say that it does not matter so much if the rumours are exaggerated, since it makes "you stay away" and avoid the notorious place: "They don't, like, dare to go to Opaltorget just because the stereotype is, like, 'If you go there, you'll get hurt.'" Gothenburg's most dangerous place was said to be without a doubt their own area of Tynnered – "it was even said in the newspaper". This does not mean, however, that it is dangerous for them.

All of the young people relate to the "suburbs", whether they live there or not. Amongst the suburban youths, degrees of social support get importance in their discussions via the difference between "we who live here" and "those from outside". Trust in the people in the area and knowledge of its social codes creates security. One young man illustrates how safe he is where he lives: "I could take my sleeping bag and lie down in the centre and sleep all night without, like, being robbed .... Because I know everyone." Those who know one another are assumed not to hurt one another but rather to help each other if there is any trouble that comes from the outside: "You know almost everyone and then you feel safe. Because you know you have people behind you in case something happens." Besides this feeling of community, unlike the anonymity of the centre of the city, the experience of safety in well-known areas also comes from an experience of being able to control any dangers. The residents are not afraid because they believe they know which unpredictable people or groups "you should stay away from". Even if they consider their areas safe, they point out that young people from other areas ought to avoid seeming cocky or scared: "A bloke who's cocky, shouldn't come [where] I live, and act all cocky, because then he'll get it." Young people here express ideas of territorialism and protecting their space – they defend "their" area – which can mean that someone who tries to trespass "will get a beating". By talking about external and internal threats as something they can personally handle, at the same time as they describe their own area as unsafe for other young people, they position themselves as dangerous, capable and brave.

Even if all the young people talk about fear in different ways – and say that "everyone is scared sometimes" – they use the city space to a larger extent than other age groups. They use a variety of more or less conscious individual strategies to minimise their vulnerability and increase their safety.[4] Above all, they look for security in each other's presence – in community. They talk about how girls, in accordance with the stereotype, are protected by boys, how girls take care of each other, like the young women in Slottsskogen, and about how boys defend and "back up" each other. Youths' relationships to and knowledge about places change over the years as fears are conquered and new areas become well-known. Their spatial confidence is strengthened and an active usage of public space can lead to it being demystified.[5] This means that mental maps are filled with their own pictures. Experiences that define places and the social life that characterises them are less threatening than what is portrayed in local mass media discourses. Consciousness of the fact that most people who move through Gothenburg on a typical night are not subjected to violence can verify their own experiences and the geography of fear can thereby, at least on a individual level, be changed.

4. Sara Uhnoo (2008) *Ungdomars tal om rädsla för våld* (*Young people's discussions about fear of violence*). Göteborg: Tryggare och Mänskligare Göteborg.

5. Hille Koskela (1999) *Fear, control & space. Geographies of gender, fear of violence, and video surveillance.* Helsingfors: Geografiska institutionen, Helsingfors universitet.

Sara Uhnoo
works at the Department of Sociology, University of Gothenburg, and studies how young people talk about violence.

5. THE MENTAL STATES OF GOTHENBURG

Mattias Andersson

THE MENTAL STATES OF GOTHENBURG

CUT –

Manuscript collected and partially written by Mattias Andersson (selection by Helena Holgersson). Première at Angered Theatre in Gothenburg 28 September 2006.

1)

In the foyer of Angered Theatre, the expectant or sceptical audience mingles. All the actors are also there, but they do not reveal themselves; in other words, everyone believes that the actors are part of the audience.

2)

The doors to the hall open.

The audience pours in – to a completely empty room.

There are no black curtains on the walls, no stage steps, no chairs and no sign of actors, stagehands or musicians.

What is this?

The audience is standing in the middle of the large, empty room.

Nothing happens.

A long pause.

3)

After a long time in this vacuum, Mattias Andersson's voice is heard coming from above:

MATTIAS: Hi. I'm Mattias Andersson and I'm the director and a partial playwright of this performance. Ten randomly chosen youths between the ages of 17 and 21, who live in different parts of Gothenburg in 2006, answered a number of questions that I formulated and that I'm currently interested in. In-depth interviews regarding these questions were carried out by three sociologists and were recorded on tapes and then carefully transcribed. 81 percent of the performance that will soon start is comprised of these interviews, word-for-word, and 13 percent is made of totally subjective scenes I myself wrote. The remaining 6 percent is paraphrases of scenes from our modern mythology. The Mental States of Gothenburg 2006. Please step in!

4)

People who are part of the performance (actors or stage-hands?) have taken about 90 chairs from storage and now put them in four rows that create a square. They show that people should sit down.

When everyone has taken a spot in the square, alone on his or her own chair, it is quiet again, for a long time.

Everyone sees everyone who is sitting there.

Who is an actor and who is the audience?

5)

From this complete nothingness, the first voices begin to speak. Two people make contact, the first interview, a fumbling start...

CUT -

8)

SOCIOLOGIST + LASZLO

SOCIOLOGIST: So, let's see... (fiddling with an mp3 player)

LASZLO: (laughs)

LASZLO: I'm just so worried that I'm going to leave here and there'll be no sound on the recording. (Turns on the microphone.) So...there. I thought I'd start with some simple questions. What's your name?

LASZLO: Laszlo.

SOCIOLOGIST: And how old are you?

LASZLO: I'm 17, and will turn 18 this year.

LASZLO: Where do you live?

LASZLO: I live in Bergsjön.

SOCIOLOGIST: Where did you grow up?

LASZLO: Where I grew up? Well, I grew up in... Hisingen, I grew up. Then when I was 9 I moved to Bergsjön, to my sister's place. So you can say, anyway, that I grew up in Hisingen.

SOCIOLOGIST: But in Gothenburg anyhow?

LASZLO: Yes.

SOCIOLOGIST: What do your parents do?

LASZLO: My parents. My dad...I, my mu- I lost my mum when I was six. And my dad, he does nothing, he's a pensioner. Retired, so he is home.

SOCIOLOGIST: And you live in Bergsjön?

LASZLO: Mm.

SOCIOLOGIST: Mm. So that was, like, the opening questions. And this is going to be a theatre play, that's the plan, so, we shall try-, we will talk about different events that have been important for you in your life and things like that. And, a question that I will come back to in the end is what event in your life you think people could perform on a stage.

LASZLO: Okay…?

SOCIOLOGIST: Or make a play out of.

LASZLO: Okay…?

SOCIOLOGIST: A scene.

LASZLO: Okay…?

SOCIOLOGIST: So is there anything you can think of before we start talking?

LASZLO: Yeah, actually.

SOCIOLOGIST: Already?

LASZLO: Yeah.

SOCIOLOGIST: Tell me.

LASZLO: I will tell…I will tell you. You could make a film of my life, you could…

SOCIOLOGIST: A special event, day or night, Laszlo…?

LASZLO: … about something. So I came home after training…

SOCIOLOGIST: Football?

LASZLO: Yeah. And after training I'm so hungry…so I come in, home, that was at my dad's house, I lived with my dad then. So I open the fridge, and there's, like, no food. I mean, there's food, but like nothing you can eat. There was cheese, but no bread, you see? Soo… I, I got really annoyed, you… if you're angry and there's no food…I got really, really angry, so I began taking chairs and breaking them and stuff like that, you know? So my dad came home. "What did you do?" and this and that, this and that. Soo… he didn't hit me, but he locked me in the bathroom for an hour, two hours… So I got used to it, I fell asleep, I didn't go to the toilet. So there wasn't a… you know, it was like a… regular thing. Sooo… when I came out, my sister was home, she's the one I moved in with later. So she was at home… and, ehhh… with her husband, Sammy is his name. And when my mum was alive, there was a man named Josef… also Hungarian, he often came over to our place, he knew my mum too, and… when he was 19 and my sister was 15, I think, he really fell in love with her and she fell in love with him. So it was already lo-, well, love for the two of them. Soo… when I come out of the bathroom I see my sister sitting there, and Sammy sitting there, and my dad too. They are drinking wine and all that, it was like seven p.m., they were drinking and so, they were having fun, so I… I didn't care, I went and sat down and watched TV. Who comes in? Josef comes in! Through the door. He comes in. Soo… he also sits down and begins to drink with them, you know. So you know, my dad, "What is it", you know, "that's going on now?", you see? Sort of "What is it… what is… my daughter is sitting here with, with two men", you know. It was a little strange for my dad. I understood him. So Sammy began to argue about Katja and all that… It was crazy! So they began to sort of get going, and like and "What do you want?", you see? And like that. And then my father flipped out, took my sister, looked her in the room. "If you come out, I'll beat you!" he said. So he closed the door. So my father took… both those two… and threw them out of the flat. And he locked the door. But the outer door, the doorknob… it was, like, broken. If you pulled, pulled on it, they came, came out, you see? So he pulled it out, so, so no one could come in. And those two were standing by the mailbox, like, "Let us in!" and they began shouting for Katja. So Katja, she came out, she was, "Let me out! I want to go out!" and all that, so, so my… my dad started to hit her… Really, he was just, "You're staying here!", and "No, no, I want to go out!" So he beat her, he really beat her. She began bleeding, and… I, I, I just stood there and cried… didn't understand anything.

SOCIOLOGIST: Because you were just standing and looking at everything?

LASZLO: Yeah, I couldn't do anything! I was, you know, youn-, I wasn't youn-, I was young, but I understood anyway. I couldn't do anything. If I stood in the middle, I would get beaten too, so I just stood there and watched, you know, "What's going on?" And when my sister... He hit my sister I remember. And Sammy and Josef had gone down to the yard, so that was how it was. And then my brother came, he came home after, I don't know... he'd been tanning or something, I don't remember. So he comes up. And he had, he had the kind of key, so if you put it in the doorknob and you could twist it and you could open the door. And so he did it... So he sees how my dad is hitting my sister. So my da-, my brother took my dad, took him away from there, and took down my sister... Took down, I mean, carried her down. And he took the doorknob and locked it again, so no one could come in or out... So he carried her down. So he had the doorknob in his hand. And there was blood everywhere... So he came out in the yard, and the police and ambulance and all that come. Soo... my brother got in trouble then, like "Let her go!" They took out their weapons and he was just, "No, I haven't done anything!" and all that. And they took him. So my sister said, "It... he hasn't done anything," and all that. So they let my brother go, and then Sammy and Josef ran up again, after my sister. And when they came in, my dad started beating them too... My dad was beating them to death too... But then Josef runs down and Sammy stays up there, he got hit, I remember. So... (laughs) Josef runs down, and the police are there, and he begins to fight with the police and the police took him. Took him to jail, I think it was, and then my dad disappeared... with his wife. They disappeared somewhere...

SOCIOLOGIST: Had she been in the flat the whole time it happened too?

LASZLO: Yeah, exactly. But she hadn't done anything either, she just screamed, and all that, like a woman does... So they just, they disappeared.

SOCIOLOGIST: And her son? Or daughter?

LASZLO: Her son wasn't home. Her son was out playing in the

yard, I remember. And when I was down in the yard, crying, I didn't know what to do. So after an hour, after, like, after... not after an hour but when I went down to the yard, I sat on the swing. So I had a blackout (snaps with fingers), sort of, I saw nothing. I fell asleep, sort of. So I woke up, it was like, this happened in the summer... it was around nine, but it wasn't so dark. So I look around and all that, then I went up... to my flat. So it says "Police Barricade"... And they have put on a new lock and things, I couldn't get in, knocked like hell on the door. "What's going on?"...

SOCIOLOGIST: About how old were you?

LASZLO: I don't want to lie to you. This was, I was around ten, eleven maybe...

SOCIOLOGIST: Yes.

LASZLO: So I stood there and knocked on the door. No one opened, nothing, sooo... And it was just, it was this way. My sister had a little dog, a little, little dog. And I heard him inside...

SOCIOLOGIST: The dog was inside?

LASZLO: Yeah. Because they locked him in the bathroom, so nothing would happen to him... or her. Soo, so I heard, so I just... It was a little Pekingese! Really small. So I was pounding on the door and no one opened! I, I felt such... it was, it was really... it hurt so much, inside... So I see that my, that is, my dad's wife's son, coming up. Eight years old... he's coming up, just "What's happened?" It was panic, uproar... And I, I, I... I didn't know what I should do, I, well, I had a blackout. Because really I can, you know, get on the tram and go to my other sister or something. But I hadn't thought of it. So I look down at the yard, and so I see the neighb-, because we knew all the neighbours, you know, they were really nice to us. Sometimes they took us up and... we got to eat buns and drink juice and all that. So we were, so they... they came down, it was two, two women. "Ah, Laszlo, we have seen everything that's happened. They disappeared and everything.

You two can come and sleep at our place if you want." So just, "Okay, okay. Really nice of you." So we went up to their flat, so we were there and so... (snaps fingers)... Then I said to her, "Yes, but our dog is still in there!" So she called the police and everything. So the police came and opened the door, and we got to get the dog. So she came up, so we were there. So I thought I'd call my other sister... Because these women refused to let me go somewhere. You know, I was, "I have to get to my other sister and tell her what has happened!" "No, you're not going anywhere!", you know. So I was, "Okay, what the hell should I do?" you know. So I began to look in the telephone directory for her number, didn't find it... So I slept (pants), I couldn't sleep that night. But Johnny, he slept right away, my step-brother, he slept right away. Sooo... I woke up... I fell asleep at like six in the morning, woke up at eleven, twelve. So I go out with the dog, take the dog for a walk... So I see my brother coming (breathes out), feeling relieved you know! "Oh, what's happened?" and so, I hugged him and so, everything... When nothing happened, around two, he took me and my step-brother, so we went to... my dad's friend, who lived by... near, a kilometre away. So we went there, so my dad and my dad's wife were sitting there and they were drinking coffee and all that. So... I, I... they have never told me what happened. Where they went to, nothing, I don't remember. But so... It was then my oldest sister came and took me, took care of me, I got to live there. Three, five months... So, then my other sister came, the one who'd been beaten. But it was strange that... like two days, three days after that, my sister and my dad sat there with each other and were talking... You understand? So it was crazy! So, so it was then she said, like, "Laszlo's going with us!" and all that, so I got to live there. So that was that. That has really affected me... Then I saw how my dad was, how my sister is, and how my brother is... You see? I saw them in that moment, how they reacted. And that affected me a lot too. An event in my life really...

SOCIOLOGIST: I can see why you remember it (laughs).

LASZLO: Mm.

SOCIOLOGIST: Yeees…

CUT -

17)

SOCIOLOGIST + ASTRID

SOCIOLOGIST: So, then, it's just a few… a few questions first. What is your name?

ASTRID: Astrid.

SOCIOLOGIST: And so, how old are you?

ASTRID: Just turned 21.

SOCIOLOGIST: Mm… and where did you grow up?

ASTRID: By Kungssten, past Majorna, towards Långedrag. Between there, somewhere. I've lived in the same row house my whole life. But now I've moved to my own flat, on Stampgatan, near Ullevi…

SOCIOLOGIST: Mm. What do your parents do?

ASTRID: My dad is a politician. And my mum works at a day care.

SOCIOLOGIST: What schools have you attended?

ASTRID: Hagaskolan, I went to Påvelundsskolan for senior compulsory school, Schillerska secondary school then, for secondary school, and then… now I go to Gothenburg University, studying social work…

SOCIOLOGIST: Mm. Uhh… (looks at her interview guide) Yeah, then there is what you do now, but you just told me you study sociology, or will be a social worker. Just like me!

ASTRID: Yeah, social work. And I have my placement at this youth centre.

SOCIOLOGIST: Right. How many weeks?

ASTRID: The whole term.

SOCIOLOGIST: But then: is there anything missing from your life?

ASTRID: Not really... Well, maybe, nah... Well, maybe I, I would probably like to take a longer trip. Yes, but there hasn't really been time...

SOCIOLOGIST: What kind of trip?

ASTRID: I don't know. I interrailed around Eastern Europe a few years ago... Which was totally wonderful! That, yeah, maybe it wouldn't be so fun to do that again... no, it would probably be lots of fun to do it again! But maybe you'd do something different, take another trip, I don't really know how. And then there are so many people who go away, "Yeah, now we're going to..." the almost obligatory trip to Asia for young people today, and that, that would surely be really fun. But it also seems boring somehow... because everyone does it.

SOCIOLOGIST: But when you feel like you want to go, it isn't that obligatory trip, but something else, right?

ASTRID: Yeah, because I... The reason why I haven't gone anywhere is that I don't really know where I want to go, and then I don't want to go because you should go! So it's turned into... partly I haven't had time and I haven't had money. But also that, you want to go somewhere you really want to go to. Even if sure, you can go out and travel around a lot and not be one hundred percent sure of... where you want to go, it isn't that you want to go on your dream trip! But it feels a little like, "Yeah, now you should go travel"...

SOCIOLOGIST: (laughs)

ASTRID: But it would be cool, like, something, it is still something I want...

SOCIOLOGIST: Mm. Do you believe in God?

ASTRID: Nah... I am a little doubtful about that actually. It feels like I am a little doubtful about all these...questions actually! (laughs)

SOCIOLOGIST: (laughs)

ASTRID: But, still... purely, common sense, it feels really illogical in some way! Ehh...

SOCIOLOGIST: Did you grow up with...?

ASTRID: No, not at all.

SOCIOLOGIST: No...

ASTRID: So, it is really hard to say. I am, I am probably not someone... who can talk about it really...

SOCIOLOGIST: It isn't anything that plays a big role in your life?

ASTRID: No.

SOCIOLOGIST: Is there anything in life that is worth dying for?

ASTRID: That is, for... That is, I can't, nothing like, a higher power, or, well, but... Ah, I, that is, for other people... who are... first and foremost more than what I am. If you say that, if my life stops, or if my life is sacrificed so others can live, who are... I'm like... so if there are more people, than what I am...ehh... And then also if it's someone close, that makes a difference too. I sort of wish that it was, that it... it would be cool if you... if there were more things like, that you really burned for something, that is really amazing. But it feels like, I don't know, you're shaped by the fact that it is pretty safe and... nice in Sweden and all that, that, it isn't really like... like...

CUT ---------------------------------------

21)

SOCIOLOGIST + LOVISA

LOVISA: My name is Lovisa Aronsson and I'm 21 years old. Right now I live in my own flat on Södra Vägen in the city, but I grew up in Örgryte. I went to primary school and senior compulsory school in Örgryte in a school... Casa de Bambini, it's called. And then Sigrid Rudebeck for secondary school, in the city...

SOCIOLOGIST: What do your parents do?

LOVISA: Now... at... my dad has his own company and my mum works there too. She had her own company before but... So, they work for themselves, within PR/Marketing you can say...

SOCIOLOGIST: What do you do now?

LOVISA: Right now, yes, I'm doing a lot right now. It's so that I... study in Switzerland and have studied in Switzerland for almost two years...

SOCIOLOGIST: Okay...

LOVISA: I study something called Hospitality Management. Which means that for half the year we have to go out and work, and then it's that... Last year I was in China, working, but now, this half-year I should have gone back to China, but it didn't work out for various reasons... And, so, I came back to Gothenburg, which wasn't planned. So I work, for my parents now, to earn money. And then... I've applied for a job at Elite Hotel, which I hope I get...

SOCIOLOGIST: Okay... what kind of job is it?

LOVISA: It's in the front office, like the reception, you could say...

SOCIOLOGIST: Okay. But what was it you did in Switzerland? What type of programme was it?

LOVISA: It is Hospitality Management, that is hotel management, you could say... And you study, all hotel programmes are focused on different things. Some are practical, while we focus more on business operations and... management...

SOCIOLOGIST: What makes you happy?

LOVISA: Mmm... Yeah, I have to say social interactions, friends....Family, friends, relatives, my boyfriend. Yeah, of course, like, when we're not fighting... (laughs) Having people around you that you care about and like, and can be yourself with...

SOCIOLOGIST: What makes you unhappy?

LOVISA: Eh, yeah, conflicts of course… And that is also related to family, friends and all that. Fights, unnecessary fuss, that is, jealousy, egotism and things like that. You're vulnerable to that. And even I sometimes… have made myself unhappy because I myself have been like that. It has felt like, "But God, what am I doing, really?" So it's those things, that I have… Loneliness has been very, very negative, I have trouble with it…

SOCIOLOGIST: In what kind of situation?

LOVISA: Well… I have trouble, I think, cooling down, I don't know… It is probably this safety I might need, but to, you know, one evening sit by myself and just feel, "Damn, everything's good," like, I have trouble with that. So it makes me unhappy…

SOCIOLOGIST: Okay…

LOVISA: And then envy and all that…

SOCIOLOGIST: Have you experienced that, so…?

LOVISA: Yes, I really have!

SOCIOLOGIST: Tell me about it!

LOVISA: Yeah, it is like an… an envy that is in society today in general, so that people shouldn't have a better life than others and, like, like that you can't wish each other happiness. And that makes me really unhappy. I've experienced that, from friends… But it isn't like if, when, that people have a nicer car or that… people have a better TV. Not at all that way. But rather it's about… that people feel good, for example. That maybe you come and say, "God damn, I feel good today, what a good day I've had…" "Ha, yeah, it's, like, all working for you. You ought to know how things are for me…" Like that. And you see that in some way every day. And it… it makes me really unhappy…

SOCIOLOGIST: Who has been your role model in life?

LOVISA: Nah, that is, my… that is, some people would say their parents, but I don't say that at all. Because I want to be very different from them. Because I feel, like, if there is something one should learn, it is really, and it sounds like a cliché, but, learn from their mistakes. Therefore I don't want to see them like models, but on the other hand I want to feel like I can learn from them. And there is no one else, nah…

SOCIOLOGIST: You say their mistakes and it makes me curious. What kind?

LOVISA: Their mistakes, it is… My parents have fought a lot, when I was growing up. We have a really open family relationship and I don't think it's always so good… I don't think, that is, it's so hard when you're little, you know, and, you are involved and there are heated discussions and it is open communication and you, everyone, like, I'm the kind of person… I don't like to fight. I can discuss and all that, but the loud, a little shouting, I don't like that at all. I don't want to do that again. My parents have… fought a lot. They, I think they were also too young to have children, too… I don't think they were really ready, to be totally honest. I'm sorry, Mum and Dad, if you see this play, it's true. And they know it too. There are… everyone makes mistakes in life…

\- CUT

23)

MATTIAS ANDERSSON (PLAYWRIGHT/DIRECTOR) + LISA & GUNILLA (WHO WORK AT ANGERED THEATRE'S OFFICE) + MEHMET & ASTRID & LASZLO (INTERVIEWEES)

\- CUT

LISA: But you think the poster looks good?

MATTIAS: Yes, well… I like the colours and the idea. What

I'm thinking about is my name. I mean, "director Mattias Andersson", but "script Mattias Andersson"… I mean, how does it look, really?

LISA: But you have put everything together.

MATTIAS: But it isn't my words, not everything, or absolutely not everything, so you cannot say that I have, like, written a play. What would be the most fun would be if one wrote exactly, 13 percent of the script by Mattias Andersson, and the rest "words after" and then listed the names of the interviewed young people in a long row, but you probably can't do that… But then I have worked like a pig on this and cut and pasted, and also added a lot so… Write "Script and direction Mattias Andersson" on the poster, so…

Gunilla comes in from the next room.

GUNILLA: Mattias, there are some people who want to talk to you.

MATTIAS: Oh really?

GUNILLA: Some of the young people from the project here.

MATTIAS: "Young people from the project"? What the hell do you mean "young people from the project"?

GUNILLA: The interviewees.

MATTIAS: You're joking!

GUNILLA: No. They're in the next room.

MATTIAS: What the hell… are they doing here? Who brought them here?

GUNILLA: No idea…They're just sitting there.

MATTIAS: Really?

Mattias goes out to the next room, where Laszlo, Mehmet and Astrid are.

MATTIAS: Hi…

LASZLO: Hello! Are you Mattias?

MATTIAS: Yes, that's right.

LASZLO: (shaking hands) Laszlo.

MATTIAS: Hi.

ASTRID: (shaking hands) Astrid.

MEHMET: (shaking hands) Mehmet.

MATTIAS: Hey, hey. Hi, hi.

LASZLO: No, we… Mehmet and I are, like, friends of friends and so we happened to hear that we were both part of this theatre production, and then Astrid here has her placement at Mehmet's youth centre. And so she thought it would be fun, or, a good thing to come here and check things out.

MATTIAS: Of course! Great! But we haven't gotten so far yet, so… It's probably better if you come a little later.

LASZLO: Tickets for the première?

MATTIAS: No, that's no problem. Absolutely no problem.

ASTRID: But can we read in advance what is going to be included? Or can we come and look in advance?

MATTIAS: Yes, absolutely.

ASTRID: But do you have a script now, or?

MATTIAS: It's in progress and all that and…You can in a few weeks, absolutely in a few weeks… But you have to trust me. There are no names, you won't be able to recognise anyone. It is excellent material and great actors, so you can trust that nothing will be strange there.

LASZLO: I think it seems really awesome, I do.

MEHMET: It seems cool.

MATTIAS: Okay, guys, then… see you at the première.

LASZLO: Bye, Mattias!

MEHMET: Bye!

ASTRID: But I wonder anyway (giggles) just for fun, like… Would you yourself have been able to answer these questions?

MATTIAS: Absolutely.

ASTRID: At that age?

MATTIAS: Yeah. Or no. No, maybe not.

ASTRID: You wouldn't? (giggles)

MATTIAS: Well, it... Of course I could have.

ASTRID: Okay. So you... Do you believe in God?

MATTIAS: Look, the interviews took place in totally different conditions. During three hours, alone with the interviewer.

ASTRID: Okay. Mehmet, Laszlo! Can you go ahead? I'll come along later. So we'll be alone here.

MATTIAS: What the hell...?

LASZLO: Sure, Astrid. See you tomorrow or something. Are you working at the centre tomorrow?

ASTRID: No, just Wednesdays and Fridays.

LASZLO: Or, we'll wait outside. We'll have a fag in the meantime.

ASTRID: Okay. Cool.

Laszlo and Mehmet leave.
Astrid and Mattias are alone.

ASTRID: So... (puts an MP3 player on a table) So I get sound and... So. Now then... What is your name?

MATTIAS: Mattias Andersson.. But seriously...

ASTRID: This is just for fun...How old are you?

MATTIAS: 36, but come on now, it...

ASTRID: Where did you grow up?

MATTIAS: In Västra Frölunda here in Gothenburg, but...

ASTRID: Is there any particular event in your life that you would like to see performed on a stage or in a film, Mattias?

MATTIAS: Well, I... I'm playwright, goddamn it. That's, like, what I do, putting scenes from my life on a stage.

ASTRID: But this is different, right? Then no one knows if you made it up or if it is totally true. Is there a specific and *true* event that you want to talk about?

MATTIAS: Well... yes, well... Okay then. If it's that way, so... It can be more from teenage years or childhood then and... But event, event, there is so much that... But maybe one thing. That just comes up now is… I was bullied, throughout my whole time in primary school and, yeah, for several reasons, so, yeah, I never told my mum then and, we had a strange relationship and there was a feeling that I was ashamed in some way and… Yes, didn't trust her either, I think… Then I had another type of, what can I call it, medical problem rather late and… God, this is so embarrassing! But…Yeah, we were going on a school trip with the class then, out in the forest and were to stay a few people in some huts then and so…

Laszlo suddenly sticks his head in.

LASZLO: Astrid, do you have a fag?
ASTRID: (to Mattias) Wait a little! (to Laszlo) Sure.
LASZLO: Can I take one or two? Mehmet also wants one.
ASTRID: No prob. Here. (Throws the pack.)
LASZLO: (Catches it.) Okay. Thanks.
ASTRID: Or I'll come along. Really dying for a fag.
LASZLO: What? You're coming with us? You're letting this go, or?
ASTRID: Yeah, it… No problem, Mattias. We'll let it go now.
MATTIAS: But I started…
ASTRID: But I understand. See you at the première instead.
LASZLO: See you at the première!
MEHMET: (Who also peeked in.) See you at the première, Mattias.

All three go out, leaving Mattias alone.

MATTIAS: Yes, well… See you… at the première…

Mattias Andersson is a dramatist and director, working as Artistic Director at the Backa Theatre in Gothenburg. In his productions the contemporary city is often depicted from an adolescent perspective.

CUT

Helena Holgersson

SOCIOLOGY AS THEATRE | THEATRE AS SOCIOLOGY

There are many occupations that involve describing society: authors, playwrights, film-makers, photographers, journalists, artists, and human and social scientists. Our portrayals are different and aimed to a certain extent at different audiences. But we frequently comment on the same phenomena. In the theatre project *The Mental States of Gothenburg*, my assignment, together with two other sociologists, was to interview youths from different parts of Gothenburg.[1] Based on our transcripts, the script-writer and director Mattias Andersson would then stage a theatre performance. Both the "playwright" and the "sociologist" became characters in the play, which prompted new thoughts in me about my own practice and the difficulties of describing a segregated city, regardless of the genre one uses to do so.[2]

1. The interviews were carried out by the undersigned, Rebecka Andrén and Elin Wikström.

2. For a more detailed discussion of how conditions can be different in these genres, see Howard Becker (2007) *Telling about society*. Chicago: University of Chicago Press.

* * *

According to the poster for the play *The Mental States of Gothenburg*, 87 % of the text was comprised of direct quotes from interviews with youths in Gothenburg. Three from the north-eastern "immigrant-dense" concrete suburbs, three from the picturesque former working-class neighbourhoods in the centre, and three from the well-to-do villa suburbs in the south, near the sea. The interviews took place during the spring of 2006. They were about the meaning of life, what makes a person into who she or he is and what one wants to achieve here on earth. In the end, the play was also to a large degree about research ethics. The process by which the stories came about and issues regarding the goal of achieving authenticity became central to the play itself. The poster that advertised the play displayed the following text, an extract from the script where Andersson himself, as a character in the play, raises questions about this:

> ... and I mean, I have nothing to hide. I'm not cheating anyone, everyone knows what it's about and the sociologists think it is completely ethically correct. At the same time, a situation can arise, I don't know, regarding money, or whose words they are really and all that, you never know, and I gave everyone a letter with my mobile number and email address and "if you want to be anonymous or if you want to take back something you've said, contact me" and all that, I have been completely open ...

The performance opens and closes with acts where the youths' stories are in some way placed in the centre. In between, we stop for a moment at the Angered Theatre's office, where the playwright is stressed and agonising over his relationship to the people whose stories his play is built on. Can one really say that one has *written* a script when most of it is comprised of interview transcripts? Maybe one can call it a play with a chapter on methodology?

Before I handed in my first transcript, Andersson was worried about whether ten interviews would provide enough material. When he had read it through, however, he got in touch, completely overwhelmed. He would, he thought, be able to write an entire play based only on this one bloke's tale, and the interviewee became two characters in the play in the end. This confirmed something that I, as a sociologist, have always been fascinated by, namely that people in these contexts are often prepared to share deeply personal stories with a completely unknown person. For Andersson, the problem turned out not to be the material itself, but rather how it should be managed. In this regard, he had the same difficulty as everyone else who wants to comment on or describe a cross-section of society by means of interviews.

I do not believe that before the project started, Andersson imagined that research ethics would be one of the main themes of the play. Certain reviewers thought he should have stuck to the young people's stories. Maybe some schoolchildren who saw the performance agreed. It is not unusual for reflections on methodology to receive such a reaction. They can be experienced on the one hand as boring and "off the topic", and on the other hand as provocative, since they relativise the interviewees' stories. However, I think it was very exciting that during work on the script, Andersson felt the need to bring this meta-discussion into the play. The sociologist Diana Mulinari once called qualitative research a "terribly violent activity".[3] In projects where one only works with interviews, one can somewhat pointedly describe the process as one in which you meet someone you did not know before, introduce yourself and your research project, turn on the tape-recorder and ask him or her about private things, only to then press "stop", thank the person and go back to the office to analyse what the person said. In *The Mental States of Gothenburg*, we sociologists and Mattias Andersson shared this assignment between us. What Andersson gained by working with "real" material was the chance to use a new perspective to address issues regarding power relationships in society and in the city. Then both the "sociologist" and the "playwright" had to be on stage.

3. Diana Mulinari (1999), cited in Hanna Wikström (2007) *(O)möjliga positioner. Familjer från Iran och postkoloniala reflektioner ((Im) possible positions. Families from Iran and postcolonial reflections)*. Göteborg: Göteborgs universitet, Institutionen för Socialt arbete, p. 86.

* * *

As soon as I and the other sociologists who had taken part in the project got in the car having seen the première of *The Mental States of Gothenburg*, we began discussing how much the characters that Mattias Andersson created were like their real models. We were, of course, the only people in the project who had met the youths face to face. Andersson had only received our transcripts. "He was not nearly so defensive"; "She was much calmer"; "She was more of a hip-hop girl", we said. Until a colleague we had invited to the performance exclaimed, "And you know how they *really* are then?" As sociologists, we are used to having complete control over our material. We talk about "our" interview subjects and we have sole right to interpret what they tell us. Still, we hesitate to let them comment on our analyses until we are finished. That they should agree with us in our interpretations of why they have said what they have said is no requirement.

The experience of seeing "my" interview subjects become characters in *The Mental States of Gothenburg* was not a pleasant one. The situation sometimes felt uncomfortable. I found two of the characters in the play very different from the people I had created an image of during the interviews and the transcription work. Here the issue of who has the right of interpretation became essential. What was it that made me think that I could describe them in a way that was closer to "reality"? How could I presume that, with the help of sociological and scientific tools, I could represent them in a way they would have been more satisfied with? Why did I assume that those who had been interviewed would agree that they were not represented on stage the way they "really" were?

Several of the interviewees came to see the play. At the première, we identified some of them in the audience. They looked at "themselves" and my colleagues and I looked at them. How did they experience this? The borders between the "real" and the "fictive" were moved and recreated around us. Several weeks later, we heard from Andersson that "my" suburban bloke returned several times, with various friends and relatives.

On the one hand, I understood why: in many ways, he can be viewed as the hero of *The Mental States of Gothenburg*. On the other hand, it surprised me, since the long passage from his interview that make up one the play's first scenes is about a family quarrel that degenerates into abuse so that the police get involved. As a sociologist, I would have been afraid of "exposing" him to an analysis of this event, and worried about how he would experience it. However, to see it dramatised on stage seems to have been an uplifting experience for him.

But it was not primarily the portrayal of "my" suburban bloke that bothered me, but rather how Andersson used "my" middle-class girl and "my" upper-class boy in his story. A drama requires a number of different characters. I felt that the story he wanted to tell about a segregated Gothenburg needed, besides a charismatic suburban hero, a defensive and over-theorising girl from the city centre and an unconcerned medical student from the villa suburbs.

* * *

A person can be portrayed in a number of different ways, even if one has stuck closely to the transcript. In a scientific article, the result depends on a theoretical perspective, the point one is choosing to make, and how one transcribes spoken language. On the stage, it depends on the choice of actors, clothes, body language, tones and pauses. Some time into the rehearsals, Andersson asked for the tape recordings of the interviews. Later, when I asked if they had helped him, he explained that by that stage the ensemble had already sketched out the characters, and did not get much use out of the tapes. The question is, then, how a sociological study is different from a play. Don't we sociologists to a certain extent also turn our interview subjects into fictional characters? And ourselves?

In *The Mental States of Gothenburg*, the sociologist is not a person the audience can identify with. This character's function is another one. With the help of her patronising/naive/distancing way of interacting with the interview subjects, Andersson was able to highlight the power problematic that is part and parcel of qualitative sociological practice. With crossed arms and sceptical, squinting eyes, the young people she interviews show their resistance to everything she represents. On stage, they seemed hardly to want to reply to her questions. This aroused a feeling in me that I could, with the help of my recordings, prove that Andersson's descriptions of the interview situations were biased, and that I could show how it *really* was. I remember that after the play, I frustratedly emphasised to my friends that, "We actually had a *nice* time."

In scientific publications, when one includes quotes from interviews, one often also includes one's own questions, so that the reader can get a picture of how the interaction between interviewer and interviewee was, and in what context a person said what. *Director's cut* here is equivalent to *researcher's cut*. However, the researcher is obviously not keen to portray him or herself in a negative light. Or at least not in the *wrong* type of negative light. One is expected to mention and reflect on slightly leading questions. That is seen as good sociology. Good theatre is something else. For example, Andersson was fascinated from the beginning by how my colleagues and I – as we had been taught – transcribed everything from the moment the recording started, even if the interview took a while to really get going, until we pressed the stop button. In the final production, there are several scenes where the sociologist tests if the microphone works and makes sure that the tape is rolling. The playwright's room for manoeuvre is different from the sociologist's. That I too make myself and the people I interview into characters in my publications does not mean that sociology is theatre. Andersson had a different sort of space to create a story based on what the young people say than I would have had in a research report. Our respective audiences have different expectations and different demands.

* * *

In the last act of the play, Andersson places the upper class against the middle class and the working class. A story about a crushed knee that puts an end to a football career but leads to medical studies is woven together with a story about anorexia and parents who do not see, and a story about a rape trial where the prosecuted is a the step-father of a good friend of the victim. The public is expected to understand them based on where in Gothenburg the people grew up. After *The Mental States of Gothenburg*, I have thought a lot about how the differences and similarities between people are presented in various portrayals of urban life. As sociologists, we know that it is not a matter of chance who leaves school, who becomes a vegetarian and who studies abroad. But at the same time: Where do the mothers with cancer live? Where do girlfriends break up? And where do people dream of a football career? Telling about a segregated city is unbelievably difficult, but there are many of us who continue to try. In theses, plays, articles, installations, films, photo series and novels. With the development of art and science more and more often from the same type of material, but still on different terms.

Helena Holgersson works at the Department of Sociology, University of Gothenburg. Her research focuses on non-citizenship, exclusion and urban experiences of everyday life.